Ethnic Conflict
A Global Perspective

D0050397

Stefan Wolff is Professor of Political Science at the University of Nottingham and a consultant to governments and international organizations. He has published extensively on ethnic conflict and conflict resolution and is editor of the journal *Ethnopolitics*. For more information about the author, see www.stefanwolff.com.

Ethnic Conflict

A Global Perspective

Stefan Wolff

OXFORD
UNIVERSITY PRESS

*This book has been printed digitally and produced in a standard specification
in order to ensure its continuing availability*

OXFORD
UNIVERSITY PRESS

Great Clarendon Street, Oxford OX2 6DP

Oxford University Press is a department of the University of Oxford.
It furthers the University's objective of excellence in research, scholarship,
and education by publishing worldwide in

Oxford New York

Auckland   Cape Town Dar es Salaam   Hong Kong   Karachi
Kuala Lumpur Madrid Melbourne Mexico City   Nairobi
New Delhi Shanghai Taipei Toronto
With offices in
Argentina Austria Brazil Chile Czech Republic France Greece
Guatemala Hungary Italy Japan South Korea Poland Portugal
Singapore Switzerland Thailand Turkey Ukraine Vietnam

Oxford is a registered trade mark of Oxford University Press
in the UK and in certain other countries

Published in the United States
by Oxford University Press Inc., New York

© Stefan Wolff 2006

The moral rights of the author have been asserted

Database right Oxford University Press (maker)

Reprinted 2010

ISBN 978-0-19-280588-1

Why do the nations so furiously rage together,
and why do the people imagine a vain thing?

Georg Friedrich Händel, *The Messiah*

To LPM, my true north.

Preface to the Paperback Edition

Since completing the hardcover edition of *Ethnic Conflict: A Global Perspective* in August 2005, ethnic conflicts have remained in the headlines, and mostly for the wrong reasons. (In-)human behaviour in ethnic conflicts has not lost its ability to shock even those who have studied them for many years. From Darfur to Sri Lanka, from Iraq to the Basque Country, from the Middle East to Somalia, prospects for stable and lasting peace remain remote.

Analysing and illustrating the causes, dynamics, and responses to these and other ethnic conflicts requires looking behind the headlines of media coverage. This book illustrates why nationalism and ethnicity are such powerful forces in mobilizing people, turning neighbour against neighbour, and inflicting such enormous human and material costs on the societies in which the resulting violent conflicts occur. It also clarifies the complex links between ethnic conflicts, organized crime, and international terrorism and demonstrates the need to address these conflicts early and in a decisive manner to prevent them from developing into major humanitarian crises and global security threats.

There is no automatism that leads from the existence of different ethnic groups to violent conflict between them. In other words, ethnic identity is not a problem in itself, it is what leaders and their followers make of it that determines whether there will be bloody civil war. Yet, while the outbreak of ethnic conflict is mostly a local affair, its resolution is most decidedly not. Just as much as early intervention by the international community can minimize the civilian suffering and material destruction, delayed, indecisive, or poorly resourced crisis management contributes significantly to the unfolding of humanitarian disasters. The longer ethnic conflicts are allowed to last in the face of international inaction, the more mutual hatred grows on the ground, the more human rights violations intensify, and the more the suffering of civilians increases. What is more, the longer an ethnic conflict lasts the more criminal and political objectives become closely intertwined, further complicating any attempts at conflict resolution.

Effective conflict management alleviates humanitarian crises in the short term and eliminates their root causes in the longer term. Even where conflict resolution efforts succeed, post-conflict reconstruction remains a formidable task. For it to be successful, there has to be constructive and meaningful cooperation between international and local, private and public, governmental and non-governmental actors. This requires recognition by all sides that non-governmental organizations have an important role to play in minimizing the impact of humanitarian crises and in building peaceful democratic societies, and that the private sector, too, has significant potential, and responsibility, to contribute to peace and prosperity in war-torn societies.

All of this is to highlight one of the important themes that is further elaborated throughout the book. Ethnic conflicts are man-made disasters—starting, continuing, and ending them (or not) are decisions made by individuals. Be they leaders or followers, politicians in governments or in international organizations, business executives or human rights activists, human beings always have a choice. While the people directly engaged in the conflict in most cases bear the ultimate responsibility for whether there is violent conflict or not, they are also its first victims. Yet, choice, and with it responsibility, extends beyond conflict zones to international organizations and their member states, multinational corporations and NGOs. In a globalized world in which information is instantaneous and in which the knowledge and resources are available to stop the suffering of innocent civilians, inaction is impossible to justify.

The recent and not so recent history of ethnic conflicts has some very important lessons to offer. Complex phenomena as they may be, ethnic conflicts are not necessarily difficult to understand. Their complexity merely means that there is a lot to understand about them. The complexity of ethnic conflicts also means not only that simplistic, mono-causal explanations are most likely wrong but that they will lead to simplistic 'solutions' that are unlikely to work. Ethnic conflicts can be resolved, but they hardly ever do so by themselves. Yet with skills, resources, and persistence individuals can, and must, make a difference to end senseless human suffering—quickly, decisively, and permanently.

Nottingham, January 2007   Stefan Wolff

Acknowledgements

Writing this book has been easy and difficult at the same time. It has been easy because I have studied ethnic conflicts in all their complexity for over a decade, travelling to many of the conflict zones featured in this book, and speaking with victims and perpetrators, as well as politicians and analysts. It has been a very difficult experience too. In my attempt to capture the many facets of ethnic conflict so as to describe and analyse a wide range of conflicts in different regions of the world, I have had to engage with the individual stories and personal suffering that ethnic conflicts bring with them and from which most of my academic writing and policy analysis had allowed me a modicum of distance. This was eye-opening in some cases, and absolutely harrowing in others. This book tries to capture and share some of the scale of this man-made misery.

The support and encouragement that I received along the way from friends and colleagues has been invaluable. Many people have helped me over the years to try to understand the complexity and nature of ethnic conflict, and not all of them can be listed here. My thanks go to Fiona Adamson, Ingolfur Blühdorn, Anna Bull, Karl Cordell, Roger Eatwell, Chris Gilligan, Colin Irwin, Walter Kemp, Alan Kuperman, Timothy Less, Jenny Medcalf, Karoline von Oppen, Donald Rothchild, Ulrich Schneckener, Elizabeth Teague, and Scott Thomas. Over the years, I have benefited in particular from numerous conversations with Maya Chadda, Elisabeth Nauclér, Pieter van Houten, Wolfgang Danspeckgruber, and John Packer. John McGarry and Brendan O'Leary have been exceptional in their support over many years. Marc Weller has always been an inspiration—as a scholar, practitioner, and friend. I am also indebted to Durjoy Bhattacharjya and Kenneth Cukier for a long and helpful dinner conversation in Oxford.

Without a doubt, this book would not have been possible had it not been for the help and advice from Melissa Rosati and the enthusiasm with which Marsha Filion, Chris Wheeler, Rachel Woodforde, Matthew Cotton, and many others at Oxford University Press took on this project and guided me through the whole process from proposal to complete manuscript with all their experience.

No words will ever quite capture how much I owe to Lucy Marcus.

Contents

Illustrations

Maps

The Balkans
1... Krajina
2...Eastern Slavonia
3...Vojvodina
4...Kosovo
5...BOSNIA & HERZEGOVINA
6...SERBIA & MONTENEGRO
7...MACEDONIA
8...CROATIA

Europe

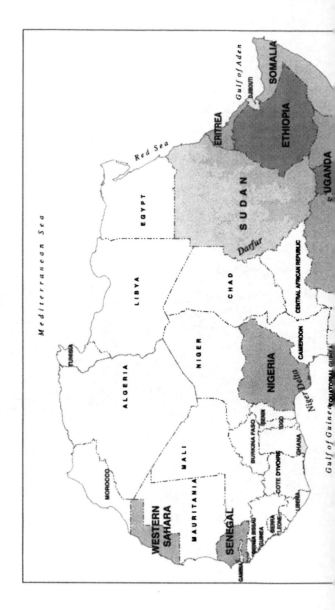

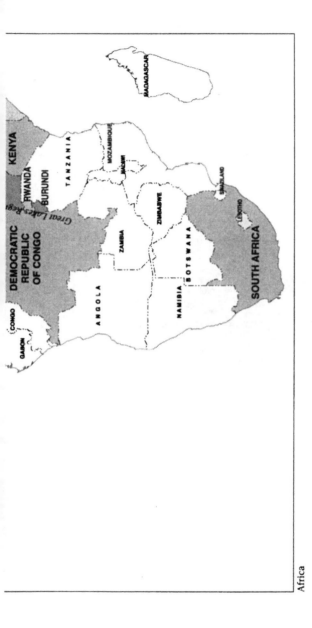

Africa

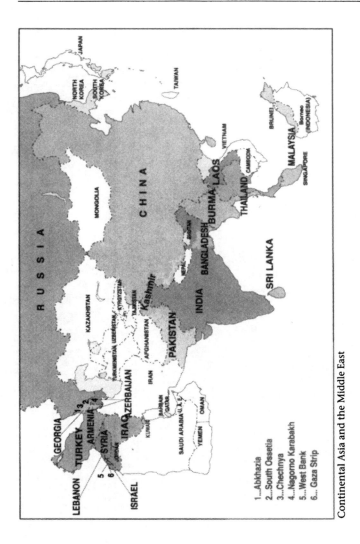

Continental Asia and the Middle East

1...Abkhazia
2...South Ossetia
3...Chechnya
4...Nagorno Karabakh
5...West Bank
6...Gaza Strip

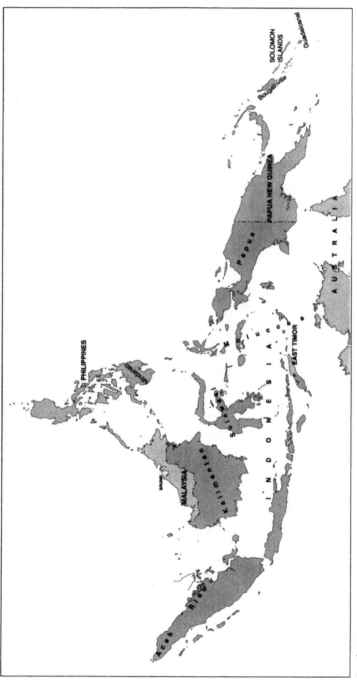

Pacific Asia

Introduction

Ethnopolitics: Conflict versus cooperation

On 18 April 2005, the BBC reported several pieces of good news. Voters in the Turkish Republic of northern Cyprus had voted for Mehmet Ali Talat, the (non-recognized) country's Prime Minister and a strong supporter of reunification with the south, in presidential elections. Talat had campaigned on a platform of reconciliation and rapprochement with the Greek-dominated part of the island and promised to initiate fresh talks with Greek Cypriot leaders. Thousands of miles to the east, peace talks were reported to have resumed between the government of the Philippines and the Moro Islamic Liberation Front. Held at a secret location in Malaysia, negotiations centred on finding workable compromises on issues such as access to land and a fairer distribution of the income generated from the natural resources in the southern Philippines. In Helsinki, meanwhile, former Finnish president Martti Ahtisaari let it be known that talks to end the conflict in Aceh of over three decades had ended on a positive note, with another round scheduled for May. Finally, at the conclusion of an Indo-Pakistani summit in New Delhi, the Pakistani President and the Indian Prime Minister released a statement saying that peace between the two countries would be irreversible and agreed to open more trade and transport links in Kashmir, with the aim of bringing this dispute of more than half a century to a permanent and peaceful settlement.

What all these developments have in common is that they are meant to address long-running conflicts that have seen more than their fair share of human suffering. Generally speaking, the term 'conflict' describes a situation in which two or more actors pursue incompatible, yet from their individual perspectives entirely just, goals. Ethnic conflicts are one particular form of such conflict: that in which the goals of at least one conflict party are defined in (exclusively) ethnic terms, and in which the primary fault line of confrontation is one of ethnic distinctions. Whatever the concrete issues over which conflict erupts, at least one of the conflict parties will explain its dissatisfaction in ethnic terms—that is, one party to the conflict will claim that its distinct ethnic identity is the reason why its members cannot realise their interests, why they do not have the same rights, or why their claims are not satisfied. Thus, ethnic conflicts are a form of group conflict in which at least one of the parties involved interprets the conflict, its causes, and potential remedies along an actually existing or perceived discriminating ethnic divide.

Empirically, it is relatively easy to determine which conflict is an ethnic one: one knows them when one sees them. Few would dispute that Northern Ireland, Kosovo, Cyprus, the Israeli–Palestinian dispute, the genocide in Rwanda, the civil war in the Democratic Republic of Congo (DRC), Kashmir, and Sri Lanka are all, in one way or another, ethnic conflicts. This is so because their manifestations are violent and their causes and consequences obviously ethnic. Yet, although all of these conflicts have been violent, violence in each of them was of different degrees of intensity. Leaving aside, for the moment, considerations of relativity (Cyprus is, after all, smaller and has fewer inhabitants than the DRC), in 30 years of violence, some 3,500 people were killed in Northern Ireland, roughly the same number during three months of conflict in Kosovo after the start of NATO's air campaign, and a single day during the genocide in Rwanda could have easily seen that many people killed in just one place.

In contrast to such violent ethnic conflicts, relationships between Estonians and Russians in Estonia and the complex dynamics of interaction between the different linguistic groups in Canada, Belgium, and France are also predominantly based on distinct ethnic identities and (incompatible) interest structures, yet their manifestations are less violent, and it is far less common to describe these situations as ethnic conflicts. Rather, terms such as 'tension', 'dispute', and 'unease' are used. Finally, there are situations in which various ethnic groups have different, and more or less frequently conflicting, interest structures, but hardly ever is the term 'tensions', let alone 'conflict', used to describe them, such as in relation to Switzerland or Catalonia, where conflicts of interest are handled within fairly stable and legitimate political institutions. Thus, not every ethnic conflict is characterized by violence, but, as we will see in the following chapters, inter-ethnic violence is always a sign of underlying conflict.

Violence does not spontaneously erupt between otherwise peacefully coexisting ethnic groups. However, 'ethnicity is not the ultimate, irreducible source of violent conflict in such cases'.[1] Power and material gain can be equally strong motivations, for leaders and followers alike, to choose conflict over cooperation, violence over negotiations. For a proper understanding of the dynamics of different ethnic conflicts it is, therefore, not enough simply to look at the degree of violence present. Rather, it is necessary carefully to analyse the different actors and factors that are at work in each conflict and the way in which they combine to lead to violent escalation or constructive conflict management and settlement. Thus, it would be mistaken to assume that ethnopolitics is only a matter of confrontation between different politically mobilized groups and states. On the contrary, there is a range of examples where ethnopolitics is pursued in a spirit of compromise and cooperation. This is a generally hopeful indication that the presence of different ethnic groups in the same country or region does not inevitably have to lead to violent conflict, and it is therefore useful to explore briefly the reasons for interethnic cooperation.

At the most basic level, it is often the realization of different ethnic groups that cooperation is more beneficial than conflict, i.e. that the diverse aims that each of the groups has are more easy to achieve in a joint effort. For obvious reasons, this limits cooperation to cases where political agendas are not mutually incompatible, where they can be transformed into a state of compatibility, or where the groups at least agree to put incompatible aims to one side and not to seek to realize them at all cost, while focusing on those elements of their individual political agendas that can be pursued jointly and with mutual benefit. This does not mean that ethnic identity has lost its salience; on the contrary, it often continues to play an important part in day-to-day politics and has often even been politically institutionalized through different systems of proportional allocation of funds, jobs, and seats in parliaments, and/or through qualified voting procedures in legislative and executive organs at the relevant national and regional levels. Although these examples underline the fact that ethnicity-based politics is not in itself a source of conflict and violence, it leaves open the question of why its 'civilized' conduct is possible in some cases but not others.

Recognizing the grave consequences of ethnic conflicts for civilians directly affected by them, as well as for regional and international security more generally, the international donor community has, over the past decade alone, pledged some $US60 billion on a vast range of projects to settle ethnic conflicts and help rebuild war-torn societies.[2] Despite this significant financial commitment and the involvement of many highly skilled people, ethnic conflict remains a threat to peace, stability, and prosperity. But why is it that Catholics and Protestants in Northern Ireland have been in perpetual conflict over the past several decades, when they can live and prosper together elsewhere? Why was there a bloody civil war in Bosnia when Croats, Serbs, and Muslims had lived there mostly peacefully over centuries, with their ethnicity hardly a matter at all in daily life? Why did nobody see and act upon the warning signs of an ensuing genocide in Rwanda that eventually killed close to a million people in a matter of weeks? What is it that makes Kashmir potentially worth a nuclear war between India and Pakistan? Why do a few militants in the Basque country reserve the right for themselves to carry out a campaign of killing and maiming in the name of the Basque people, when the overwhelming majority of this same people want nothing more than an end to the senseless violence?

The picture painted above seems bleak, but there is another way of looking at ethnic conflict, one that is more optimistic. Between 1946 and 2001, there have been around 50 ethnically motivated conflicts worldwide; by 2003, all but 16 of them had been settled. What has made it possible for so many conflicts to be resolved? Ethnic conflicts in the Balkans—from Bosnia to Kosovo to Macedonia—were hailed as successes of international intervention without border changes, whilst the secession of East Timor from Indonesia and of Eritrea from Ethiopia indicated that the creation of new states to settle ethnic conflicts was, in specific cases, still accepted as a potentially viable solution. More recently, ethnic conflicts in southern Sudan and Senegal are among those that appear to have been resolved, similar conflicts in Bougainville and Mindanao seem to be nearing settlements, and violence has at least been suspended in Aceh, Indonesia, and Sri Lanka. What accounts for these successes? Are there lessons from the resolution of these conflicts that could be applied elsewhere? Why and where and how are they applied or not?

To find answers to these questions will be the main task of this book. This is neither easy nor straightforward, for there is no single explanation of the dynamics of ethnic conflict and its management, settlement, and prevention. Although there are some general trends and commonalities that cut across a whole range of different conflicts, it is often very specific local dynamics that provide the key to understanding a particular conflict. Both aspects, however, need to be understood to offer at least some satisfactory explanations about ethnic conflicts, and the chapters that follow will, therefore, combine general analysis with specific cases. We shall first examine the historical origins and contemporary manifestations of the ideas of nationalism and ethnicity. This will help us understand why and how ethnicity has become such a powerful mobilizing force that can plunge societies into years of civil war and what, if anything, distinguishes it from nationalism.

Neither ethnicity nor nationalism in itself causes ethnic conflict. Rather, the stakes in ethnic conflicts are extremely diverse, ranging from legitimate political, social, cultural, and economic grievances of disadvantaged ethnic groups to predatory agendas of states and small cartels of elites, to so-called national security interests, to name but a few. As organized ethnic groups confront each other, minorities and majorities alike, with and without the backing of state institutions, an important question is to what extent ethnic conflicts are actually about ethnicity and to what extent ethnicity is merely a convenient common denominator to organize conflict groups in the struggle over resources, land, or power.

Understanding the causes of ethnic conflicts will help in some way to explain who fights in ethnic conflicts and how. It is important to bear in mind that ethnic conflicts do not just exist or come into being. They are the product of deliberate choices of people to pursue certain goals with violent means. This is true for domestic conflict parties, as much as for the actors involved in ethnic conflicts that are external to the country or region in which the conflict emerges. As a result of the threat to international security and stability, international organizations, neighbouring states, and regional and world powers may all have their own interests in particular conflicts. The range of conflict parties extends further beyond states and state organizations to diasporas of economically better-off brethren elsewhere in the world, willing and able to support their ethnic cousins' struggle with money, arms, and political lobbying. More recently, 'religious cousins' have become significant players in many ethnic conflicts as well. The menace of al-Qaeda and the terrorist cells that it has created around the world has become an additional complicating factor in a number of ethnic conflicts. Legitimate grievances that many Muslim minorities have in non-Muslim countries have been hijacked by religious fundamentalists, whose long-term agenda is often very different from those of local insurgents fighting for political rights, civil liberties, and equal economic opportunities.

A history of ethnic conflict in the twentieth century illustrates that there are only very few cases of such conflict that permanently elude any, even temporary, resolution. But this does not mean that solutions are always self-evident, readily embraced by the conflict parties, and easily implemented, even with significant international aid and assistance. Why is it that resolution of ethnic conflicts is such a complicated process, fraught with difficulty and often frustration for those offering their good offices in support? Is it the unreasonable intransigence of individual agents, more interested in their aggrandizement than in peace and prosperity for their followers? Why the lack of attention of the international community to conflicts where the parties are entrapped in a vicious cycle of violence from which they cannot break free without outside help? Is it the lack of resources and skills to find and implement solutions that satisfy all parties? These are the questions that need to be addressed in order to understand different approaches to how best to solve ethnic conflicts, the strengths and weaknesses that they have, and above all their dependence upon the concrete situation to which they should be applied.

Settlement agreements and peace deals supposedly signed by the conflict parties in good faith are many; those that are successfully implemented and lead to stable peace are far fewer. In many cases, the settlement achieved is only a temporary reprieve before violence escalates anew. As a consequence, there has been an increasing realization that ethnic conflicts do not simply end whenever a peace agreement has been concluded. Rather, the international community has been confronted by complex post-agreement scenarios in the Balkans, the Middle East, Northern Ireland, Africa, and south-east Asia, but success in sustaining peace has often eluded those who managed to forge the original agreement. Increasingly, therefore, post-conflict reconstruction is seen as an integral part of the conflict settlement process. Once an agreement has been signed, especially if it was reached with international mediation, programmes and projects are launched to aid the transition from war to peace, democracy, and prosperity. This involves building acceptable, accountable, and transparent institutions, to generate self-sustaining economic growth, and to create a civil society with free and independent media, civic organizations, and a general climate in which people once again begin to trust each other and are willing to live together peacefully.

No journey to explore ethnic conflict would be complete without highlighting its human dimension—a dimension that is primarily one of endless, and often senseless, suffering. People who die in ethnic conflict are more than just statistics. They often die horrible deaths. They leave behind grieving and frequently vengeful families who have to try to survive amid continuing violence that gradually but surely destroys the very social, political, and economic foundations of their lives. Yet, human beings are not only the passive, innocent, and unfortunate victims of torture, rape, looting, and killing in ethnic conflicts. They are also the ones who commit these very atrocities, leading others (by example) and following often too willingly. The accounts of victims and perpetrators often provide disturbing testimony to the depths to which human beings can sink. Yet if there is anything optimistic in the realization that ethnic conflict is not a natural but a man-made disaster, it is the fact that human beings are able to learn—not only about how to kill and torture more effectively, but also about tools to resolve ethnic conflicts and help the societies in which they occur to rebuild and embark on a road towards sustainable peace and development. Ethnic conflicts are likely to stay with us for some time, but understanding their causes, consequences, and dynamics can equip us to deal with them earlier and more effectively in the future.

1

The human dimension

Facts, figures, and stories of ethnic conflict

Among the events shaping international affairs, ethnic conflict is one that seems particularly difficult to grasp for many people in the western world. Not only does it seem irrational to kill people or force them from their homelands just because they belong to a different ethnic group, it also appears so wasteful of human and material resources in the light of the problems and challenges faced by most of the countries in which such conflicts occur, especially in the developing world. Would it not be so much better to spend the income gained from diamonds, oil, or precious minerals on education, housing, and healthcare, instead of buying guns and paying soldiers to rape, pillage, and loot? Is there no better way for political leaders to use their talents than to incite their followers to hate, expel, and kill the supporters of political opponents? Do common people not have the sense to see that civil war wrecks their country's prospects to achieve peace, stability, and prosperity, often for generations to come? Why, when given the opportunity to throw out the rascals, do they continue to vote for them? And why does the plight of refugees and survivors of massacres not move the so-called international community to speedy intervention to stop the killing, punish the perpetrators, and rebuild the country affected? These are legitimate questions and satisfactory answers to them are few and far between. What is more, attempts to understand ethnic conflicts and do something about them that does not make things worse have often been marred by the perpetuation of various myths. The most common of these are: ethnic conflicts are a new phenomenon that exploded on to the world stage with the end of the Cold War some 15 years ago; since then, conflict within states has become more prevalent than conflict between states; ethnic conflicts are based on ancient hatreds between the groups fighting in them and that, therefore, nothing can really be done about them; and ethnic conflicts do not really affect 'us' in the West anyway.

Myths always have a grain of truth in them, and sometimes even more than that. So let us begin with examining some of the facts about ethnic conflict. According to data collected by researchers at the International Peace Research Institute in Oslo and the Department of Peace and Conflict Research at Uppsala University,[1] there were approximately 50 ethnic conflicts with more than 25 people killed per year between 1946 and 2001. Of these, around 60 per cent started, and in some cases ended, before 1990 whilst the other 40 per cent dated in the post-1990 period. Although this clearly means that ethnic conflicts pre-date the end of the Cold War, it also highlights that proportionally speaking more ethnic conflicts began in the last decade of the twentieth century than in any other. With the end of the bipolar world order and the constraints on international action that it had brought with it largely removed, the post-1990 period also saw more media coverage of such conflicts and of international efforts to resolve them. Post-1990 conflicts also happened 'closer to home' for many in the western world—the Balkans are, after all, part of Europe. The 1990s also saw unprecedented atrocities committed in ethnic conflicts. The genocide in Rwanda, the siege of Sarajevo, the massacres of Srebrenica and Racak, and the endless treks of refugees from Kosovo produced images not seen in the western media for decades. By 2003 a slightly different picture had emerged. Of 16 ongoing ethnic conflicts in that year, 10 had started before 1990. The longest lasting of them is the struggle between the government of Burma (Myanmar) and the Karen National Union, which began in 1949. Of the post-1990 ethnic conflicts, Darfur in western Sudan was the latest addition.

What, if anything, can we learn from these statistics? Ethnic conflicts are not an exclusive post-Cold War phenomenon, but they have become more important factors in international relations over the past decade and a half. Moreover, many conflicts that predated the end of the Cold War have been resolved, as have quite a number of those that began after 1990. Thus, important lessons may be gleaned from looking at both pre- and post-1990 conflict resolution successes.

What about the notion that conflict within states has become more prevalent than conflict between states since the end of the Cold War? Again, there is quite a lot of truth in this, but also a good deal of misperception. Between 1946 and 2001, there were some 40 conflicts between states, compared with 50 ethnic conflicts and a good deal of 'ideological' conflicts within states in which the struggle for political power between different factions—often between left and right—escalated into violence. So already for the half century since the end of the Second World War, the statement is questionable. On the other hand, if we look at the figures in a slightly different way, there is, at least implicitly, more credibility to them. Since 1990, there has only been one inter-state war in Europe: between 1992 and 1994, Armenia and Azerbaijan fought over the territory of Nagorno-Karabakh, an Armenian-populated enclave in Azerbaijan. Clearly, this war had strong ethnic overtones and could also be described as an ethnic conflict that spilled across borders and dragged another state into an initially internal conflict. The break-up of Yugoslavia in the first half of the 1990s is a somewhat special case. With the recognition of Slovenia and Croatia, and later of Bosnia and Herzegovina, as independent states, the wars fought on their territories were, to some extent, inter-state wars. Yet, describing these conflicts in this way does not do their nature justice: they all were ethnic conflicts *par excellence*. Even before 1990, inter-state wars in Europe were few and far between: in 1946, the UK and Albania fought over the Korfu Channel, in 1956 the Soviet Union invaded Hungary, and in 1974 Turkey conducted a military operation against Cyprus, occupying large parts of the island and triggering a process of large-scale ethnic cleansing that created two almost completely homogeneous parts—the ethnically Turkish north and the ethnically Greek south. More importantly, however, the perception that conflict within states has become more prevalent than conflict between states since the end of the Cold War has been shaped by the fact that most of these internal conflicts in Europe are in fact post-1990 affairs. Before 1990, there were only a few such internal conflicts in Europe. In Cyprus, Greek Cypriots and Turkish Cypriots clashed in inter-communal fighting after the collapse of the power-sharing constitution in 1963. In France, as a fall-out from the Algerian War of Independence between 1954 and 1962, the government faced challenges from commandos of the pro-independence Front de Libération Nationale (FLN) as well as the Organisation de l'Armée Secrète (OAS), a terrorist group of French colonists and army officers opposed to Algerian independence. In Greece, communists and non-communists faced off against each other in a civil war between 1946 and 1949. In Estonia, Latvia, Lithuania, and Ukraine, the Soviet government eventually overcame the resistance of anti-Soviet forces in the late 1940s. Spain has seen a long-lasting and violent conflict with Basque separatists that continues to date. From the mid-1960s onwards, Northern Ireland experienced over 30 years of violence between extremists unable to agree whether the region should remain part of the UK or unite with the Republic of Ireland. In stark contrast, since 1990, there have been 18 new internal conflicts in Europe, of which 11 have been ethnic conflicts.

In the Middle East, there have been 12 inter-state wars since 1946, only three of which fall into the post-Cold War period (Kuwait, Afghanistan, and Iraq). In Asia, this ratio is 14:1, the one being the continuous quarrels between India and Pakistan over Kashmir, which have been ongoing since 1947 and led to a fourth war between the two countries in 1999. In Africa, the ratio is 13:5. Thus, if anything, what we can say is that inter-state wars have decreased in frequency or, more drastically put, they have become even less prevalent since 1990 than they were before.

What is perhaps more important than the distinction between inter-state wars and internal wars is to point out that many of the so-called internal wars may not be inter-state wars, but they are not internal wars either in the sense that they are not confined within the borders of just one state. The conflict in Chechnya involves Georgia, used as a supply base and route for Chechen rebels, and has destabilized neighbouring regions in Russia. In turn, Georgia's two ethnic separatist conflicts—South Ossetia and Abkhazia—are marked by significant Russian involvement and support for the separatists. The conflict in the eastern part of the Democratic Republic of Congo (DRC) has, over time, involved several neighbouring countries, including Rwanda, Burundi, and Uganda. The conflicts in the Balkans—Bosnia and Herzegovina, Macedonia, Kosovo, and Serbia and Montenegro—are inseparably linked. The conflict in and over Nagorno-Karabakh has involved Azerbaijan and Armenia, and will not be resolved unless the two states find a mutually acceptable solution to their territorial dispute. Similarly, the disputed territory of Kashmir has been partitioned among China, India, and Pakistan, and the latter two have gone to war with each other four times since 1947. India, in the meantime, has also been dragged, to some extent willingly, into the conflict in Sri Lanka, partly because of its own large Tamil population who are ethnic cousins of the Sri Lankan Tamils, and partly because it led an ill-conceived peace-keeping mission to Sri Lanka in an attempt to resolve the long-lasting conflict there. The conflict in the Solomon Islands escalated, in part, because of an ongoing conflict in neighbouring Bougainville, itself part of Papua New Guinea. Thus, a more accurate way to phrase the point about the increasing importance of internal compared with inter-state wars would be this: rather than being fought between regular armies of recognized states, most of the conflicts of the post-Cold War era involve non-state armed groups, often defined on the basis of ethnic identities, that straddle state boundaries and give many of today's ethnic conflicts a distinct regional dimension. In addition, the shift from inter-state warfare between regular armed forces to internal and regional conflicts, involving, if not exclusively, a large number of irregular and often poorly disciplined and controlled non-state forces, has also meant a massive increase in civilian casualties in

13

such conflicts. At the beginning of the twentieth century only about 10 per cent of war casualties were civilians, while by the end of the century the figure was closer to 95 per cent.

The impression that nothing can be done about ethnic conflicts is based on the assumption that they are mostly the product of the actions of irrational or mad leaders and their followers who conceive of today's world through the prism of 'ancient hatreds'.[2] Consequently, nothing really was done about many, if not most, post-1990 ethnic conflicts, at least not for some time. UN peace-keepers were sent to Bosnia and Herzegovina with no peace to keep and a weak mandate; there were too few of them; and they were not well equipped. With close to 40,000 military personnel and at a cost of over $US4.5 billion, the UN Protection Force in the former Yugoslavia managed to break the siege of Sarajevo in 1994 only with the help of NATO (North Atlantic Treaty Organization). The UN safe area of Srebrenica was overrun by Bosnian Serb forces in 1995, leading to the massacre of several thousand Bosnian Muslim men despite the presence of a Dutch troop contingent in the town. In the end, only massive air strikes by NATO in support of Bosnian and Croat ground forces brought Serbs to the negotiation table in Dayton, Ohio. Spending $US1.6 billion and involving some 22,000 military personnel, the UN Mission to Somalia from March 1993 to March 1995 did not even see a negotiated end to the tribal warfare in the country but left with most of its mission unaccomplished. In another example, $US450 million was the price for failing to prevent the genocide in Rwanda.

To the credit of the organized international community, there have also been some successes of late, which means that something can be done, at least about some ethnic conflicts. The Australian-led UN intervention in East Timor in 1999, following the fighting that broke out between pro- and anti-Indonesian forces after a majority of East Timorese voted for independence in a referendum, must be judged as one of the few relatively unambiguous success stories. Similarly, a UN-authorized and again Australian-led Regional Assistance Mission to the Solomon Islands in 2003 has been able to bring peace and stability to this country. The UN

Office in Burundi, established after a 1993 coup that killed the first democratically elected Hutu president in a country traditionally controlled by its Tutsi minority, succeeded in preventing a civil war of similarly genocidal proportions to the one in neighbouring Rwanda. The UN Mission in Cyprus, created in 1964, may have failed to prevent the partition of the island in 1974, but it has at least been able to maintain peace on the island for the past three decades, even if it has so far been unable to achieve resolution of the conflict. Following the NATO intervention in the Kosovo conflict in 1999, the UN, Organization for Security and Cooperation in Europe (OSCE), European Union (EU), and NATO have undertaken the tremendous task of rebuilding the conflict-torn territory—not as unambiguous a success as the mission in East Timor, but so far clearly less of a failure than earlier efforts in Bosnia and Herzegovina. Finally, decisive EU and NATO intervention in Macedonia prevented a significant escalation of the conflict between ethnic Albanians and Macedonians in this other successor state of the former Yugoslavia. The aftermath of the violence in 2001 and the difficult implementation of the EU- and NATO-brokered Ohrid Agreement of August in that year have not been free from problems, but Macedonia has embarked on a path to peace and stability, rather than continuing on the brink of civil war. Thus, the international community can do something about ethnic conflicts. It may not always succeed, often because of self-imposed limitations, but it is not condemned to either perpetual failure or constant inaction.

But do ethnic conflicts in far-away places like central Africa, the South Pacific, or even the Caucasus and the Balkans really have an effect on people living in the developed countries of western Europe or North America, Australia, or Japan? The fact that people get killed, maimed, and raped in the conflicts may be perceived as tragic, and seeing pictures on TV and in newspapers and magazines of atrocities in Rwanda or Bosnia and Herzegovina may be disturbing, but it has little direct impact on people's lives. So, is there no reason to be concerned, or for any intervention to be made motivated purely by humanitarian considerations for the victims of ethnic conflicts? Hardly. The consequences of ethnic conflicts have a very direct effect far beyond their epicentres.

Ethnic conflicts create instability, refugees, and conditions in which organized crime and increasingly international terrorism can fester. Ethnic conflicts, or their resolution, also create other ethnic conflicts in the same country or elsewhere in the region, and at times they draw neighbouring states into the conflict leading to inter-state war. During Africa's 'first world war' in the DRC, regular and irregular combatants from many neighbouring countries were involved in the fighting. Next door, the ethnic geography of Hutu and Tutsi groups in Rwanda and Burundi has linked both countries and the conflicts in them. For example, in 1972 a rebellion of Hutu against the military regime of Tutsi in Burundi killed about 100,000 Hutu and turned twice as many into refugees, most of them escaping to neighbouring Rwanda, where, since the first elections after the country's independence in 1962, Hutu ruled over the Tutsi minority. So in 1972, the plight of their ethnic cousins 'inspired' Rwanda's Hutu to take it out on the country's Tutsi population with arson, looting, and beatings, rather than with the quasi-genocidal massacres that had been regularly conducted between 1959 and 1964. In Sudan, however, it was the impending resolution of the long-standing conflict between the government in Khartoum and rebels in the south of the country that was seen by other ethnic groups in the country as too exclusive. Learning the lesson that violence can lead to a favourable peace deal, armed groups based among the African population in the western region of Darfur challenged the central government, dominated by the country's Arabic population, and a new conflict erupted leading to tens of thousands killed and several times as many displaced from their homes.

All these conflicts led to a very large number of people being displaced in their home countries and becoming refugees in neighbouring countries. This has created a situation in which one-third of the world's 15 million refugees can be found in Africa, alongside an additional 15 million internally displaced people on the continent. Given the desperate conditions in which these people live, it is surprising neither that many casualties of Africa's ethnic conflicts die of the consequences of ethnic conflicts—starvation, exposure, lack of healthcare—rather than from actual fighting, nor that this leads to a perpetuation of conflicts as refugee camps become the bases from which armed groups begin to operate. Regional instability thus becomes a consequence as much as a source of ethnic conflicts.

This is not only an 'African problem'; similar dynamics can be observed elsewhere—in the Balkans, the Caucasus, and Asia. Conflict in and over Kashmir has led to four wars between India and Pakistan to date. Now that both countries have nuclear capabilities, a fifth war between them is not really a prospect for anyone to look forward to, regardless of how distant geographically they may live from Kashmir. The conflict in Chechnya is a major source of instability in the entire post-Soviet region, stretching all the way to the central Asian successor states and attracting radical Islamist fighters to Chechnya who not only fight Russian forces in the separatist province but have also taken hostages in a Moscow theatre and in a school in the neighbouring Republic of North Ossetia-Alania in the Russian Federation. Chechen rebels have also been accused of downing Russian passenger jets and igniting bombs in Moscow apartment blocks. The ethnic conflicts in the Balkans in the 1990s created hundreds of thousands of refugees and displaced people, not only in the region itself, but also across Europe as a whole.

The instability that many of these conflicts create in individual states and entire regions creates conditions in which organized crime can fester. The Balkans have become a major trafficking route for illegal immigrants, women forced into prostitution, and guns and drugs destined for western Europe. Areas in northern and western Afghanistan, controlled by tribal leaders and often beyond the control of the government in Kabul, produce almost 90 per cent of the opium sold in the UK. Ethnic conflicts in Africa are partly, and often largely, financed by diamonds, precious metals, and other commodities extracted in areas under the control of rival armed groups. The export of oil particularly from the Caspian Sea Basin

17

is largely dependent on stability in the south Caucasus, Turkey, Central Asia, and Afghanistan. Significant levels of ethnic conflict in any of these regions could seriously hamper access to the region's large oil and gas reserves, and increase the dependence of major economies on the oil-exporting countries in the Middle East, itself a region prone to conflict and war.

These facts and figures tell a compelling story about the menace of ethnic conflict. They are important statistics helping us understand the scale of the problem, its spread across the globe, and its consequences for the countries directly affected and their near and distant neighbours. What these statistics do not tell us much about, however, is the human tragedy of ethnic conflict. Individual suffering disappears behind faceless statistics. To understand ethnic conflict as a phenomenon of relationships between human beings is essential in order to assess properly its causes and consequences, and the potential remedies on offer. Successful prevention of ethnic conflicts, conflict resolution, and the rebuilding of conflict-torn societies make it necessary to embark on a journey that is mostly filled with the horror of murder, torture, rape, arson, and looting. Very little in this journey offers hope—the Schindlers and Wallenbergs who tried to save Jews during the Nazi Holocaust were few and far between then, and their number has not increased significantly since. Nor has the number of politicians and community leaders grown whose vision of the future for their troubled countries goes beyond accumulating power and amassing personal riches.

Let us begin our journey in Kosovo in March 1998. Long-simmering tensions between ethnic Albanians and Serbian security forces were beginning to escalate into violence with the rise of the Kosovo Liberation Army and its first systematic attacks on Serbian government forces in the area. This had been preceded by decades of often-violent repression of ethnic Albanians in a province in which they then outnumbered Serbs by four to one and had led to their complete disenfranchisement shortly after Slobodan Milosevic had come to power. The bloody disintegration of the Yugoslav federation and the failure of the international community to take seriously the non-violent independence movement among Kosovo Albanians added to the gradual escalation. Certain that he could crack down on the emerging militant resistance movement among the Albanians in Kosovo with the usual impunity, Milosevic gave the go-ahead to a campaign of terror against suspected rebels, their families, and alleged supporters—in short against the ethnic Albanian population of Kosovo. This campaign reached an early climax in March 1998 in the Drenica village of Kosovo, with attacks on the villages of Likosane, Cirez, Donji Prekaz, and Glodjane, killing over 120 people, including women and children. Amnesty International documented the attacks, relying on eyewitness accounts of those who were fortunate enough to survive—but had to live with the memories of seeing their loved ones killed in cold blood, as did this 70-year-old woman who gave an account of her son's murder to Amnesty International:

When we arrived at the door of the yard he said to me 'Let me help you'. . . . When we went out of the yard my son held me. He told me 'okay mother let's go', the only thing which I know from him. In front of the house when we were stopped they [the police] took my son from me. . . . I told him go and leave me here because nothing will happen to me. He didn't say anything to me and they took my son from me until I turned my eyes to him . . . they ordered my son to lay down then they searched him and ordered him to get up again and he did that. Again to lay down, they did not find anything, no weapons. I saw with my eyes how they prepared their automatic weapons, two of them, one on one side and another on the other, they shot him between the shoulders I saw that with my eyes and screamed at that moment 'Please God, I rely on you!' . . . I didn't know what else I could say. I held those two walking sticks. I felt that my feet were completely cold. I could not feel them, I didn't know that they were mine. I saw how he was still, he didn't move he seemed to be sleeping. I thought to go and to see him one of the police ordered me: 'Don't move!' He did not let me and I was just staying and looking. Then I wanted again to go and to cover him. I wanted to take this [her scarf] off and one of them turned a gun to me, but he didn't let me.[3]

This was not an isolated incident that could be blamed on an over-zealous local commander trying to please his superiors by carrying out a particularly thorough 'counter-insurgency' operation. Over the months such attacks intensified, as did the fighting between ethnic Albanian guerrillas and Serb security forces. Both sides committed human rights violations, kidnapping, killing, and torturing people suspected as rebels or collaborators. Eventually, after a proposal by the international community to resolve the crisis with non-military means was rejected by the Serbian side, NATO launched an air campaign against Serbia and quickly defeated Milosevic's forces, and a UN administration was established in Kosovo.

Other parts of the world have been less 'lucky'. This account of atrocities in Darfur could have been recorded in Kosovo as well:

It was early in the morning, people were sleeping. About 400 armed people cordoned the village, with military uniforms, the same ones worn by the army, with vehicles and guns. A plane came later, to see if the operation was successful. At least 82 people were killed during the first attack. Some were shot and others, such as children and elderly, were burnt alive in their houses.[4]

Determined international action in aid of the civilian population of this region in western Sudan has, however, been only slowly forthcoming. And so the violation of human rights continued unabated, as this refugee reported:

During the first attack the village was burnt, some people were killed by gun shots. Others, like children and the old, were burnt. We didn't have time to protect ourselves. Women are often attacked, their cloths are taken from them and they are left naked; men are killed and women are raped; they are tortured, raped and beaten.[5]

The humanitarian crisis in Darfur may be the latest ethnic conflict that has grabbed the attention of the world's media. This is not surprising as the crack-down by the central government's armed forces and their allied Arab militias—the Janjaweed—has cost the lives of tens of thousands of civilians and displaced hundreds of thousands more. Yet, even at this scale, Darfur is by far not the worst of recent ethnic conflicts. Ten years earlier, also in Africa, the world was shocked by the attempted genocide of the minority Tutsi population by the Hutu majority in Rwanda. The systematic and organized killing of some 800,000 Tutsi, and a number of moderate Hutu, was shocking not only because of the brutality with which the genocide was pursued but also because of the degree to which it involved ordinary people and turned them into killers. Some joined the killing squads willingly, others were forced to kill—as this woman who testified to Amnesty International:

I killed three people, three men. I knew them, they were my neighbours ... I didn't have any alternative. When I refused to kill, the government soldiers banged a gun on my child's head and she died. She was six weeks old.[6]

A Hutu man who also took part in the genocide told the BBC:

On the morning of 15 April 1994, each one of us woke up knowing what to do and where to go because we had made a plan the previous night. In the morning we woke up and started walking towards the church. . . . People who had grenades detonated them. The Tutsis started screaming for help. As they were screaming, those who had guns started to shoot inside. . . . I entered and when I met a man I hit him with a club and he died. . . . Some people did not even find someone to kill because there were more killers than victims. When we moved in, it was as if we were competing over the killing. We entered and each one of us began killing their own. . . . Those you cut were just not saying anything. . . . I saw people whose hands had been amputated, those with no legs, and others with no heads. I saw everything. Especially seeing people rolling around and screaming in agony, with no arms, no legs. People died in very bad conditions.[7]

Yet there is little indication that he, like many others participating in the genocide, accepts responsibility for his actions:

It was as if we were taken over by Satan. We were taken over by Satan. When Satan is using you, you lose your mind. We were not ourselves. Beginning with me, I don't think I was normal. You wouldn't be normal if you start butchering people for no reason. We had been attacked by the devil.[8]

One woman survived this particular episode in the genocide because her 'body had been drenched in blood and it was getting dry on me so the killers thought I had been cut all over. They thought I was dead'.[8]

Barely a year after the Rwandan genocide had ended another atrocity shocked the world—the massacre of several thousand Bosnian Muslim men in Srebrenica after this so-called UN-protected safe zone had been captured by the Bosnian Serb Army. Not only did this incident expose the failures of the UN mission in Bosnia and Herzegovina during the war, but it continues to serve as a symbol of human tragedy well beyond the actual massacre. Shocking as this incident of mass killing under the very eyes of the international community may be in itself, the suffering of surviving family members of those killed is as powerful an indication of the lasting personal tragedies brought about by ethnic conflict:

When I counted later, 25 members of my close family, my nearest and dearest family, all gone. And that wounds me terribly. All sorts of ideas come into my head. I don't have the people I used to sit around with, the people I used to talk to. . . . I had everything—house, land and all that, but the most severe pain is close family, when you lose that. Your house, buildings, or apartment, that can all be compensated for, but your family, never. It's lost forever. And now, let me tell you, I feel such grief that I don't know what to do with myself.[9]

Although some cases of ethnic conflict hit the headlines of the international media, the human suffering occurring in many others remains under-reported, and few cases attract constant media attention. Despite continuous fighting, they drop from the horizon as initially exceptional tragedies become routine elements of life in conflict zones. Turkey's counter-insurgency against Kurdish separatists had been ongoing for decades, but it was mostly human rights organizations who, to little effect, covered human rights violations committed by the Turkish government, similar to and worse than the one illustrated in this victim's statement:

During the first interrogation they grabbed me by the hair and punched my head against the wall. I was thrown to the ground. They kicked me and one officer put his boot into my mouth. . . . I was spitting blood. They pressed a wooden truncheon against my genitals and twisted it. They laughed, saying: 'She is enjoying this.'[10]

Back in Africa, much of the violence that has continued since the official 'end' of the war in the DRC has gone unreported outside a small community of human rights activists. Especially in the eastern part of the country, fighting between forces of the transitional government in Kinshasa and rebel groups and their backers in neighbouring countries has particularly affected civilians. In May and June of 2004, Bukavu, the provincial capital of South Kivu, was the scene of fighting between pro- and anti-government forces. As control over the town switched between forces, so different groups of civilians were exposed to violence. Initially, pro-government forces took control of the city and carried out reprisals against the minority Banyamulenge ethnic group after one of the pro-government soldiers was killed. Several days later, opposition forces captured the town, allegedly to prevent further massacres against their fellow Banyamulenge. This noble cause, however, did not stop them from committing their own crimes against the civilian population, as this man told Human Rights Watch:

On Thursday June 3 two Banyamulenge soldiers came to my house. They pointed their gun at my head and asked for money. We were five men in the house, and my little sisters were in the back room. They asked for phones, and demanded $100 from each of the men. So I gave them $75 and a telephone, because we had heard there had been other killings. . . . Then they locked the men in a room and went to the girls' room. They attacked my seventeen-year-old sister. I heard her screaming. . . . One soldier came back into the room and said: 'until you accept the Banyamulenge as Congolese, there will be no calm in Bukavu. Mbuza Mabe killed our mothers, sister and uncles. We leave you with that message. . . .'[11]

From Rwanda to Bosnia and Herzegovina, from Kosovo to the DRC, the stories of human suffering are easily interchangeable. Similar stories could also be told about the conflicts in Nagorno-Karabakh or South Ossetia, in East Timor, Sri Lanka, or Aceh. People are prepared to kill and to die because they see themselves as ethnically different from others, because they are told that this is a difference of life and death, and because they often only too willingly accept such 'explanations'. As a consequence of such 'logic', many more suffer and many more decide to stand by and let the suffering continue or become willing accomplices in the slaughter. As much as one would like to think otherwise, ethnic conflicts are stories about deliberate choices made by human beings about action or inaction. Above all, however, they are stories of human suffering.

2

Ethnicity and nationalism

Let us begin our exploration of ethnicity and nationalism with two tales to illustrate how ethnic identities 'come into being' and contribute to the formation of groups that, in some but by no means even the majority of cases, eventually engage in violent conflict with one another. Our first tale begins in Rwanda around 2000 BC. By then the first inhabitants of the territory of today's Rwanda had arrived in the area. They were hunter–gatherers and forest dwellers. Although the oldest of Rwanda's inhabitants, their present-day descendants, the Twa, are only a very small minority of around 1 per cent of Rwanda's total population. About 1,000 years later, farmers began to migrate to the area. Clearing forests and cultivating the land, they quickly grew in numbers, partially displacing the original settlers. Today, their descendants, the Hutu, make up around 85 per cent of Rwanda's population. Another two centuries later, the third of present-day Rwanda's ethnic groups came to the area—Tutsi, who reared cattle, migrated in large numbers from the north, and gradually gained control of the area through conquest and assimilation. Hutu and Tutsi spoke the same language, shared many traditions and customs, intermarried, and lived together unsegregated.

What distinguished the two main groups was occupational status. Tutsi, originally cattle herders, had also become soldiers and civil servants. Hutu remained mostly farmers. Even though the occupational status of Tutsi gave them a dominant position in society, the existing clan system cut across group membership, and several clans included members of all three groups. Clan identification was often more important than what was later to become the main social cleavage—ethnic identity. Within this clan system, patron–client relationships involved reciprocal bonds of loyalty within and between groups. However, it also created a hierarchical system, in which patrons were mostly Tutsi and clients mostly Hutu. As the hierarchy was multi-layered, some Tutsi were also clients, but rarely of Hutu. These social structures, eventually, created Tutsi-dominated political and economic structures, which were reinforced first by German and then by Belgian colonial rulers from the late nineteenth century onwards, and provided the institutions within which ethnic difference became the most important social cleavage in the post-colonial era.

Already in the mid-1950s, political demands were formulated in ethnic terms. Hutu called for decolonization and democratization, denying that Tutsi were anything but immigrants with no place in a Rwandan nation. Tutsi, on the other hand, drew very different inferences from history and rejected any Hutu role in the running of the emerging country because of their own superiority. Little wonder then that political parties, created in the 1950s in preparation for the country's independence, were formed along ethnic lines and reinforced the already existing deep divisions. Given the numerical supremacy of Hutu—85 per cent over 15 per cent Tutsi—the first parliamentary elections in 1961 returned a clear Hutu majority. As a consequence of intra-Hutu rivalries and Hutu–Tutsi conflict, Rwanda had become a one-party state by the mid-1960s in which Hutu rule had replaced Tutsi domination. As Hutu leaders appealed more and more to ethnic sentiments, drawing on their past inferior status and exploitation by Tutsi, a Hutu ethnic identity solidified alongside that of an already existing Tutsi group identity. Over the next three decades, these identities were further consolidated and, by the time of the genocide in 1994, they had become the most significant reference points for members of both groups, reinforced also by frequent anti-Tutsi violence over the decades and regular incursions by Tutsi militias based in refugee camps in neighbouring states.

Bosnia and Herzegovina tells a different story. If comparisons of this kind can be made at all, the country today is probably as deeply divided as a society as Rwanda. As a result of a three-and-a-half-year war between 1992 and 1995, which had a number of quasi-genocidal episodes involving significant ethnic cleansing, over 200,000 of the country's almost 4.5 million pre-war residents are dead or missing and almost a third were driven from their homes. The war, and the peace settlement reached at its end, have left the country divided territorially, politically, and socially, with ethnic splits among Serbs, Croats, and Muslims being the primary fault line. The viciousness with which the war was fought and the emotionally intense way in which most members of the three groups interpret its causes, conduct, and consequences suggest that, similar to Rwanda, there has been a long history of inter-ethnic animosities and hostilities that culminated in a bloody civil war in the early 1990s. Although the myth of 'ancient hatreds' has long been done away with, the evolution of ethnic identities among the three groups living in today's Bosnia and Herzegovina is nevertheless vital in understanding the meaning of ethnicity and nationalism in a broader context.

The year 1992 marked the beginning of a fundamentally different period in the history of Bosnia and Herzegovina—its existence as an independent state. Before that, the territories of present-day Bosnia and Herzegovina had belonged to empires—to the Ottoman Empire from the middle of the fifteenth century onwards, to the Habsburg realm, *de facto* since 1878 and *de jure* since 1908, and to the various incarnations of Yugoslavia from the end of the First World War to 1992. Throughout this period of several centuries, ethnicity was politically of little relevance in the territories of present-day Bosnia and Herzegovina, where members of all three national groups spoke the same language and lived together peacefully and without clear territorial borders separating them. If anything, religion was the main distinguishing feature among the three communities—Muslims, Orthodox Serbs, and Catholic Croats—and began to become a component of emerging national identities. Although Serbs and Croats could always be identified ethnically, the ethnic origin of Muslims remains disputed. Serbs and Croats claimed Muslims, respectively, as converted under the Ottoman Empire, whereas Muslims traced their origins to a pre-Ottoman Bosnian kingdom. Muslims in the Ottoman Empire did enjoy a number of privileges, whereas non-Muslim populations were excluded politically and socially, not least through the millet system, which, however, offered them some autonomy in the regulation of their religious, cultural, and educational affairs. Thus, although the upper echelons of power were occupied exclusively by Muslims, Serbs, Croats, and Muslims were all represented among the socially and economically disadvantaged lower strata of society. Emerging ethnic group identities were thus based on a mixture of distinctive features—religion, status, and origin.

The control, and subsequent annexation, of Bosnia and Herzegovina by the Habsburg Empire contributed further to a consolidation of ethnic distinctiveness. Initially welcomed only by Croats hoping for unification with other Croatian parts within the Empire, Vienna was smart enough to try to win over the Muslim élite as the most numerous and, after four centuries of Ottoman rule, also the most powerful community in Bosnia and Herzegovina. Despite this accommodative approach, large numbers of Muslims left Bosnia and Herzegovina and Serbs became the numerically dominant group. Nevertheless, Habsburg cooperation with Muslims continued, and Bosnia and Herzegovina soon came to be known as the most loyal province of the Empire.

With much delay compared with other areas of the Balkans, a national movement in Bosnia and Herzegovina emerged only in the late nineteenth and early twentieth century. It was not, however, a unified national movement as in Serbia or Albania, for example, but split along the lines of its population groups. These divisions were further enforced in the first constitution of Bosnia and Herzegovina in 1910, introducing specific group rights, autonomy, and a system of rotation in the highest offices in the province. Elections also held in 1910 contributed to the consolidation of these differences as well, operating a system according to which seats in the new assembly were allocated according to religion—to

Orthodox Christians, Muslims, Catholics, and Jews—and in proportion to each religious group's share in the overall population. This encouraged the formation of political parties along those religious lines that corresponded, for the most part, to the three main ethnic identities in Bosnia and Herzegovina.[1]

The First World War brought an end to Habsburg rule and the creation of the first of many Yugoslav states—the Kingdom of Serbs, Croats, and Slovenes. Even though Muslims were not recognized as one of the constituent peoples, Muslim parties existed in Bosnia and Herzegovina and attracted, just as their Serb and Croat counterparts, a share of the vote largely equivalent to their share in the population.[2]

An inner-Yugoslav compromise between Serbs and Croats in 1939 included Croat-inhabited parts of Bosnia and Herzegovina into a Croat province, which was to enjoy substantial autonomy. German and Italian military advances into the Balkans and the territorial reorganization during the subsequent occupation annexed all of Bosnia and Herzegovina to the fascist Croatian state established under German protection. A guerrilla war soon embroiled the entire region, with Communist resistance forces emerging as the most effective, attracting support from all ethnic groups in the region. After the victory of the Partisans, a socialist and federal state was established in Yugoslavia in which Bosnia and Herzegovina became a constituent republic, endowed as were all the other republics of socialist Yugoslavia with a qualified right to secession. Although the territorial entity of Bosnia and Herzegovina was recognised as such, the recognition of Muslims as a constituent people happened only in 1968 and contributed to affirming the existence of a separate Muslim ethnic identity. This manifested itself in a revival and strengthening of this identity—many of those who had previously identified as Yugoslavs now 'switched' their ethnic identification to Muslim, changing the demography of Bosnia and Herzegovina to a society with a plurality of Muslims, followed by Serbs and the much smaller Croat community. What did not change, however, was that the defining characteristic of Bosnia and Herzegovina remained its constitution by three distinct groups—Muslims, Serbs, and Croats—who lived together without conflict or clear territorial borders between them. This was even more remarkable given that Serbs throughout Bosnia and Herzegovina and Yugoslavia more generally occupied a disproportionate share of high offices in state administration and the Communist Party.

The death of Yugoslavia's post-war leader, Josip Broz Tito, in 1980 marked the beginning of the end of multi-ethnic society in Yugoslavia as a whole. With Tito gone, leaving behind a strongly decentralized state, the constituent republics became increasingly important power centres. This had particularly devastating consequences for Bosnia and Herzegovina, the most ethnically diverse of all the former Yugoslav republics, as ethnically based nationalism began to emerge in the late 1980s. Three of the five political parties contesting the first multi-party elections in Bosnia and Herzegovina at the end of 1990 were explicitly mono-ethnic and sought to appeal to 'their' respective ethnic communities. As moderates within them were sidelined and the three parties cooperated in undermining the two multiethnic parties, ethnic identification became increasingly important and eventually emerged as the dominant point of reference for most people living in Bosnia and Herzegovina. As with elections under the Habsburg Empire and in the 'first' Yugoslavia, these three ethnically defined parties carried most of the votes in the 1990 elections and the composition of the two chambers of parliament and of local assemblies accurately reflected census results.

It is important to emphasise again that the three ethno-nationalist parties continued to cooperate after the elections and that inter-ethnic tensions, inasmuch as they existed at all, were minor and did not involve any violence. Yet, as the conflict in the wider Yugoslavia escalated with the secession of Slovenia and the war in Croatia, the competing visions that each of the ethnic groups had for a future Bosnia and Herzegovina proved too much for the political structures just established in the republic. When attempts to rescue Yugoslavia, even in a territorially smaller and more decentralized version, failed, Croats and Muslims favoured independence for Bosnia and Herzegovina, whereas Serbs resisted it strongly. Fearing marginalization and discrimination, Serbs and Croats began to establish their own self-rule in areas in which they dominated numerically, thus pre-empting in some ways the subsequent territorial divisions of Bosnia and Herzegovina established in the Dayton Accords of 1995. When a referendum on 29 February and 1 March 1992, boycotted by Serbs, returned an almost 100 per cent majority in favour of independence the fate of Bosnia and Herzegovina was sealed. Within a period of only a few years, centuries of peaceful inter-ethnic relationships had been wiped out and a war was to begin in which atrocities would be committed unseen in Europe since the Second World War.

If anything, these two accounts enable us to understand how powerful a resource ethnicity can be in politics. Perhaps more importantly, they also highlight that ethnicity is not always the most relevant means by which people organize themselves in a society, or are categorized by others and, even if it is, that this need not cause bloodshed on the scale of the Rwandan genocide or the war in Bosnia and Herzegovina. As ethnicity, above all, means identity with one's own ethnic group—English, German, French, Kurd, Chechen, and so on—everyone has an ethnic identity. Yet, people have many other identities, too, as speakers of distinct languages, believers in different religions, professionals, members of certain age groups, men or women. In different contexts, different identities are more important—we are more aware of some than of others. Ethnicity acquires enormous power to mobilize people when it becomes a predominant identity and means more than just a particular ethnic origin; it comes to define people as speakers of a certain language, belonging to a particular religion, being able to pursue some careers but not others, being able to preserve and express their cultural heritage, having access to positions of power and wealth or not. In short, when ethnicity becomes politically relevant and determines the life prospects of people belonging to distinct ethnic groups, it is possible to mobilize group members to change a situation of apparently perpetual discrimination and disadvantage or in defence of a valued status quo.

Nationalism, on the other hand, is at the same time a narrower and a broader concept. At its most basic, it is an ideology that puts the nation first before all other forms of social or political organization. More to the point, however, nationalism has occurred, and continues to occur, in different varieties. Chechen, Kurdish, and Palestinian nationalisms are state seeking. Hutu nationalism in the mid-1990s in Rwanda, and German nationalism in the 1930s, manifested themselves in attempted genocide. Nationalism among Serbs, Croats, Bosnian Muslims, ethnic Albanians, and ethnic Macedonians in the Balkans had occasional genocidal tendencies, but was mostly aimed at building ethnically 'pure' homelands through what became infamously known as ethnic cleansing. All these types of nationalism are primarily ethnic based—that is, they define the nation in ethnic terms and exclude from it anyone who is not a member of the same ethnic group—by means of genocide, ethnic cleansing, disenfranchisement, and so on. Civic nationalism, in contrast, finds its expression in a definition of the nation on a territorial basis: everyone who is a citizen of France is French, albeit not necessarily in an ethnic or linguistic sense. Although not always as conflict prone as ethnic nationalism, civic nationalism may be discriminatory as well, if only in the sense that it does not acknowledge ethnic differences and thus potentially deprives members of ethnic communities other than a country's dominant group from opportunities to preserve, express, and develop their distinct identities.

Ethnicity and nationalism are not mutually exclusive concepts. In fact, there are only a few cases in which there are no clear links between the two. The USA, essentially an immigrant society, may be one of the few examples in which an overarching national identity exists almost completely independently from individuals' ethnic identity. This is not to say that ethnic identities, or some of their components, such as language or religion, do not matter. On the contrary, affirmative action programmes are perhaps the most obvious indication that ethnicity is politically relevant. However, different ethnic identities do not stop people from identifying themselves and others as 'fellow Americans'. This is obviously in stark contrast to the links between ethnicity and nationalism that made up the deadly compounds creating the conditions in which the Balkan wars of the 1990s, the genocide in Rwanda, and many other conflicts around the world have become possible. In order to understand why ethnicity and nationalism have this powerful capacity to mobilize people, we need to begin by taking a closer look at each of the two concepts in turn.

The origins of the term 'ethnicity' go back to the Greek word for nation—'ethnos'. In Ancient Greek this was used to describe a community of common descent[3]—in other words, 'ethnos' is used to describe a kinship group linked by ties of blood. The roots of the word, and even its original meaning, are widely agreed. Yet, because of its increasingly politicized nature, and the more contemporary meaning of ethnicity, and its implications for the relationships between people and between them and the states in which they live, definitions of ethnicity vary greatly and are hotly disputed among academics as well as among politicians. The definitional chaos that has engulfed the academic study of ethnicity and informed (and at times ill-informed) the public and policy debates on ethnicity and its political consequences may be intriguing in itself, but without a minimum of order it is not helpful to clarify what lies at the heart of ethnicity and if and how its core components relate to ethnic conflict. In order to achieve some clarity on these matters, it is useful to make some basic distinctions between different schools of thought on ethnicity. The so-called primordial school holds that ethnicity is so deeply ingrained in human history and experience that it cannot be denied that it exists, objectively and subjectively, and that it should therefore be considered a fact of life in the relations between individuals and groups who all have an ethnic identity. In contrast to this view, the instrumentalist school argues that ethnicity is by no means an indisputable historical fact. Rather, instrumentalists suggest that ethnicity is first and foremost a resource in the hands of leaders to mobilize and organize followers in the pursuit of other interests, such as physical security, economic gain, or political power.

What both schools agree on is that ethnicity has a number of tangible aspects, such as a common history, customs, traditions, language, or religion. These are important components of an individual's ethnic identity because they allow more easily the drawing of boundaries between those who belong to the same group and those who do not. In other words, these markers make it possible to establish differences not only between individuals, but also between groups. However, these are two distinct, albeit closely related, matters. It is one thing to determine whether I have the same ethnic identity as someone else; it is quite another thing to turn this into an issue of group membership, even more so if such group membership becomes socially, economically, and politically relevant. Thus, even though everyone has an ethnic identity, this does not mean that every aspect of people's lives has to be organized on the basis of ethnic in-groups and out-groups, or that access to jobs, education, and public office will be determined according to ethnic group membership. To organize society on such principles is a conscious and deliberate choice made by some and often accepted by many. Yet, even if we accept that tangible aspects of ethnicity exist, they cannot fully explain the phenomenon in relation to the intense emotions that 'ethnic issues' generate. We thus have to explore the issue of groups and group dynamics more in order to arrive at a satisfactory explanation.

Before 1871, there had never been a unified German state with a strong central government. A certain fiction of it—the Holy Roman Empire of the German Nation—had been kept alive for some 1,000 years, but its hollow nature, weakened by a multitude of disparate and conflicting particularistic interests, unable and unwilling to unite for a common cause, had been exposed by the defeat that it suffered at the hands of Napoleon in 1806. As so often in history, defeat marked the beginning of recovery, or more precisely of discovery. And this 'discovery' was of the common bonds that united all the people of a future Germany to be. The German Romantic movement, which had been around for some time, was now able to turn its cultural project of discovering what united all Germans—primarily language, culture, and descent—into a political project of self-determination. And thus the first modern ethno-nationalist movement was born not as an exclusive or racist one, bent on genocide or ethnic cleansing, but one with a truly liberal and liberational agenda: to defeat Napoleon and create a German nation-state in which rights of citizenship did not derive from a social status acquired at birth but from ethnic belonging. To be sure, the German Romantics defined Germany and the Germans probably as much in opposition to France and the French as they defined them on the basis of common cultural traits. Yet, while initially all Germans were meant to be equal citizens of this new state, much later some concluded, from the fact that Germans were a distinct ethnic group, that they were in fact more equal than others and many only too willingly believed this. When they did, they used a very specific interpretation of this Romantic view of the German nation to exclude from it everyone not deemed 'racially adequate'. In a frenzy of pseudo-scientific, and above all politically motivated, 'purification', German Jews in particular were singled out as 'alien' to the German nation, completely disregarding that they were probably the most assimilated of all Jews living in the diaspora and had contributed enormously to German economic and political power and to its cultural wealth as a nation. As a group, they were dissimilated and persecuted, and eventually an attempt was made to kill all of them in Germany and most other parts of Europe under German control.

The German case illustrates the extremes of the prevalent approach to defining an ethnic group—what its members have in common and what distinguishes them from others—commonly adopted by advocates of various 'national projects'. The typical 'us' versus 'them' requires activists to define the in-group both in itself and as opposed to the out-group. The more confrontational the definitions—that is, the more 'our' poor situation is a result of 'their' oppression, or the more superior 'we' are compared with 'them'—the more likely are inter-group relations to take a turn for the worse. The creation of such images among group members about themselves and others does not always stand at the beginning of a nationalist project. Rather, as the Holocaust, the Rwandan genocide, and the ethnic cleansing in the Balkans indicate, such negative images are more likely to be invoked at times when they appear politically convenient—in pursuit of an extreme racist agenda, in attempts to hold on to power, or during, and with the purpose of, the disintegration of multinational states.

The point about the earlier brief excursion into German history is not to single out Germans for inventing ethnonationalism and blaming them not only for driving the political implications of this doctrine to its genocidal extreme, but also for equipping extremists in other parts of the world from central Africa to the Balkans, to the Caucasus and to south-east Asia with an ideology that continues to wreak havoc. Rather, there are two important insights that we can gain from this exploration of German history. First, ethnic groups can be both self-defined—the German Romantics defining the German nation—and other defined—as in the case of the dissimilation of German Jews. Most commonly, self-definition and other-definition coexist. Second, ethnicity is only partly based on culture, myths of descent, historical memories, religion, customs, traditions, language, a specific homeland, or institutions; it is just as much based on what people believe, or are made to believe, to create a sense of solidarity among those who are members of a particular ethnic group, excluding, and at times directed against, those who are not.[4]

This link between tangible and intangible aspects is extremely important for understanding the political implications of ethnic identity and of the formation of conflict groups based on ethnicity. Tangible characteristics of ethnicity are important only inasmuch as they 'contribute to this notion or sense of a group's self-identity and uniqueness'.[5] In turn, then, a threat to, or opportunity for, these tangibles, real or perceived, is considered as a threat to, or opportunity for, self-identity and uniqueness. Confronting this threat or taking this opportunity leads to ethnicity being politicized—that is, to the ethnic group becoming a political actor by virtue of its shared ethnic identity. From this perspective, the debate between primordialists and instrumentalists over what ethnicity really is may very well be a false one altogether, and ethnic identity should perhaps rather be seen as something that has roots in a group's culture, and historical experiences and traditions, but that is also dependent upon contemporary opportunities that can be a useful instrument for mobilizing people for social, political, or economic purposes that may or may not be related directly to their ethnic origins.[6]

This convergence of past experiences and present opportunities manifests itself in the different claims that leaders of ethnic groups make, supposedly on their constituents' behalf. These are generally related to one or more of the following closely linked areas. At the broadest level, ethnic groups seek self-determination, a demand that is often, but not always correctly, equated with the desire for independent statehood: nationalism, defined in ethnic terms, seeking its fulfilment. Generally perceived as less threatening by the international community, but not necessarily more willingly granted by the state in question, some ethnic groups are content living as minorities in a given state, provided that their linguistic, religious, and cultural distinctiveness is respected and that they are granted adequate rights to preserve, express, and develop their identity in a society with a dominant culture that is not their own. In other cases again, ethnic groups are happy to assimilate into such a society and not stake any specific claims for rights related to their cultural, linguistic, or religious distinctiveness, but merely demand equality of opportunity. In other words, they want to be treated exactly the same as any other citizen and not experience any discrimination because of their distinct ethnic identity. Depending on their actual situation, ethnic groups make these claims vis-à-vis the state in which they live, vis-à-vis their kin-state or other kin-groups abroad, and vis-à-vis other external actors, such as international organizations and individual states which may be sought out and lobbied to assume a patron role.

Claims for self-determination by ethnic groups are often seen as the most threatening by states because they suggest, implicitly, that a particular group seeks to establish its own independent state. But this equation of self-determination with secession is questionable. Empirically, there is very little evidence that ethnic conflicts are about, or resolved by granting, independence. Outside the decolonialization context, which saw independent statehood granted to most of the colonial possessions of European powers such as Britain, France, Spain, Portugal, Belgium, and the Netherlands, the period since 1945 has seen only one other major wave of new state formations, namely in the aftermath of the collapse of communism. The dissolution of the Soviet Union and the so-called velvet divorce of Czechoslovakia were both consensual, whilst Yugoslavia disintegrated in a sequence of bloody wars. To be sure, there are other examples, too. Eritrea negotiated its secession from Ethiopia, after Eritrean and Ethiopian rebels jointly ousted the dictatorship of Mengistu Haile Mariam. East Timor, on the other hand, achieved its independence after Indonesia was forced to hold a referendum on the issue and to accept its results. East Timor may well have been the last but one case of decolonialization, with only Western Sahara, currently occupied by Morocco in contravention of international law, left to be resolved. Arguably, all of these cases had an ethnic or ethno-national dimension to them, but with the exception of the former Yugoslavia and East Timor, as well as Western Sahara, there was very little if any violent conflict involved that could be directly traced back to competing ethnic identities.

Furthermore, if we consider the vast range of other ethnic conflicts in which groups claim the right to self-determination, not all of them equate independent statehood with such claims, and in virtually none does the organized international community endorse unilateral declarations of independence or recognize entities controlled by ethnic groups as a result of their military strength as independent states. Thus, for example, the predominant position of the international community in Kosovo remains that further boundary changes are acceptable only if they are achieved consensually, and the so-called Turkish Republic of Northern Cyprus has not been recognized by any country other than Turkey. Despite this poor track record, in a number of cases ethnic groups demand outright independence, such as in Spain's Basque country, in Corsica, Kosovo, Chechnya, the Transdniestria region of Moldova, and Sri Lanka. Importantly, it is not always the case that all sections of a particular ethnic group share these demands, nor, as is evident in many other cases, is establishing a state of their own what ethnic groups actually desire. Although they may still seek a greater level of self-determination, many such claims stop short of demands for independence and rather seek higher degrees of autonomy within the boundaries of an existing state. This is true, for example, for the Chittagong Hill people in Bangladesh, for tribal people in Burma, for the Tripuras, Bodos, and Nagas in India's Assam province, for Uighurs in China's Xinjiang province, for Moros in the Mindanao region of the Philippines, for the Casamance region of Senegal, and for the Miskito Indians in Nicaragua. All of these groups are united by one specific feature that often makes them look like a particular threat to governments: they live in compact settlements, often in their traditional homelands, and frequently in peripheral regions. Thus, even if their demands are 'only' for greater autonomy, governments tend to see this as the beginning of a slippery slope towards independence and thus a serious threat to the territorial integrity of what they consider, rightly or wrongly, their state.

Take the example of Indonesia. After the fall of its long-term military dictator Suharto on 21 May 1998, the new Indonesian government bowed to long-standing international pressure and agreed to hold a referendum in East Timor in which the population could decide on whether to remain part of Indonesia or become an independent state. Illegally occupied since 1975, the territory had been subjected to fierce fighting between government forces and rebels, killing close to a quarter of a million people over three decades. East Timor, however, has not been the only independence-minded province of the world's largest Muslim country. Thus, acceding to East Timor's demands was a risky strategy for Indonesia, and in the wake of the referendum in 1999 violence not only escalated there but in other parts of Indonesia as well, most notably in Aceh. Yet, rather than seeking long-term accommodation with other separatist groups, the Indonesian government relied on the use of force, and the collapse of a peace deal with the Free Aceh Movement in 2003 seemed to confirm, in the eyes of the government in Jakarta, that violent repression is the only viable strategy to keep the ethnically highly diverse country together. In the wake of the tsunami disaster in December 2004, there was quite considerable movement on both sides and it seemed that negotiations on a peaceful resolution could be resumed.

Yet, between these two options of independence and bloody repression, illustrated by the two extremes of East Timor and Aceh, there is no dearth of conflict resolution options available to governments and ethnic groups in such similar situations. The key is for individual leaders to recognize and use the opportunities that exist for settling their differences without recourse to violence. Weighing, and shaping, present opportunities in the context of the past experiences of an ethnic group is a responsibility that leaders in situations of potential or actual ethnic conflict cannot simply abdicate. The fact that ethnic identity has its roots in the past and present is thus a curse as well as a blessing. People cannot escape the fact that ethnic differences exist, but what they make of these differences is in their hands, and those of their leaders.

Not all ethnic groups are in a situation in which independent statehood or increased autonomy within an existing state is a possible or desirable option. They may be impossible, or at least difficult, to achieve because members of the group live dispersed across the state's territory. They may seem undesirable because group members are relatively well integrated into the social, political, and economic life of the country in which they live. In neither situation, however, does this imply complete cultural assimilation. Even a well-integrated ethnic minority may take pride in the preservation of its cultural heritage, wish to pass it on to following generations, and be able to express its ethno-cultural distinctiveness without fear of discrimination. This then leads to demands for specific linguistic, religious, or cultural rights that allow members of the ethnic group to do just that. The development of often-extensive minority rights legislation, which recognizes and protects difference, has helped avoid violent conflict in a number of countries. This is very obvious if we consider a number of recent examples in the European context. Not only are there international instruments such as the Council of Europe's Framework Convention on Minority Rights and the Charter for Regional or Minority Languages, but countries like Slovenia and Hungary, and to a lesser extent Slovakia, Poland, Romania, Bulgaria, and the three Baltic states have gone to some lengths to accommodate minority demands for linguistic, religious, or cultural rights.

Even more widespread, and more easily conceded, are demands for equal access to resources and equality of opportunity for members of ethnic minorities, in short for non-discrimination on ethnic grounds. Laws banning discrimination are commonplace in most democratic states, but even there they are often difficult to enforce outside the public sphere. Take the example of the Roma minorities in central and eastern Europe. Despite attempts by governments, non-governmental organizations (NGOs), and international organizations to address the often desperate social and economic situation of Roma in countries such as Bulgaria, Romania, Slovakia, the Czech Republic, and Hungary, their efforts often fail because of widespread social prejudice that penetrates all levels of state and society, including the police, social services, and the education system. Existing prejudice becomes a self-fulfilling prophecy: the state fails in its duty to provide public services, minority groups see their perception of discrimination confirmed and disengage or try to force the issue, whilst majorities feel confirmed in their belief that minorities are essentially 'enemies of the state' who do not deserve any special rights.

The test for non-discrimination legislation as well as for specific laws on minority rights is not merely their existence in the statute book, but the degree to which they are implemented and meaningful in everyday life. Where they fail this litmus test, demands are likely to increase and the means with which their realization is sought can easily escalate. This also means that the nature of demands made by ethnic groups is not necessarily an indicator of the strength and cohesiveness of the ethnic identity of group members, but rather a reflection of the degree of threat under which group identity is perceived to be. Current perceptions and past experiences often function as an escalator in this context—the worse a group's historical experience within a particular state and the more threatening current state policies are perceived to be to the identity of the group and its members, the more likely will demands be high and the means with which they are realized be indiscriminate, including violence. In the Chechen conflict, so-called Black Widows—young female suicide bombers—have become more common only since the escalation of violence in this restive region of Russia as a result of which large numbers of civilians were killed by Russian armed forces in a conflict in which hardliners on both sides insist on the realization of their maximum demands, independence, and subordination under Moscow's rule, respectively. In contrast, other regions in Russia, such as Dagestan, Tatarstan, and Bashkiria, have managed to negotiate extensive autonomy arrangements with Moscow satisfying the regions' concerns, and violence has consequently been largely absent. A long tradition of accommodation and by-and-large peaceful dispute resolution has so far prevented violent escalations in Canada over the issue of Quebec and in Belgium, where stakes are equally high, including some secessionist demands. By the same token, and even though there was sporadic violence, demands of French speakers in Switzerland's predominantly German-speaking Bern canton, after a struggle that lasted over 30 years and, which also had socioeconomic dimensions, led to the formation of a new Jura canton in 1978. None of this can be taken to suggest that the degree of violence with which ethnic claims are pursued corresponds to the strength of ethnic identity that a particular group feels. Rather, it emphasizes that there is no automatism that leads from the existence of ethnic differences to violent conflict between different groups or between groups and the state. In other words, the existence of different ethnic identities within the same state is not a problem in itself; it is what people—leaders as well as their followers—make of it that determines whether claims based on such different identities can be accommodated peacefully or whether they will lead to bloody civil wars.

There is one additional issue that, although it can be a prominent feature of ethnic identity and almost always overlaps to some extent with ethnicity, needs to be considered for a better understanding of inter-ethnic relations—territory. Its significance stems from the fact that it can be used as a defining criterion in relation to citizenship rights and identities, the basis of political entities from states, to regions and local communities, and a potent source of mass mobilization in the form of regionalism and nationalism. All these functions can also be performed by ethnicity, and often territorial components form a significant dimension of ethnic identities, primarily in the form of actual, and sometimes mythical, homelands to which a given ethnic group traces its origins. Nevertheless, it is important to distinguish between ethnicity and territory as key factors in the dynamics of interethnic relations.

For states and ethnic groups alike, territory possesses certain values in and of itself. These include ownership of natural resources, such as water, iron, coal, oil, or gas; they extend to the goods and services produced by the population living in this territory, and they can comprise military or strategic advantages in terms of natural boundaries, access to the open sea, and control over terrestrial transport routes and waterways, as well as communication channels. Thus, throughout history wars have been fought over territories; territories have changed hands as a result of wars and new wars have arisen as a consequence of that. Yet, all of that took place largely without consideration of the people living in these territories, and it was only with the advent of nationalism that the issues of state, nation, and territory became linked. True, there are some early examples from Europe of peace treaties and territorial settlements in which, to use modern terminology, minority rights provisions were included. These include the Treaty of Perpetual Union between the King of France and the Helvetic state (1516), the Peace of Westphalia (1648), and the Final Act of the Congress of Vienna (1815). But, by and large, concern for the populations living in the territories that the Great Powers used to maintain a basic balance of power in Europe was not very high on the agenda of diplomats. Nor should it necessarily have been, given that notions of national identity, especially in its ethnic variety, began to emerge more broadly only in the course of the nineteenth century. Once they did, however, they became powerful forces to dominate not only European power politics throughout the 'long nineteenth century', which effectively ended only with the post-First World

War peace settlements, but also far beyond and into the post-Cold War world order.

The European vision of the territorial nation state was also superimposed on other parts of the world, recreating many of the problems of incompatible political and ethnic borders that Europe had experienced itself. And just as European states were unable, or unwilling, to resolve the resulting conflicts peacefully through accommodation, so the states modelled in the European image during the decolonialization process in Asia and Africa found it difficult to provide security, liberty, and prosperity to all their citizens on an equal basis. Some, like India, managed this process relatively more successfully and experienced less conflict; others like Pakistan and Nigeria, for example, had to go through prolonged and bloody civil wars to establish credible sovereign institutions, albeit with quite different outcomes: West Pakistan, now Bangladesh, asserted its independence (after an Indian military intervention), while the Nigerian central government prevailed in the secessionist conflict with the northern state of Biafra and maintained the country's territorial integrity.

As a result of the significance of territory as a symbol of individual and collective identities, its political, economic, and social importance for the constitution of states, and its strategic value as a source of control and influence, states and ethnic groups alike make claims to territories that they consider essential from any one of these perspectives. Some claims to territory are justified with reference to history. Albanians in Kosovo see themselves as descendants of the ancient Ilyrian people who first settled in this area. But Albanians and Serbs also both employ more recent history: the cradle of the Serbian Orthodox church is said to be Pec in western Kosovo, whilst the birthplace of the Albanian national movement is Prizren in the south. Some Israeli Jews, on the other hand, rely on a different kind of history and cite the divine rights that they have to the land of Israel according to the Bible. Settlers and colonists, to give a third example, often justify their claims to territory in disputes with indigenous groups, or 'first nations', by referring to their own cultural superiority or to that of their methods of production and exploitation. In this reading, claims to territory are legitimate if claimants can prove that they use, and use better, the resources that the disputed territory has, be they agricultural, mineral, water, and so on.[7]

Regardless of these or any other reasons given in their justification, territorial claims can occur in different guises. They can be secessionist, irredentist, or autonomist. Secessionism is best understood as the political movement of an ethnic group that hopes to succeed in establishing an independent state of its own on the territory on which it lives. This has been the pattern of demands across much of the Balkans and the Caucasus. In contrast to such a group-based movement, irredentism is primarily a state-based movement that seeks to enlarge its own territory by laying claim to territories in neighbouring states, which are normally inhabited by members of the same ethnic group. In the case of Serb irredentism in relation to Serb-inhabited areas of Croatia and Bosnia and Herzegovina, irredentism and secessionism went hand in hand. Abkhaz and South Ossetian desires to secede from Georgia and unite with Russia were predominantly driven by the secessionists, with little if any irredentist desires on the part of Moscow. In contrast, the Armenian 'national project' comfortably accommodates secessionism in Nagorno-Karabakh and irredentist demands within Armenia to this part of the territory of neighbouring Azerbaijan.

Among territorial claims, the demand for autonomy is the only one that does not seek changes to existing international boundaries, but expresses the desire of a particular ethnic group to gain a measure of self-governance within its homeland, which it recognises to be part of an existing state. In some cases, this is chosen as a second-best option by ethnic groups who recognize that their claims to independent statehood are unlikely to be fulfilled or who realise that their ability to survive as an independent state or to provide essential services to their citizens would be limited. In addition, because of its less 'disruptive' impact on the existing system of states, the international community has long since been an advocate of autonomy as a viable compromise between existing states and some of the ethnic groups living within them. This is reflected, for example, in the Dayton constitution for Bosnia and Herzegovina, in the settlement reached in Moldova between ethnic Moldovans and the Gagauz minority in the country, and in the agreement between the Sudanese government in Khartoum and the rebels in the south of the country.

Disputed territories can thus simultaneously be a phenomenon of inter-state, inter-ethnic, and group-state relations. What is important to note in this context is that inter-group relations must be conceived of more broadly than the traditional pattern of minority–majority relations when territorial aspects are considered. Quite often, disputed territories are inhabited by members of more than one ethnic group with an interest and opportunity structures in relation to the territory in question, which are most likely to be different and thus have the potential to spark further ethnic conflicts. Take the example of so-called 'orphans of secession'—ethnic groups that find themselves on the wrong side of the border after changes to international boundaries.[8] The unilateral declarations of independence by Croatia and Bosnia and Herzegovina, and their subsequent international recognition, sparked serious fears among the two countries' Serb populations about their future. Manipulated by nationalist leaders on all sides, these fears quickly escalated and violence ensued leading to all-out war among Serbia, Croatia, and Bosnia and Herzegovina.

Cyprus is a similarly instructive example concerning the significance of ethnic and territorial claims and the dynamics to which they give rise. Here, a coup attempt in 1974, instigated and supported by the then military regime in Greece, was aimed at over-throwing the Cypriot President, Archbishop Makarios, and bringing about the unification of Cyprus with Greece. With a recent history of inter-ethnic violence between Greek and Turkish Cypriots that was barely contained by a fragile and eventually collapsing power-sharing regime, Turkish Cypriots would have suddenly found themselves an even smaller minority in a Greek state that, even as a democracy, let alone a military dictatorship, had a poor record of minority protection. Subsequent events were heavily influenced by the different interpretations of the Treaty of

Guarantee signed by Greece, Turkey, and the former colonial power Great Britain, which had backed the power-sharing settlement to end the civil war in Cyprus in 1960. Article 1 clearly stated that the Republic of Cyprus would ensure the maintenance of its independence, not participate in any political or economic union with any other state, and prohibit all activity promoting either such unification or partition of the island. In Article 2, Greece, Turkey, and the UK recognized and guaranteed the independence and territorial integrity of Cyprus, and assured each other that they, too, would prohibit any attempt to change the sovereign status of Cyprus. Crucially, Article 3 provided that, in case of any breach of these provisions, the three guarantor powers would seek to take joint action to restore that status quo. However, each of the three states also reserved the right in Article 3 to take unilateral action if no common position could be achieved. Thus, the Greek-backed coup against Archbishop Makarios was a clear infringement of the Treaty by both Greek Cypriots and the Greek military junta, and Turkey was arguably in its rights under the Treaty of Guarantee to invade the island in an attempt to restore the democratically elected government of Cyprus. However, what followed the invasion was also in clear breach of the Treaty—Turkish forces occupied a large part of the island, massive ethnic cleansing on both sides created two ethnically almost completely homogeneous parts of the island, and the introduction of a UN peace-keeping force and subsequent creation of the Turkish Republic of Northern Cyprus, recognized only by Turkey, effectively partitioned Cyprus. Although these events in 1974 have spelled an end to ethnic conflict on the island, they have not resolved any of the underlying issues that led to it in the first place, nor have they done anything to mitigate the political significance of ethnic identity in the relations between the two main groups on the island. Ethnicity and territory remain the main focus of each group's identity and it has been impossible to achieve any breakthrough in negotiations over nearly three decades because so far no formula has been found that can simultaneously accommodate both groups' ethnic and territorial claims.

In both of these cases—Cyprus and the former Yugoslavia—the

significance of territory lies primarily in its symbolic and historical importance for the relevant groups' ethnic identities, regardless of the extent to which claims match up with the historical record, and in the groups' expectations if sovereignty over their homeland changes to a different state. A Croatia without Eastern Slavonia and Krajina was unthinkable for most Croats, whereas local Serbs feared repression and forced assimilation if they became part of an independent Croatian state and were deprived of the protection of a central government in Belgrade. Kosovo has great historical significance for Serbs and Albanians alike, yet local Serbs are fearful of minority status in an independent Kosovo, although it is equally impossible for most Kosovo Albanians to accept Belgrade's sovereignty again. Turkish Cypriots, and Turkey as a guarantee power, were unwilling to accept the prospect of the island's unification with Greece, whereas Greek Cypriots are unable to contemplate partition. Similar cases exist elsewhere in Europe and Asia. Abkhaz and South Ossetians in Georgia are almost classic examples of orphans of secessions. Georgian independence exposed them to growing majority nationalism in the newly independent state of Georgia without the balancing protection of Moscow—hence their desire to remain part of Russia. In the South Ossetian case, separation from their ethnic brethren in North Ossetia was an additional factor that made being part of Georgia rather unattractive. The dynamics of the conflict in and over Nagorno-Karabakh are almost identical. Azeris consider the area an integral part of Azerbaijan, and to hold on to it, or at least to the hope of restoring their country's territorial integrity, has become one of the most important components of an Azerbaijani (ethno-)national identity. Armenians, on the other hand, point to the fact that the area is predominantly Armenian in its ethnic make-up, even more so after a sustained period of ethnic cleansing and homogenization, and should therefore be considered part of an Armenian territorial state. In the disputed territory of Kashmir, partitioned among India, Pakistan, and China, a local conflict between Hindus and Muslims is overshadowed by the rivalry between India and Pakistan.

Yet, there are also a number of cases in which claims to territory are less related to its symbolic value or to the consequences of changes in sovereignty, but more related to the material value of territory. Take the example of the Niger Delta. Since the early 1990s, there has been constant conflict in this region of Nigeria that is the source of most of the country's oil wealth, killing around 1,000 people per year. There are over seven million people who live in the region, belonging to five main ethnic groups. These groups are variously in conflict with oil multinationals, including Chevron, ExxonMobil, and Shell, over land and compensation for environmental damage, with the government over the share that they receive in their homeland's oil wealth, and with each other over land ownership of oil exploitation areas.

Although the case of the Niger Delta may seem rather complex in its amalgamation of ethnic and territorial claims, domestic politics, and international business, it pales in comparison to the war in the so-called Democratic Republic of Congo (DRC). Involving seven nations, and therefore often described as Africa's first 'world war', at least three million people have died, most of them civilians and most of them from preventable and curable diseases and starvation, rather than as a direct consequence of the fighting. More than another two million people have been displaced from their homes within the DRC or in neighbouring countries, many of whom have no access to any outside humanitarian assistance. The fighting that broke out in 1998 was temporarily halted by the Lusaka peace agreement of 1999, which finally collapsed with the assassination of then DRC president Laurent Kabila in 2001. Angola, Zimbabwe, and Namibia have since then supported the Congolese government under Joseph Kabila, who succeeded his father in the same year, against rebels who were backed by the governments of Uganda and Rwanda—themselves both former allies of Kabila—and Burundi.

The reasons that have brought different countries into this war are complex. Rwanda, for example, has had intermittently up to 20,000 troops in the DRC, officially claiming to secure its borders against incursions by Hutu militias who, after carrying out most of the massacres in the 1994 Rwandan genocide, fled to the eastern

DRC. Yet, this significant troop presence and the limited capacity of the Congolese state to assert its authority across the entirety of this territory also enabled the Rwandan army to take control of diamond mines and precious mineral resources. All other major players, including the government of the DRC itself, also have economic interests related to the country's rich resource base, comprising, among others, water, diamonds, coltan (a rare mineral used in computers and mobile phones), tin, copper, and timber. As in the Niger Delta, competition over land and the resources that it holds extends beyond the level of the states involved to local ethnic groups, creating constantly shifting alliances between these groups and their external backers to maximize the profits of economic exploitation.[9]

The war in the DRC has all the hallmarks of so-called new wars that became prevalent in the 1990s and show remarkable similarities with the events in the former Yugoslavia and many other contemporary ethnic conflicts: the targeting of civilians with killing, torture, and rape; disruption of humanitarian assistance; widespread looting and pillage during incursions of 'enemy' territory; and ethnic cleansing, albeit the last following an agenda aimed at resource exploitation rather than the territorial aggrandizement of a mythical ethnic homeland. Foreign powers, such as Rwanda and Uganda, have thus deliberately promoted inter-ethnic conflicts in the eastern DRC and the accompanying mass killings as a means of maintaining their control over economically valuable territory.

What emerges from this discussion is that a combination of ethnic and territorial claims seems a particularly explosive mix for the occurrence of violent ethnic conflict. In other words, where groups have clearly formed ethnic identities that are in part based on claims to the same stretch of territory, violent escalation of their disputes over rights and self-determination is more likely. This is also borne out if we look at cases in which conflict was averted or settled. For example, the conflict in and over Papua New Guinea's Bougainville province was settled once the conflict parties agreed on a formula that detached ethnic from territorial claims and postponed a final resolution of the claim to independent statehood, which part of the Bougainvillians had made, to a referendum after a period of 10 to 15 years of substantive autonomy within Papua New Guinea. Similar strategies have been applied in Northern Ireland and in Moldova in relation to Gagauzia. In Northern Ireland, the population north and south of the border between the two parts of the island, created as a result of a unilateral partition in 1920, were asked to approve a settlement in 1998, creating new structures of government within Northern Ireland that provided for fair power sharing between the regions' two main communities, as well as new arrangements between Northern Ireland and the Republic of Ireland and between the Republic and the UK and its constituent parts. In addition, and this is the crucial point, the agreement of 1998 also provides a mechanism by which, at regular intervals, the population will be consulted on changes to the state border now existing on the island. Should a majority decide in favour of a change—that is, in favour of Irish reunification—both governments in London and Dublin have committed themselves to accepting such an outcome and facilitating the necessary constitutional changes. The option for a change of existing international borders is also part of the deal struck between Moldova and its Gagauz minority. In exchange for Gagauz acceptance of Moldovan sovereignty, the minority gained a significant measure of autonomy from the government in Chisinau and the option to hold a referendum on independence should Moldova ever decide to unite with Romania, a country with which a majority population of Moldovans share a common ethnic identity and a history of common statehood. In the north–south peace deal in Sudan, concluded in January 2005 after a 30-year civil war, a similar provision was included: after six years, during which both conflict parties commit themselves to working genuinely towards making the agreed autonomy regime work, there will be a referendum on independence to be held in the southern states, the result of which will be accepted by the government in Khartoum and its erstwhile opponents in the south.

Another way of looking at the links between ethnicity and territory is through the spectrum of nationalism. Most commonly, nationalism is seen as an ideology that advocates that each nation should have its own state. Yet, this is not the whole story of nationalism. First of all, nationalism embodies the desire to gain political power for a group that believes that it constitutes a nation. This power is then used to gain or preserve the ability of the group to shape its own future, express, preserve, and develop its identity, and maintain its unity. Informed by the principle of self-determination, national movements make claims on behalf of people. Yet, the implications of these claims are very often of a territorial nature—at one end of the spectrum demands are raised for local or regional autonomy and, at the other, secessionist movements become active or irredentist policies are pursued.

Nationalism is not necessarily tied to ethnicity. From this perspective, we could distinguish between civic and ethnic varieties of nationalism. This differentiation often goes hand in hand with a moral judgement—civic nationalism is deemed to be more virtuous and liberal, whereas ethnic nationalism is generally seen as dangerous and exclusive. French nationalism is often considered as the prime example of civic nationalism: all citizens of the Republic are French, regardless of their ethnic, cultural, religious, or linguistic background, and have the same rights and responsibilities. The state is, so to speak, blind to difference in allocating resources and everyone is treated the same by virtue of being a citizen. The other side of the medal, however, is that such an approach does not recognize difference and, in fact, denies that existing differences are in any way politically relevant. This classically liberal approach advocates the minimal and, in a broader sense, secular state, where everyone is equal in the public sphere, and where religion, language, ethnicity, etc., are a strictly private matter. Yet, this alleged egalitarian approach is open to question. Civic nationalism by default advantages majority cultures: their language, traditions, customs become 'official' whereas those of minorities are relegated to the private sphere, and it is the responsibility and choice of individuals whether or not they want to maintain certain aspects of their identity that 'diverge' from the national identity, which, although defined as civic, is in fact nothing but the majority's ethnic identity writ large. Civic nationalism thus has some very strong assimilationist and possibly exclusivist tendencies. Despite claims to the contrary, these can easily lead to ethnic conflict, as the example of Corsica in France demonstrates. As a result of the difficulty that civic nationalism has with the recognition of difference, such conflicts are hard to resolve as successive French governments have experienced when attempts to grant Corsica greater autonomy were struck down by the French Constitutional Council.

Ethnic nationalism traces its origins back to the German Romantic movement and philosophers like Herder and Fichte. At a time when modern nation states did not yet exist in central and eastern Europe, cultural markers, and particularly language, were seen as the embodiment of a people's 'essence'. Struggling to overcome the particularism that had divided Germany into some 200 principalities, counties, and kingdoms with a weak central power, the German Romantics of the late eighteenth and early nineteenth centuries were hardly racist in their views, but had a political agenda of state-seeking nationalism built on ethno-cultural distinctions. Although ethnic nationalism may thus be founded on the very recognition of difference that civic nationalism denies, it is not necessarily a better or a worse kind of nationalism. In many ways it is both better and worse at the same time. It is worse in that it is far less accommodating of difference because it often does not allow for equality in the public sphere and discriminates against members of ethnic groups other than the dominant group because they are different. The twentieth century is full of the extremes to which this form of nationalism can be taken: from the Holocaust of the Jews and the organized extermination of Roma by the Nazis to the ethnic cleansing in the 1990 Balkan wars and the Rwandan genocide and to the Apartheid system in South Africa. On the other hand, the recognition of difference can be the first step to address the consequences of difference and thus mitigate their potentially dangerous impact on multi-ethnic societies. Minority rights legislation, autonomy and federal arrangements, and many complex forms of power sharing have been instituted to do just that. Canada, Switzerland, Belgium, Spain, India, Nigeria, and South Africa are all ethnically diverse societies with often very deep splits on the basis of language, religion, and other ethnic 'markers' that have attempted, and in many cases succeeded, to restore and preserve inter-ethnic peace and stability by recognizing difference and managing it in a respectful and meaningful way.

This discussion about the different varieties of nationalism also raises another question, namely about the primacy of ethnicity and nationalism. This can be looked at from two perspectives. Which of the two came first? And which of the two is politically more important? The first of these two questions is the one that can be answered more easily, and in a sense more definitively. Historically, ethnic groups precede nations. In fact, nations are often nothing but state-seeking or state-controlling ethnic groups. Thus, the key distinction between ethnic groups and nations lies in their relationship to the state. Nations, by definition, require a state to fulfil their potential; ethnic groups do not and historically have not. This is not to say that ethnic groups have always existed or that the make-up of their identity does not change over time. If we assume that some components of ethnic identity are 'objective', such as language, cultural traditions, and religion, then we have to accept that these exist independently of the group's awareness of them. In this sense, one could argue that ethnic groups exist whether or not they know it. It is then up to individuals to 'awaken' their fellow group members to the fact that they share certain characteristics with each other but not with other people. In this way, ethnic identities are as much created as they are based on objectively identifiable, if often small, differences between groups of people. The subjective element within ethnic identities—the perception that people have of differences that matter and those that do not—allows for a certain degree of fluidity of group membership. Ethnic identities change over time and so do the criteria of group membership and vice versa. In this fluidity of boundaries, ethnic groups are in no way different from nations, regardless of whether they are ethnically defined or adhere to some notion of civic identity. Yet, in the same way in which ethnic groups and nations are distinguishable from each other in their relationship to the state, so their political relevance can be determined, at least in the contemporary world of nation states. Ethnicity does not have to matter politically; nationalism always does. Different ethnic identities can, and in many cases do, peacefully coexist in the same state; different nationalisms cannot. The former Yugoslavia is a case in point. Since the country was founded at the end of the First World War—as the Kingdom of Serbs, Croats, and Slovenes—there has never been a dispute between its constituent groups about the fact that they had very different ethnic identities: language distinguished Slovenes from Croats and Serbs, the use of the Cyrillic rather than Latin alphabet set Serbs apart from Croats and Slovenes, religion was a marker on the basis of which one could differentiate Croats and Serbs, and so on. Yet this recognition of ethnic difference did not prevent the emergence of an overarching sense of national identity as Yugoslavs—in some ways 'facilitated' by the suppression of ethnically based nationalism, in others genuinely growing out of intermarriage or a belief in the Yugoslav project. It was only when political leaders invoked ethnic nationalism to create or consolidate their own powerbase that the unity of the state was threatened and ultimately destroyed: temporarily during the Second World War under German and Italian 'tutelage', and permanently in the aftermath of the Cold War. The success of multi-ethnic states is thus predicated on their ability to prevent the emergence of state-seeking nationalisms among their constituent groups—a resounding and unquestionable success in the USA and Switzerland, a clear failure in the cases of Yugoslavia, the Soviet Union, and Czechoslovakia. Other cases are more ambivalent: Quebec may yet decide to secede from Canada; Belgium may, at some point, dissolve. Only constant, and successful, renegotiations between ethnic groups and between them and the state have been able to keep the two states together. In other cases, secession or state disintegration has been stopped only through brutal repression of secessionist movements: Chechnya, Sri Lanka and Indonesia spring to mind as contemporary cases, as do India, Burma, Bangladesh, Nigeria, and Sudan, which all have past and present track records of using force in defending their territorial integrity.

What is thus essentially at stake for ethnic groups is political, economic, and social participation in, and at times control of, the state in which they live. The modern state is, for the most part, a nation state—that is, a state that normally has one dominant ethnic group in which other such groups do or do not have certain rights. Although some may dispute on moral grounds that the nation-state is the best form of political organization of peoples and territories, it remains the predominant one and is coveted by majorities and minorities alike. This may be so, but we should not overlook the fact that the very idea of the nation state is built upon the fiction of either ethnic homogeneity or the willing acceptance by ethnic minorities of living in a state that is not 'theirs'. The more the state is contested in its particular existence—its territorial extent and the people whom it does or does not include—the higher the risk of conflict. For some time now, many ethnic Albanians in Kosovo found it difficult to accept living in the same state as Serbs and that large numbers of their ethnic cousins remain in southern Serbia or Macedonia. As a consequence, demands for Kosovo's independence persist, even more strongly after five years of limbo status under UN administration, irredentist claims to Albanian communities in the south of Serbia and the west of Macedonia are occasionally quite seriously voiced, and the return of Serb refugees from Kosovo remains, at best, very difficult to achieve. Thus, while the modern nation state remains by and large the undisputed form of political organization in the contemporary world, it is in some ways more likely to create problems than to resolve them. Of course, the state in itself is not the problem. It is merely a set of institutions that exist over time and are used to exert control over people and territory—that is, to uphold state sovereignty and maintain territorial integrity. Although sovereignty is a right of states, inasmuch as they can be a holder of rights, it has more recently also been interpreted as a responsibility. States need to provide their citizens above all with security—physical, but also economic, social, environmental, etc. These services, of course, should normally extend to all citizens regardless of ethnic identity. Many multi-ethnic states have gone to great lengths to ensure equality of all their citizens in all walks of life—by recognizing differences and making provisions in law and policy so that difference does not result in discrimination. Complex power sharing and self-governance regimes, including federal solutions, minority rights systems, non-discrimination legislation, and many more measures already discussed above prove the ability of states to accommodate different ethnic groups.

At the same time, however, states may also serve as instruments to ensure the dominance of one ethnic group and enable it to retain its leaders' grip on power. Apartheid in South Africa, segregation in some of the southern states of the USA, the dominance of Protestant Unionists in Northern Ireland for half a century after the partition of the island of Ireland in 1920, and the implicit and explicit discrimination that ethnic minorities in Israel, Kurds in Turkey, and Tamils in Sri Lanka face in their daily lives illustrates the different degrees to which the state can be abused by dominant groups. Importantly, too, we should note that democracies are not immune from such tendencies.

Where does this leave us in our story of ethnic conflict? Perhaps the best way to sum up the discussion so far is to accept that ethnic identity, after all, remains a fact of life. However, we also need to acknowledge that it is what people make of it and how they use it that decides whether there is ethnic conflict or not.

3

What causes ethnic conflicts?

The province of Bougainville in Papua New Guinea comprises two large islands—Buka and Bougainville—as well as a number of smaller groups of islands, and hosts a population of a little more than 150,000 people. It is one of the country's most remote provinces, being located some 600 miles from Port Moresby, the capital of Papua New Guinea. Although Bougainvilleans can be broadly characterized as Melanesians, unlike the rest of Papua New Guinea's citizens they bear an unmistakable mark of distinction from them in that the colour of their skin is much darker. Easily insulted and discriminated against because of this, Bougainvilleans share this trait with the inhabitants of the Solomon Islands, a country barely 15 miles to the south of Bougainville. Although this suggests a degree of distinctiveness that sets Bougainvilleans apart from the rest of Papua New Guineans, it is not the only reason for the ethnic conflict that escalated into violence in the late 1980s and took a decade to resolve.

The communities that make up Papua New Guinea today have only a weak, if any, sense of shared national identity. Made up of some 700 linguistic groups within a population of only about five million people, Papua New Guinea is highly fragmented. In addition to distinct linguistic identities, regional identification also plays a significant role, often cutting across language groups, and vice versa. The reason for this amazing diversity lies in the colonial imposition of territorial structures on disparate communities that had existed separately from each other for centuries. Just as in Africa, the arbitrary nature of the resulting boundaries had its source in the strength and reach of the colonial powers rather than in any broader consideration of the wishes of the indigenous population. Thus, the eastern half of the island of New Guinea was divided between Germany and Britain in 1885. In the twentieth century, Australia gradually took over as the administrative power. The UK transferred its half of the island in 1902, and the Australians occupied the remaining portion during the First World War. When Papua New Guinea became a trust territory, Australia continued to administer both areas jointly until 1975.

Already during the period of the trusteeship, Bougainville's economic, social, and political development was neglected. There was little investment on the part of the Australian government, who even 'outsourced' the establishment of schools to missionaries. Unsurprisingly, Bougainvilleans became increasingly frustrated and calls for the independence of their islands began to emerge in the early 1960s. Although the demand for independence was not universally and equally shared among all Bougainvilleans—some were happy to settle for autonomy within Papua New Guinea—from the mid-1960s onwards, one particular development acted as a catalyst to unite them into a strong ethno-nationalist movement. This was the arrival of an Australian mining company in 1964, which, after a successful exploration, established the world's largest open-pit copper and gold mine. Shares were split 80:20 between the mining company and the government of Papua New Guinea; the owners of the land on which the mine was built were compensated with only small royalties. Added to the environmental damage from the mine's operation, traditional Bougainvillean cultural and social life was also disrupted by settlers from mainland Papua New Guinea who were brought in as labourers. Further consolidated by the murder of two Bougainvillean civil servants, the ethno-nationalist movement among Bougainvilleans became focused on secession as the only solution to their plight. When attempts by moderate Bougainvillean leaders to establish a far-reaching autonomy regime within Papua New Guinea failed before the country's independence in 1975, Bougainville unilaterally declared its own independence on 1 September 1975, two weeks before the official date set for Papua New Guinea to become an independent state. Neither the government in Port Moresby nor any other government around the world recognized the Bougainvillean declaration of independence. The central government subsequently dissolved the provincial government in Bougainville and began to withhold Bougainville's share of the mining profits. By June 1976 the situation escalated—Bougainvilleans attacked and destroyed government offices on the island; the central government responded by sending in riot police. Further escalation into all-out civil war, however, could be prevented by direct negotiations between Bougainvillean leaders and the central government, leading to the restoration of the provincial government. More than 10 years passed, without any major incident, but also without any substantial improvements in the situation for the Bougainvilleans—environmental degradation accelerated, tensions between indigenous people and settlers continued, no adequate compensation was paid to Bougainvilleans, and no real investment was made into the islands' development. A new generation of Bougainvilleans was less and less willing to put up with this situation, and became more aggressive in its demands and means. When their representations did not lead anywhere either, they decided to attack the mining company and its employees directly in 1988. The crisis escalated further when, in early 1989, tit-for-tat killings between Bougainvilleans and settlers spiralled out of control and into several days of riots. As the central government brought in troops, Bougainvillean opponents of the mine organized themselves into the so-called Bougainville Revolutionary Army, and a 10-year civil war ensued, killing thousands of civilians.

When the conflict in Bougainville had been all but settled in the late 1990s, historical and cultural differences between the ethnic groups in the neighbouring Solomon Islands contributed to the rapid and violent escalation of the ethnic conflict there.[1] The former British protectorate, an island group in the south-west Pacific, north east of Australia, has a population of less than half a million and is, like its northern neighbour, Papua New Guinea, linguistically very diverse. The main island is Guadalcanal with an ethnically relatively homogeneous rural population of some 60,000 and about an additional 50,000 people of diverse ethnic backgrounds living in the country's capital, Honiara, also located on Guadalcanal. The more populous island, with over 120,000 residents, is Malaita. Friction between the different groups began to arise during and after the Second World War, when Malaitans proved more flexible in making use of the economic opportunities offered by an American military presence and the subsequent British development of the country's capital. However, as long as the Solomon Islands remained a British protectorate, tensions between the indigenous groups paled in comparison to the misgivings that all Solomon Islanders had about the British administration of the islands. Independence in 1978 gradually began to change this and tensions started building up, primarily between Malaitans, the economically and politically dominant majority, and rural inhabitants of Guadalcanal who resented the Malaitans' success and accused them of discrimination and exploitation. Leaders of indigenous groups on Guadalcanal complained, not unjustly, about illegally appropriated land, excessive migration of Malaitans to Guadalcanal, the impunity with which Malaitans were able to commit crimes, including murder, against the indigenous population of Guadalcanal, and the unfair distribution of the economic wealth generated on Guadalcanal.

The inability and unwillingness of successive Malaitan-dominated governments to address these issues led to an escalation of tensions into inter-ethnic violence in the late 1990s. Loosely organized armed gangs of indigenous residents of Guadalcanal started a campaign of terror against settlers from other islands of the country, killing and maiming dozens of them, and driving some 20,000 from the land on which they had lived for a generation or more, forcing them to flee to the capital Honiara. The tactics used by these armed gangs are typical for many similar conflicts elsewhere: burning down homes, killing livestock, looting, and widespread intimidation.

An additional feature of the escalating conflict in the Solomon

Islands was the impact that the conflict in neighbouring Bougainville had. On the one hand, refugees from the violence there sought and found refuge on Guadalcanal, thus preparing the ground for Bougainville militants to use this part of the Solomon Islands as a safe haven. In exchange, they provided training to local militants and helped them to recover weapons left after the Second World War as well as to acquire new ones in raids on police stations. On the other hand, cross-border incursions by the defence forces of Papua New Guinea prompted the government of the Solomon Islands to buy sophisticated military technology, including high-powered firearms, to improve its border security. Yet these guns and other military hardware were later used by Malaitan regular and irregular forces in raids on civilians and militants in Guadalcanal. In addition, the course of the conflict in Bougainville, especially when seen through the prism of militants from the northern neighbour, provided ample 'proof' for militants in Guadalcanal that central governments could be successfully challenged, and that violence was an effective and legitimate means to do so.

Thus, militants from Guadalcanal organized themselves into the Guadalcanal Revolutionary Army—an obvious tribute to the Bougainville Revolutionary Army—and the Isatabu Freedom Fighters. Both groups later renamed themselves the Guadalcanal Liberation Front and Isatabu Freedom Movement and began to coordinate their activities more closely. The Guadalcanal militants entered the stage in 1998 as loosely organized cells without a unified command structure, but soon controlled most parts of rural Guadalcanal. Most of these groups abided by the terms of a New Zealand-brokered peace accord of October 2000, except for the Guadalcanal Liberation Front who continued fighting until August 2003 and were forced to surrender only after the terror regime that they established in the southern part of the island turned the indigenous villagers whom they claimed to represent and former allies from among the Isatabu Freedom Fighters against them.

The insurgents faced the government's paramilitary police and a quasi-elite squad, the Rapid Response Unit, later known as the Special Task and Rescue division, as well as groups of so-called

Special Constables. Similar to many other conflicts of this kind, regular security forces of the government and pro-government Malaitan militias cooperated to such an extent that they had become indistinguishable in their aims and means by the time they officially joined forces in the Malaita Eagle Force, which was soon to become notorious for its human rights violations. Emerging relatively late in the conflict in early 2000, the Malaita Eagle Force drew recruits and support from Malaitan settlers on Guadalcanal, many of whom had been displaced by Guadalcanal militants. They also enjoyed backing from former and active Malaitan members of the government's security services and from officers who were unhappy with government policy in the conflict. Succeeding with a coup against their own government in June 2000, they launched Operation Eagle Storm aimed at eliminating all Guadalcanal insurgent groups. Fighting continued for three more years, killing several hundred people, displacing thousands more, and devastating the country's economy and public services.

The combination of creed, greed, and grievances, exacerbated by poor leadership, particularistic interests, and spill-overs from conflicts in neighbouring countries, that led to conflict and violent escalation in Bougainville and the Solomon Islands is not unique. Discrimination, the persistent violation of human rights, and deliberate economic and social neglect, on the one hand, and the ability of leaders of the affected communities to capitalize on their resulting grievances, forge and appeal to their ethnic distinctiveness, and compensate some or many with actual and promised material rewards, on the other, are essential in understanding the causes of ethnic conflicts.

In Nigeria, for example, ethnic conflict is allegedly about the control of the country's vast oil reserves. In other parts of Africa, diamonds are a major source and prize of ethnic civil war. Kosovo has neither oil nor diamonds. The Albanian population there struggled for their right to self-determination, to be free from Serbian oppression, to have their own schools and universities in which students can study in Albanian, in short not to feel like second-class citizens in their ancestral homeland in which they

63

outnumbered their oppressors by a ratio of nine to one by the late 1990s. In the Israeli–Palestinian conflict, the main conflict issue is statehood—the demand of Palestinians for their own state and the demand of Israelis to have their existing state secure from a constant threat of annihilation by fundamentalist extremists. In Northern Ireland, Catholics and Protestants are almost equal in number; the province is part of one of the most highly developed industrial countries in the world and part of the country that 'invented' democracy. Compared with many poverty-stricken and war-ravaged societies, the conflict in Northern Ireland should have been resolved long ago without costing the lives of over 3,000 people over a 30-year period. Yet the visions that each community has about what a just solution of this conflict would look like are diametrically opposed and virtually incompatible—the same stretch of territory cannot, at the same time, be part of the UK and part of the Republic of Ireland.

This very brief survey reveals that, although the stakes in what is commonly referred to as ethnic conflict are extremely diverse, in each of these and other cases it is organized ethnic groups that confront each other—minorities and majorities—with and without the backing of state institutions and with or without external support. What we therefore need to do is try to bring order to this 'chaos' of diverse claims and interests, examine to what extent ethnic conflicts actually are about ethnicity, and explore to what extent ethnicity is merely a convenient common denominator to organize a conflict group in the struggle over resources, land, or power. In other words, we need to determine what causes ethnic conflicts. In the preceding chapter we explored the nature of ethnicity and nationalism and found that, although they are facts of life almost everywhere, the mere fact of people having an ethnic identity and the presence of nationalist ideologies do not necessarily and inevitably lead to conflict, let alone civil war, ethnic cleansing, and genocide. Moreover, closer examination of many conflicts labelled as 'ethnic' leads some to argue that ethnicity is sometimes no more than a convenient mechanism to organize and mobilize people into homogeneous conflict groups willing to fight each other for resources that are at best indirectly linked to their ethnic identity.

In the last months of 2000, a debate was waged in the Northern Ireland Assembly and in the Assembly Commission on whether Easter lilies should be treated on a par with poppies. Easter lilies have been historically one of the most important symbols of the Republican and Nationalist movements. They are closely connected to the 1916 Easter Rising, which stood at the beginning of a chain of events that eventually lead to the partition of Ireland, and have subsequently become a symbol of commemoration for those who have died in the struggle for a free and united Ireland, including IRA terrorists. The poppy, on the other hand, sold by the Royal British Legion in memory of the soldiers who fought for, and died in defending, the UK in war time is of particular significance for members of the Unionist and Loyalist communities because it emphasises the sacrifices made by them contributing to the British war efforts and is for them a reminder of the strong links between Northern Ireland and Great Britain. Yet, both communities not only value their own symbols very highly as intricate parts of their identities, but also take exception and offence to the other's symbol because they see it as a reminder of either oppression or of terrorist violence, respectively, inflicted upon them. Thus, proposals for outright parity between the two communities' symbols—initially manifested in a suggestion to allow the sale of Easter lilies alongside poppies in the Assembly buildings—were rejected outright by Unionists. When they were watered down to a compromise solution, to the effect that Easter lilies should become part of the flower arrangements during the Easter Recess of the Northern Ireland Assembly and approved in the Assembly Commission, some Unionists viewed the matter as so urgent that they invoked a special provision under the 1998 Agreement, according to which the Assembly had to be recalled just before Easter to discuss the matter. The irony of holding this debate on the third anniversary of the Agreement was certainly not lost on the former Lord Mayor of Belfast, Alban Maginness of the Nationalist Social Democrat and Labour Party (SDLP), who wondered 'what sort of lunacy has descended upon the Assembly that it has to be urgently reconvened over a bowl of lilies'.

Of course, many conflicts are about much more than such symbolic issues—they are about the physical security of members of a particular group and their right to live in peace and freedom on a specific stretch of land, but they are also about the control of valuable resources, such as oil, water, and diamonds, and they are about people's rights to speak their native language and practise their religion. A discussion of what is at stake in ethnic conflicts needs, therefore, to begin well before the fighting over prized symbols and valued resources has begun. Without exploring the complex web of causes of ethnic conflicts, it will not be possible to understand the intensity of emotions involved which often lead to seemingly incomprehensible conflict where the outside observer may see plenty of room for compromise.

As the literature on the causes of ethnic conflicts has grown at impressive speed over the past two decades, there are a great many theories about what causes and influences such conflicts. Clearly, any 'adequate theory of ethnic conflict should be able to explain both elite and mass behavior' and should also 'provide an explanation for the passionate, symbolic, and apprehensive aspects of ethnic conflict'.[2] From this perspective, two factors are particularly important—comparative group worth and legitimacy. Conceiving them as a joint function of group entitlement, they allow an explanation that '[e]thnic conflict arises from the common evaluative significance accorded by the groups to acknowledged group differences and then played out in public rituals of affirmation and contradiction'.[3] In other words, differences between groups assume great significance in guiding the actions of leaders and their followers. Consider the example of Easter lilies and poppies in Northern Ireland again: two communities have different traditions, symbols, and historical experiences, and interpret them and their meaning in radically different ways. As some on both sides fail to see that their own symbols carry a very different meaning for the respective other community, and vice versa, they are unable to understand how something that is undoubtedly legitimate in their view lacks the same legitimacy in the eyes of the other community and can be seen as offensive and hurtful. By the same token, differences in what people appreciate as legitimate eventually lead to claims about relative group worth: if you cannot acknowledge the value of my symbols, your culture must be inferior. In turn, then, being seen and treated as inferior—in the job market, in the allocation of public housing, in admission to university, etc.—leads the discriminated group to question the entire political system that allows such discrimination to occur and to develop an alternative, in their view more legitimate, system. The more one group challenges the status quo and the less another is prepared to allow changes in it, the more likely is it that conflict will rapidly escalate into violence. This was the case in the late 1960s in Northern Ireland when a legitimate civil rights movement led to extreme polarization and radicalization in Northern Irish society and levels of violence between the two communities that had not occurred for decades.

Similar patterns of conflict escalation could be observed some 20 years later in Kosovo. An overwhelming majority of ethnic Albanians in this province of Serbia were systematically deprived of their status and denied access to public goods—jobs, education, healthcare—by a minority of local Serbs backed, and some would argue set up, by a government in Belgrade under Slobodan Milosevic intent on manipulating existing ethnic tensions in Kosovo to tighten its grip on power in what by then was left of the former Yugoslavia. To be sure, this is not just a European phenomenon: the worsening of Tamil–Sinhalese relations in Sri Lanka before the outbreak of the civil war on the island followed a similar pattern, as did events leading to a coup against a minority Indian government in Fiji.

Such socio-psychological explanations are, however, only part of the story of ethnic conflict. At another level, ethnic conflicts also involve very rational choices made by individuals. From this perspective, we can distinguish between underlying and proximate causes of ethnic conflict and categorize the resulting conflicts 'according to whether they are triggered by elite-level or mass-level factors; and whether they are triggered by internal or external developments'.[4] The underlying causes—that is, necessary, but not sufficient conditions for the outbreak of inter-ethnic violence—comprise four different types of factor: structural, political, economic and social, and cultural and perceptual. Structural factors are conditions such as weak states (for example, states that do not exercise control on the entire territory within their boundaries), intra-state security concerns (such as about potential secessionist movements, possibly with external support from neighbouring states), and ethnic geography (including territorially concentrated groups in border areas and ethnic groups that straddle international boundaries). Political factors that need to be present for ethnic conflict to erupt include discriminatory political institutions (which pursue policies that deliberately disadvantage members of particular ethnic groups), exclusionary nationalist ideologies (that question, for example, the equality of all citizens, deny citizenship to members of particular ethnic groups, or advocate forced cultural assimilation of minorities), and contentious inter-group and intra-group politics at mass and elite levels (in other words, a political sphere that is mostly carved up between ethnic parties that compete with each other on ethnic platforms). Economic and social factors play an equally important role in setting the scene for potentially violent ethnic conflicts: economic problems, discriminatory economic systems (such as a system of cultural division of labour with job opportunities determined by ethnic background), and (uneven or preferential) economic development and modernization are factors that can contribute to the mobilization of ethnic groups and their formation into conflict groups ready to fight for equality of economic opportunity, redistribution of resources, or the preservation of a privileging status quo. Finally, cultural and perceptual factors must not be underestimated either: patterns of cultural discrimination (such as the imposition of an official state language, the systematic destruction of cultural resources and historic monuments, the outlawing of certain cultural practices and traditions) and problematic group histories (which, in their extreme, may include past instances of ethnic cleansing and attempted genocide) are all factors that have significant influence on the development of ethnic conflicts.[5]

Consider the situation in Sri Lanka in this context. Common political structures on the island were established under British colonial rule only from 1815 onwards, but, given a long prior history of cultural and political autonomy for Tamils under Portuguese and Dutch rule, the two main communities on the island have very different views on the legitimacy of the state of Sri Lanka and on the role that they should play within it, and on the rights that they should enjoy. Interestingly, however, instead of prolonged violent resistance against the British and their unification of the island, which clearly endangered the Tamil minority's autonomy, Tamils made use of the educational and entrepreneurial opportunities that followed the take-over by Britain and came to be over-represented and eventually dominant in business and the civil service. Unsurprisingly, this was not received well by the majority Sinhalese community and led them to fear that their language and religion—that is, the key determinants of their ethnic identity as Sinhalese—were in danger of being eroded in a Tamil-dominated society. The Buddhist revival among the Sinhalese in the nineteenth century hardened already existing splits between the two communities and added a clear ethnic dimension to the already entrenched status hierarchy. The Sinhalese increasingly took a view of themselves as a people who had been invested with a divine mission by Buddha. Not only did this contradict the reality of life in then British-ruled Ceylon, it also clashed with Tamil views on Ceylonese culture and history.

During the build-up to independence, the British colonial rulers introduced universal suffrage in 1931, which clearly boosted the prospects to gain political influence for the majority Sinhala community. Fearing that unitary state structures in a Sinhalese-dominated country would inevitably lead to discriminatory practices against them, and unwilling to perceive themselves as a minority after many years of privileged status, the Tamil community called for constitutional protection of their status. Although it may have been possible to achieve at least something akin to minority rights and possibly even autonomy within a political system where the colonial power still wielded significant influence, the majority democracy installed after independence in 1948 in which Sinhalese parties dominated the parliamentary system made such a project of constitutional reform not only difficult, but outright impossible. As a consequence of another wave of Sinhala Buddhist cultural revivalism in the 1950s, Tamils not only saw a change in their share in power and influence but became increasingly subjected to culturally discriminatory practices, such as those embodied in the Sinhala Only Act of 1956, according to which Sinhala replaced English as the official language for government and business, and the introduction in the early 1970s of communal quotas for university entrance that also discriminated against Tamils. The new constitution in 1972, changing the country's name from Ceylon to Sri Lanka, rejected the Tamil demand for internal self-determination and granted Buddhism the foremost place in the life of the state. Over time, political and cultural discrimination of Tamils also significantly reduced their educational and employment opportunities. With even the dimmest hopes of an eventual federalization of Sri Lanka disappearing, the Tamil community became increasingly radicalized, but remained non-violent until a hard-line government in Colombo resorted to the use of force to suppress peaceful protests in the Tamil-dominated Jaffna peninsula. This transformed tensions between the Sinhalese majority and Tamil separatists into a violent ethnic conflict in the mid-1980s in which thousands have died. As a consequence of the civil war that is still ongoing despite negotiations, facilitated by Norway, between the Sri Lankan government and the Tamil Tigers, and of the continuing and increasing 'Sinhalization' of Sri Lanka, the economic situation on the island has also deteriorated for both communities, albeit disproportionately affecting the Tamils.

This brief account of the situation in Sri Lanka highlights the importance of another dimension of the account of the causes of ethnic conflict. Apart from underlying conditions, such as political, economic, and cultural discrimination, a second set of causes is required to 'enable' the outbreak of violent ethnic conflicts.

Labelled 'proximate causes', these are factors that increase the likelihood of conflict in a situation in which all or some of the underlying 'ingredients' are present.[6] In this category of proximate causes, a distinction can be made between internal and external factors that operate at the mass level and the elite level. Internal elite-level causes are bad leaders and external ones are bad neighbours; internal mass-level causes are serious domestic problems and external ones are bad neighbourhoods. In the Sri Lankan case, the influence of bad leaders is the most significant, whilst external factors are almost completely absent. The stance that the Tamil Tigers have taken on the legitimacy of using violence against the central government and on policing their own community, and the refusal, for two decades, to accept negotiations unless the government recognizes the right of the Tamils to self-determination and implicitly to establish their own independent state on part of the island, sat uncomfortably with a central government which for a long time had refused to recognize Tamil claims, repeatedly reneged on promises and commitments, and often used excessive force, including against civilians. Although there were also some internal mass-level factors that contributed, if not to the outbreak of the conflict, at least to its prolongation (such as the revival of radical Buddhism among Sinhalese and the desperation of young Tamils in a situation in which living standards decreased constantly and positive prospects for the future, including any employment opportunities, were almost completely absent), it is fair to say that the choices that the leaders in both communities made were decisive factors in creating a situation in which, even after 20 years of fighting, there are few prospects for sustainable peace.

This view of the causes of ethnic conflict and the distinction between underlying and proximate causes also enable an explanation of why, despite similar basic conditions, not every situation of ethnic tensions leads to full-scale civil war. Take the case of the former Yugoslavia. Why did the Serb-dominated and controlled Yugoslav army not put up a big fight over Slovenia? One explanation is that the absence of a significant Serb minority in the republic greatly diminished Serbian appetite for a fight, whereas in

Croatia, Bosnia and Herzegovina, and Kosovo not only were there Serb minorities that wanted the continued protection of Belgrade and had militarily mobilized for their own 'self-defence' but, unlike Slovenia, these areas were also important for the project of a Greater Serbia and Serbian public opinion could more easily be swayed to support the war effort there. Undoubtedly, the Milosevic regime in Serbia proper was not the only one to blame. A similarly virulent form of ethnonationalism emerged in Croatia in the late 1980s/early 1990s. With a nationalist government under Franjo Tudjman that openly embraced the symbols of the war-time Ustasha regime, which had engaged in mass killings of Serb civilians, local Serbs had every reason to fear discrimination and worse at the hands of the new rulers, yet their own radicalization only contributed to the escalating spiral of violence.

Bosnia and Herzegovina suffered from very similar bad leaders and bad neighbour syndromes. Wedged between Croatia and Serbia, and large ethnic Croat and Serb minorities in the emerging country, Bosnian Muslims at times fought a two-front war against both a Greater Croatia and a Greater Serbia policy, endorsed and actively supported by foes inside and outside the country. Little wonder that the third ethnonationalist movement in the region, that for a Greater Albania, or, as some would not wrongly argue, for a Greater Kosovo, was soon to clash with the rival ideology for a Greater Serbia. Yet, what is interesting about the case of Kosovo is that independence was, for almost two decades, pursued by non-violent means alone, and only from about 1996 onwards did the conflict between Serbs and ethnic Albanians escalate into violence, precisely because the Milosevic regime saw an opportunity in manipulating the Kosovo issue such that it could strengthen its grip on power in Belgrade. Had it not been for the decisive military intervention led by NATO, this strategy may well have worked.[7]

A final point in support of an argument that places special emphasis on the role of political elites is the case of Macedonia. Situated in a bad neighbourhood comparable only to the Great Lakes Region in central Africa and the Caucasus, with several 'bad neighbours' around denying the country's choice of name (Greece), its ethno-cultural distinctiveness (Bulgaria), and questioning its borders and ultimately its statehood (Kosovo), these gloomy external conditions were easily matched by internal ones including high unemployment, political and cultural discrimination, and an ethnic geography according to which a partition of the country could have been executed without great problems. Yet, despite shortcomings and mistakes that led to significant, albeit brief, inter-ethnic violence in 2001, reasonable and responsible leaders, supported by NATO and EU facilitation, prevailed and negotiated an agreement in the summer of 2001 that saw an end to violence and the beginning of a reform process; this process has been slow to date, but has nevertheless progressed and begun to address some of the underlying causes that enabled the violent escalation of the conflict.

Yet, although leaders' choices may explain particular outcomes—prolonged war in Bosnia and Herzegovina compared with a brief spell of violence in Macedonia—one part in the explanation of causes of ethnic conflicts remains missing, and this is why some leaders choose war over peace, confrontation over accommodation. These choices, of course, remain meaningless unless leaders can mobilize sufficient numbers of followers for the one or other course of action. In order to understand the motivations of leaders and followers better, it is worthwhile considering a particular rational choice explanation of ethnic conflict that focuses on the so-called security dilemma and assumes that individuals always make rational choices, weighing the costs and benefits of their actions. David Lake and Donald Rothchild, for example, argue that 'the fundamental causes of ethnic conflict' are 'strategic interactions between and within groups'.[8] Within the realm of strategic interactions between groups, 'three strategic dilemmas can cause violence to erupt: information failures, problems of credible commitment, and incentives to use force preemptively (also known as the security dilemma)'.[9] As for within-group strategic interactions, 'ethnic activists and political entrepreneurs may make blatant ethnic appeals and attempt to outbid moderate politicians, thereby mobilizing members, polarizing society, and magnifying the intergroup dilemmas'.[10] Often exacerbated by proximate factors such as primordial identities, economic decline, regime change, and bad leaders and bad neighbours, the most significant of these strategic dilemmas is the security dilemma, which, in turn, 'rests on . . . information failures and problems of credible commitment'.[11] As a plethora of empirical evidence underlines the importance of the security dilemma in explaining the occurrence of ethnic conflict, the conditions in which security dilemmas emerge need to be investigated carefully, and in this context five 'fear-producing environments' can be identified: government breakdown; geographical isolation or vulnerability of a minority within a larger group; shifts in the political power balance between groups; changes in access to, or control over, economic resources; and forced or voluntary demobilization of partisan armies.[12] To these, one additional 'fear-producing' environment should be added: changes in external patronage or balance of power between rival patrons.

The crumbling of the Soviet Union generated fears among many ethnic minorities in the Soviet Union's republics who had relied on the control exercised by Moscow over local elites, preventing them from abusing minority groups living on their territories. The Armenians in the Nagorno-Karabakh region of Azerbaijan saw, as early as 1988, their only option of (physical and cultural) survival in breaking away from Azerbaijan. Impossible under Soviet rule, Armenian military intervention managed to achieve the annexation of the region to the 'mother country'. Similarly, the Abkhaz and South Ossetians in Georgia preferred staying with Russia after the collapse of the Soviet Union and, even though they did not fully achieve this, they were able to establish control in these two regions of Georgia and now 'enjoy' the protection of Russian peacekeepers. These three cases illustrate two important points. First, patron states do not always have to have ethnic 'ties' with the groups that they protect or by whom they are lobbied for protection. Second, patron states who intervene unilaterally, rather than seeking a consensual settlement of such disputes with the host state are unlikely to effect permanent 'solutions': the conflicts in Nagorno-Karabakh, South Ossetia, and Abkhazia are merely frozen, that is, in a lasting stalemate, but sooner or later they will need to be settled, and this will be possible only by way of agreement between both states involved—a point vividly illustrated by the 1969 South Tyrol settlement (involving Austria and Italy) and the 1998 Agreement on Northern Ireland (involving the UK and the Republic of Ireland); the way to the latter was partly paved by an earlier 1985 Anglo-Irish Agreement which did not, however, directly involve any of the political parties and paramilitary groups in Northern Ireland itself. It is also important to bear in mind that the mere prospect of cooperation between host state and patron state is not automatically greeted with great enthusiasm by their local protégés: Unionists in Northern Ireland cried foul in 1985 (and some even continued to do so after 1998), and characterized the deal struck between the governments in London and Dublin as a sell-out. Loyalists committed more acts of violence against Catholics, and sporadically against British security force. So too did the IRA, empowered by an arms shipment from Libya. Arguably, both sides, among other things, feared that agreement between the two governments would permanently prevent them from achieving their political goals—a united Ireland and no influence from Dublin in Northern Irish affairs.

Implicitly or explicitly, the notion of the security dilemma is thus at the core of a wide range of causal explanations of ethnic conflicts. The strategic, pre-emptive use of violence is generally thought to be more likely in conditions of emerging anarchy which heighten the uncertainty of identity groups about their future (physical or cultural) survival. Yet, these fears do not always and necessarily translate into actual violent conflict. In other words, there is no automatism that leads from an existing security dilemma directly into a violent ethnic conflict. To establish a relationship between an existing security dilemma and the violent escalation of a conflict, it is therefore once again useful to look at the decisions that individuals take in response to a specific security dilemma— masses that push their elites in the direction of a particular course of action; or leaders who choose a particular policy and the followers who are willingly led down a specific path.

One way to describe the essence of the security dilemma is that an increase in one person's, group's, or state's security is at the same time perceived as a threat, or decrease in security, by another actor. My acquisition of a baseball bat to protect my property from burglars decreases the physical security of the burglar to go about his 'business' and is likely to give him incentive to carry a similar or more powerful weapon as well, which in turn decreases my own security when defending my property, and may prompt me to up the stakes by acquiring a firearm, and so on. The same dynamics, albeit at different scales, work at the level of groups and states. What agents taking this course of action—as individuals, groups, or states at all three levels—have in common is a strong belief that a condition of anarchy prevails in which they cannot but rely on themselves to ensure their security. I might not trust the police to protect me from burglars, ethnic groups may not be confident that state institutions are sufficiently impartial and effective in enforcing law and order, and states will possibly have little faith in the power of the organized international community to defend them against predatory neighbours. As a result of this reliance on oneself, not only are there incentives to escalate an arms race but also such incentives exist with regard to the pre-emptive use of violence. What if my opponent in the future acquires a weapon so powerful and expensive that I cannot match it? Would I not be better off to attack now when I am still in a position of relative advantage, thus thwarting any future attacks that might catch me off-guard or under-prepared?

Following such logic of consequentiality is an all too familiar pattern in the escalation of ethnic conflicts. What distinguishes an ethnic security dilemma from 'traditional' interstate security dilemmas is that it is based on a more comprehensive view of what security is. The ethnic security dilemma thus involves elements of physical security (literal survival of group members), political security (freedom from oppressive regimes that exclude group members from meaningful participation in the political process), economic and social security (freedom from economically and socially exclusive regimes that deny equal opportunities of economic and social advancement to group members), cultural security (freedom from forced assimilation), and environmental security (freedom from environmental destruction and resource scarcity). Thus, when local Serbs took up arms in Croatia and in Bosnia and Herzegovina, they did it in part because they feared that their relative advantages over their opponents would diminish over time, leading to their physical, political, economic and social, and cultural security as members of a particular ethnic group coming under threat. The violent suppression of peaceful demonstrations in Sri Lanka and Kosovo in the 1980s followed a similar logic by state actors: crushing separatist movements before they gain greater momentum and intimidating those who might join them if the state did not send a clear message. What often additionally drives state actors is the creation of a potentially detrimental precedent: without the harsh repression of insurgents in East Timor or Aceh, in Chechnya, in Kosovo, or in Biafra, others might follow suit and the result would be the disintegration of the existing state. In other words, from the perspective of the government, the physical security of the state and its institutions is at stake.

Even though many of the predictions that state actors make in attempts to justify their violent crack-downs may prove wrong with the benefit of hindsight, it is the perceptions of an existing security dilemma that determines the course of action. Intercommunal violence in Northern Ireland in the late 1960s and early 1970s involved many incidents that in today's terminology would be called ethnic cleansing. Yet the creation of ethnically homogeneous neighbourhoods there, the forced displacement of Greek and Turkish Cypriots in 1974 on Cyprus, as well as earlier cases of expulsion and forced resettlement in the period immediately after the Second World War in east central Europe were all driven by the very same security concerns: in situations where only the group can guarantee above all physical and cultural security, an ethnically homogeneous neighbourhood, region, or state is easier to defend against threats. This logic, however, forgets that everyone living in such ethnically homogeneous areas is also more vulnerable to attack, because violence aimed at another ethnic group can be executed much more easily if they can be readily identified according to where they live. This also extends to other, non-physical aspects of security: economic and social advancement in mainstream society may be impossible for someone carrying the stigma of living in a certain neighbourhood or region that identifies him or her as belonging to a specific ethnic group; likewise, environmental security may be under threat if only one group is likely to be affected negatively by the consequences of an irrigation project, deforestation, etc.

Although the security dilemma is no doubt a very useful tool to explain the emergence of violence in ethnic conflicts, it is important to bear in mind that there are two other strategic dilemmas that can contribute to the violent escalation of ethnic conflict. Apart from the security dilemma, information failures and problems of credible commitment are important for our understanding of how and why leaders are able to mobilize their followers and radicalize them to the point where the (pre-emptive and indiscriminate) use of violence against members of a different ethnic group becomes a legitimate strategy for group survival. For leaders to succeed in mobilizing and radicalizing their followers in this way, followers need to believe in the reality of the threat to their security that leaders claim. In other words, there needs to be enough 'credible evidence' about the intentions of rival groups to execute threats for ordinary people not only to condone but also to participate actively in committing acts of violence. This evidence, however, cannot easily, or can only to a certain extent, be manufactured by leaders of one group without the 'help' of other groups. Again, the example of the wars in former Yugoslavia is instructive. Had it not been for Croat president Tudjman's embrace of the symbols of fascist Croatia and his virulent ethnonationalism, demanding independent statehood for Croatia, many local Serbs may have trusted in the ability of Yugoslav institutions to protect them, or at least in the sustainability of the multi-ethnic peace that had after all prevailed throughout the post-1945 period, and for the most part also for centuries before the beginning of the Second World War. Thus, whilst the 'problematic group history' is reduced to a single episode in history, the fear among Serbs in Croatia and Serbia proper, combined with ambiguous signals from Croatia, enabled Milosevic to hype up fears among Serbs to such an extent that local insurgency and all-out war were seen as the best options to guarantee the group's security. Uncertainty among Serbs about the real intentions of Croatia's leaders—that is, a failure to communicate them—and vice versa meant that eventually both sides felt justified in the use of violence. In other words, for security fears to lead to violent ethnic conflict it takes leaders of both groups to 'cooperate'.[13]

That such escalating spirals of fear can occur in majorities and minorities also becomes obvious if we consider ethnic conflicts in the post-Soviet periphery. In Nagorno-Karabakh, Armenian fears of being subject to genocide (grounded in a traumatic episode in Armenian history towards the end of the Ottoman Empire) and Azerbaijanian fears for the territorial integrity, and thus very much for the existence of their state, clashed during the break-up of the Soviet Union.[14] For both Armenians and Azeris, control over Nagorno-Karabakh became symbolic and existential for their survival. With each uncertain about the other's intentions and left 'alone' to resolve their problems after the dissolution of the Soviet Union, fears of ethnic violence turned into self-fulfilling prophecies.

Credible commitment problems—the third of the strategic dilemmas—manifest themselves in a somewhat different, albeit not unrelated, manner. Take the example of Northern Ireland since 1998. In the Agreement concluded that year, the British and Irish governments, and all but one of the mainstream political parties in Northern Ireland, committed themselves to a new system of government in which local parties representing both communities would exercise a wide range of powers independently of the government in London. As a result of the bonds that one part of the population—varyingly referred to as Nationalists, Republicans, or Catholics—felt with the Republic of Ireland, arrangements were also put in place for extensive cross-border cooperation between the government in Northern Ireland and its counterpart in Dublin. This

Agreement meant significant concessions from both communities: Unionists, always keen to preserve Northern Ireland's links with Great Britain in the UK, accepted power sharing with Nationalists and Republicans, who, in turn, gave up their unqualified demands for reunification with the Republic of Ireland and acknowledged that this could be brought about only through a referendum in Northern Ireland in which a majority of the population voted in favour of such a move. With a 30-year history of violent conflict, costing over 3,000 lives and injuring many thousands more, both communities had quite different ideas about what the Agreement actually meant—in other words what they had committed themselves to. For Unionists, sharing power with Nationalists and Republicans was the price to pay for peace—that is, for the decommissioning of all weapons by paramilitary organizations, especially the IRA. This link, famously expressed in the slogan 'no guns, no government' was, however, only vaguely and ambiguously established in the Agreement itself, which noted that all parties would use their best efforts to bring about paramilitary decommissioning within two years of the conclusion of the Agreement. Hence, any subsequent interpretation of the Agreement by Unionists legitimizing their refusal to share power with Sinn Féin, who are considered to be closely connected to the IRA, was based on Unionists' fears that Republicans were not seriously committed to peace because of their refusal to decommission their weapons. This, in turn, was seen by Republicans as 'clear evidence' that Unionists, too, were not committed to the Agreement, and especially not to sharing power with them, and used the decommissioning issue only as a smoke screen behind which they could hide their real intentions. Locally referred to as 'the blame game', this debate has raged on for over six years now. The UK government had to step in several times and prevent the collapse of the entire process by temporarily suspending Northern Ireland's government institutions. The latest suspension occurred in October 2002 over allegations of continued IRA intelligence gathering, which prompted Unionists once again to walk out of government. However, unlike on previous occasions, no deal was possible between Unionists and Republicans that could have enabled the restoration of government in Belfast. Subsequently, elections were held in November 2003, returning hardliners in both communities as the strongest parties in the new assembly. By December 2004, despite intensive negotiations, no agreement had been reached on a new government, and both sides continued blaming each other, in public at least, for the lack of progress and doubting the sincerity of their opponent's commitment to peace. Alleged IRA involvement in the UK's largest ever bank heist in Northern Ireland, and the murder of a Catholic man in Belfast by senior IRA members, did little to assuage Unionist fears of continued Republican paramilitary activity. Likewise, the IRA's publicly made offer to kill those who had committed the murder did not enhance the democratic credentials of the organization or portray it as a group with a firm grasp of the notion of the rule of law. Yet, a short time after this remarkable demonstration of lack of judgement, Sinn Féin President Gerry Adams called on the IRA, in a press conference on 7 April 2005, to abandon their armed struggle for good and join a peaceful and democratic campaign for a united Ireland, not, of course, without praising the IRA for holding 'the line and fac[ing] down a huge military foe, the British Crown Forces and their surrogates in the unionist death squads'.[15]

Although Northern Ireland is not a unique case in this respect, it is distinct from many other cases in that it stands on one end of a spectrum of cases in which peace agreements that were successfully concluded, and often received international praise, subsequently faltered when it came to their implementation and operation. In Northern Ireland there was no major resurgence of violence, whilst the collapse of the Oslo Accords between Israel and the PLO was followed by the second, and much more devastating, Intifada. At the most extreme, the breakdown of the Arusha power-sharing pact in Rwanda between Hutu and Tutsi led to the worst act of genocide since the Holocaust. It would obviously be wrong to blame only the lack of credible commitment on the part of the conflict parties for this, but doubts about how serious a former deadly enemy is about his commitment to sticking to a peace deal feed seamlessly into a renewed security dilemma that provides elites with a rationale, and masses with incentives, to resume violence for fear of being eventually worse off if they gave their opponents the benefit of the doubt. This is, unfortunately, too frequent a phenomenon to be brushed off lightly. In a study of almost 50 civil wars that began between 1940 and 1992 (albeit with only a small minority among them being ethnic conflicts), it was found that 'negotiated settlements that appear to have all the elements of success—a cease-fire agreement, specific arrangements for future governance, resolution of underlying issues—still fail if they lack the guarantees necessary to reassure groups to proceed with implementation'.[16]

A final important point to be made in this discussion of the causes of ethnic conflict is related to the observation that strategic dilemmas, such as those related to information failures, credible commitment, and ultimately group security, occur not only in the interactions between groups but also within them. Moderate Hutu in Rwanda were prepared to share power with Tutsi; moderate Nationalists and Unionists shared power successfully in Northern Ireland in 1974, albeit for only three months; within Israel, there are severe policy disagreements between Likud and Labour on how best to secure the future of Israel; not all Chechens favour violence and terrorism as the most suitable approach to resolve differences with Russia; in Spain's Basque country, almost every terrorist atrocity committed by ETA is followed by large public protests of moderate Basques speaking out against the use of violence; and many ordinary Tamils suffer more from the oppression that they experience at the hands of their 'own' Tamil Tiger 'liberation movement' than from counter-insurgency measures by the government in Colombo.

How is this relevant as a cause of ethnic conflicts? Obviously, intra-group competition, or even rivalry, is hardly a cause of conflict itself. At best, it would be a proximate cause, that is, a factor that makes conflict more likely in the presence of other conditions. But even this is not necessarily self-evident and it takes specific individuals to act as catalysts in making ethnic conflict more likely.[17] So-called ethnic activists, who individually feel a strong need of identification with members of their own ethnic group, can create significant and often self-intensifying and self-sustaining social pressures that lead to the polarization of societies and the formation of conflict groups based on their members' ethnicity. These pressures, obviously, work all the more effectively the more resources in a given society are accessible only on the basis of group membership. The more social life centres on activities of one's own kin group—the bars you go to, the civic organizations you join, the neighbourhoods you live in—the more so-called cross-cutting cleavages become eroded. What may begin in the purely social and private spheres soon spreads to the economic sphere—whom you work for, whom you hire for your business—and ultimately to the political—which party you join, which candidate you vote for. Very often, these processes are not sequential, but occur in parallel and at great speed. They produce and are the products of genuine fears that people have about their security now and in the future, and do not exist in a vacuum. Nor do they inevitably lead to ethnic conflict. Strongly polarized societies, such as Belgium and to a lesser extent Switzerland, have existed for long periods of time without inter-ethnic violence. Even in societies as deeply fragmented as Northern Ireland, Sri Lanka, or India, violence is not an inevitable or permanent feature of life.

A second catalyst is, therefore, often necessary to exacerbate volatile situations in such a way that security dilemmas become so acute that the pre-emptive use of violence seems the only way to secure the survival of the group. This catalyst is the political entrepreneur who, although not necessarily sharing the same emotional need for ethnic identification as the ethnic activist, has no hesitation in utilizing and manipulating ethnic identity and the social splits that it can create as a powerful tool to mobilize people, and thus create the 'human resources' deemed necessary for pursuit of political power.[18] Take the example of Slobodan Milošević—he effortlessly managed the transformation from ordinary communist apparatchik to nationalist Serbian leader once the opportunity structures for the pursuit of power radically changed in the crumbling communist regime in Yugoslavia in the late 1980s. Milošević's shift from communism to nationalism as his powerbase fundamentally changed the playing field not only within Yugoslavia but also in Serbia itself. The links that Milosevic created between the survival of the Serb nation and events in Croatia, Bosnia and Herzegovina, and ultimately Kosovo, made it all but impossible for moderate leaders to make their voices heard, let alone attract public support for different, less nationalist political agendas. This was particularly obvious during the build-up to the Kosovo conflict. Milosevic effectively managed to present himself as the guardian of the Serb nation and won significant majorities for himself and his party in relatively free elections. Moreover, even the so-called democratic opposition did not dare to challenge him on his Kosovo policies out of fear of being marginalized in the electoral contest dominated by hard-line nationalist rhetoric.

Yugoslavia is not unique in this context. This kind of ethno-nationalist mobilization and the rise of hard-line, often uncompromising, and radical leaders are phenomena that can be witnessed in many other, not only ethnic, conflicts across the world. They occur in contexts of heightened insecurity and on-going or impending regime change, but again not inevitably and not forever. The rise of Ian Paisley and his Democratic Unionists in Northern Ireland to become the strongest political party after the November 2003 elections, the electoral victory of Ariel Sharon in Israel in 2001, the political and military power amassed very quickly by the Shia cleric Moqtada al-Sadr, the dominance of Turkish Cypriot politics by Rauf Denktash for more than three decades, and the showdown between a more compromising prime minister and a more hard-line president in Sri Lanka and the perseverance of the latter and her party in elections in 2004 are all examples of these phenomena. This process of ethnic outbidding in which leaders of different political parties within one ethnic group attempt to present themselves as the only safeguards against their ethnic group being 'sold down the river' by their irresponsible rivals complements the efforts of ethnic activists. Together, ethnic activists and political entrepreneurs increase the homogeneity of existing ethnic groups and the polarization of society as a whole, thus making it more likely that tensions between groups will escalate into violence, that conflict will continue without hope of resolution, and that agreements will fail to live up to their promises.

The security dilemma and related dilemmas focusing on credible commitment problems and information failures offer a powerful explanation of the dynamics leading up to the violent escalation of ethnic conflicts. Yet not all rational choices that individuals and groups make are related to their own physical and cultural security. A number of ethnic conflicts also suggest that economic motives—greed and the opportunity to pursue greed-driven agendas—are often equally if not more significant causes, which help us understand the occurrence of ethnic conflict. Since the late 1990s, a number of scholars have tried to expand the debate on the causes of ethnic conflicts beyond the traditional grievance paradigm. In the context of debates about so-called 'new' wars, arguments about economically motivated violence gained and, to some extent, maintain significant currency. Paul Collier and Anke Hoeffler of the World Bank, for example, argue that ethnic conflict occurs if the incentive for rebellion is sufficiently large relative to its costs.[19] They maintain that the incentive for rebellion is the product of the probability of victory (the ability of the government to defeat rebels) and its consequences (the benefits of state capture or secession). Costs are seen as a combination of the opportunity cost of rebel labour (that is, loss of earnings in high-income countries makes rebellions there unlikely) and the disruption to economic activity caused by warfare (which makes both state capture and secession less attractive because it reduces the potential benefits to be reaped by the rebels). In their original 1998 study, Collier and Hoeffler found that civil war was overwhelmingly a phenomenon of low-income countries, that natural resources made things worse, unless there were plenty of them, that countries with larger populations have higher risks of war and that these wars last longer, and that it is not ethno-linguistic fractionalization as such that is damaging to societies but that degree of fractionalization that most facilitates rebel coordination (for example, very different language, culture, physical appearance, as well as relatively compact settlement areas of the groups rebelling). Several years later, Collier and Hoeffler offered a more advanced explanation of how greed affects the likelihood of ethnic conflict breaking out: exceptional opportunities for the rebel movement.[20] Indicators for the existence of such exceptional opportunities were seen in the availability of financing for a rebellion (extortion of natural resources, donations from diasporas, subventions from hostile governments) and in opportunities arising from atypically low costs (low per capita income, low rate of male secondary schooling, and low growth rates of the economy). Collier and Hoeffler also investigated the relevance of a range of other opportunities, such as the availability and cheapness of military equipment, military skills among the population at large, weak governments, and a terrain favourable to rebels (such as forests and mountains). Their findings again emphasize the importance of economic factors: the presence of natural resources that can be used in financing rebel movements, diaspora support and low costs in terms of foregone earnings, and the availability of conflict-specific capital (equipment and skills) were the most significant factors. The only significant non-economic factor that they found was ethnic dominance: where one ethnic group has monopolized the state and its resources whilst others remain excluded from meaningful political, economic, and social participation. Under such conditions, the risk of conflict nearly doubled.

Clearly, in the light of many of the examples used in this book, a purely economic explanation of ethnic conflict does not seem very satisfactory, and so it should not come as a surprise that many scholars have criticized Collier and Hoeffler's work. Among them, Karen Ballentine and Jake Sherman counter Collier and Hoeffler's sweeping generalizations with in-depth case studies.[21] They and their contributors find that economic factors are nowhere the sole factor causing outbreak of conflict: in Kosovo, Sri Lanka, and Bougainville, grievances and insecurity bred by systematic exclusion of minorities from political and economic participation had a much larger impact on the escalation towards violent ethnic conflict. In the Democratic Republic of Congo (DRC), however, conflict is clearly more economically driven, although it also has its causes in political misrule, corruption, socioeconomic deterioration, and institutional decay.

As far as the impact of economic factors on the duration of ethnic conflicts is concerned, Ballentine and Sherman and their contributors accept that access to lucrative economic resources is a more important factor, but poignantly ask whether self-enrichment is an end in itself or instrumental in funding a rebellion that has its causes in serious socioeconomic or political grievances. Others have criticized Collier and Hoeffler's studies along similar lines. Michael Pugh and Neil Cooper, for example, note that Collier and Hoeffler's selection of cases excludes all anti-colonial insurgencies, in which (political) grievances were by far the most influential factors.[22] Like Ballentine and Sherman, they also note that the false consciousness postulated by Collier, stating that 'rebel supporters are gulled into believing the discourse that self-interested rebel leaders promote'[23] may infer motives from actions, but still leaves motives in the realm of speculation, because it remains unclear whether economic agendas are primary causes of conflict—that is, whether people rebel to satisfy greed—or whether they are instrumental in order to help realize political agendas of grievance.

Importantly, this debate about the causes of ethnic conflict should not be seen in the mutually exclusive way in which it is sometimes presented by advocates of one or another line of thinking. As we see again in Chapter 4, at different levels of our analysis of the causes of ethnic conflicts different factors matter in different ways. Political leaders may be able to mobilize support for their own power games if they can convince their followers that they are in danger of annihilation. If people see concrete economic advantages in pursuing an agenda of systematically excluding members of another ethnic group from opportunities of political, economic, and social participation in a given state, they may willingly buy into a discourse of cultural survival. These are phenomena that are not only linked to areas of ethnic conflict in 'uncivilized' parts of the world; they occur in so-called advanced or post-modern societies that have supposedly moved beyond the narrow confines of ethnic nationalism as well. Debates about immigration, asylum fraud, or becoming a cultural minority in one's own homeland are widespread across western Europe, not only but especially at election times.

The often emotional responses that people have to such politically and economically highly charged issues once again underline the importance of individuals—leaders and followers alike—and the decisions that they make in determining whether conflict will occur and endure. Yet individuals do not act in a vacuum. Leaders in particular are crucial in the process of catalysing existing tensions into open warfare, but they can do so only if circumstances permit. A difficult economic situation can be talked up into an impending collapse of a country's ability to feed and shelter its citizens, a political impasse in parliament can be presented as a serious crisis, and ambiguous pronouncements by the leaders of other ethnic groups about their intentions can be used to induce fears about the inevitability of violence, but hardly ever does conflict merely 'appear' overnight. An important implication of this build-up towards violent conflict, rather than its sudden eruption, is that although violence may be temporarily prevented or contained by focusing on leaders inside and outside the country and by ameliorating the consequences of serious domestic problems, a conflict itself cannot be resolved without addressing its underlying causes.

4

Who fights in ethnic conflicts and how?

> Chechen detainees who arrived at the Russian Chernokozovo
> 'filtration' camp in January 2000 received an ominous wel-
> come. 'Welcome to hell,' the prison guards would say, and
> then force them to walk through a human corridor of baton-
> wielding guards. This was only the beginning of a ghastly cycle
> of abuse for most detainees in early 2000, who suffered system-
> atic beatings, rape, and other forms of torture. Most were
> released only after their families managed to pay large sums to
> Russian officials bent on extortion.

This is the beginning of a report by Human Rights Watch, dated
October 2000. It further details a litany of human rights abuses
committed by Russian troops in Chechnya, including mass arrests
and arbitrary detention, torture and abuse, and 'disappearances'.[1]
Such 'counter-insurgency' measures are not the only forms of gross
human rights violations committed by the Russian government
against Chechen civilians. The village of Alkhan-Yurt and the treatment of its population exemplified in many ways the plight of
civilians caught between insurgents and government troops in the
secessionist province. In November 1999, Chechen rebels were
present in Alkhan-Yurt, a strategically important village providing
a southern route to and from the Chechen capital Grozny. The
village elders wanted the rebels to leave in order to save their village, but rebel commanders refused and threatened to kill village
elders. The fighting that ensued between them and the advancing

Russian army was severe, and killed several dozens of Russian soldiers in weeks of heavy fighting, which destroyed large parts of the village. Finally, the rebels retreated and in early December Russian forces gained complete control of Alkhan-Yurt. Enraged by the weeks of fighting over the village and the loss of many of their comrades, Russian forces, rather than bringing peace to the village, went on a rampage of killing, expulsions, looting, and burning. This lasted for more than two weeks, and there was no attempt by Russian authorities to intervene.[2]

The beginning of a third phase in Sri Lanka's civil war in April 1995 was similarly marked by gross violations of human rights. According to a Human Rights Watch report, the Sri Lankan army used civilians as 'human mine detectors and shields against LTTE attacks'.[3] In July of the same year, hundreds of thousands of civilians were forced to flee from areas of the Jaffna peninsula affected by the army's 'Operation Leap Forward'. Hundreds of civilians also died during this campaign. In one particularly infamous example, the destruction of Saint Peter's Church in Navaly by government air raids resulted in hundreds of people being killed and seriously injured.[4] Similar to other conflicts, Sri Lanka has also witnessed human rights violations on a similar scale committed by insurgents. More than 50 Sinhalese civilians were killed on 18 September 1999 by the so-called Tamil Tigers, the main insurgent group in Sri Lanka seeking independence for the north-east of the country, occupied predominantly by Tamils and Muslim groups. Only three days earlier, 22 Tamil civilians had been killed in a bombing raid by the Sri Lankan Air Force. Such tit-for-tat killings of civilians have been a marked feature of the Sri Lankan civil war for a decade now.

Ethnic conflicts like those in Chechnya and Sri Lanka do not just exist or come into being overnight. As we have seen in Chapter 3, they are the result of deliberate choices of people to pursue certain goals with violent means. Often they see this as their only choice in conditions that are beyond their control. Serbs in Croatia took up arms against the newly independent Croatian state in 1992 when this state adopted a flag, currency, and political rhetoric that brought back memories of the Second World War, when the fascist Croatian Ustasha regime had conducted a policy against Serbs that was in all but name genocidal. To be sure, the violent conflict that ensued in Croatia and subsequently engulfed Bosnia and Herzegovina as well was not a sudden, unpredictable, and uncontrollable phenomenon of mass violence, but had been carefully and deliberately planned by political leaders in Belgrade, Zagreb, and Sarajevo, and their local allies on the ground.

Kosovo Albanians began to organize militarily and support violent resistance to the Serbs only when they felt that they had exhausted all other means to pursue their goal of self-determination peacefully. Clearly outgunned and outnumbered by Serb armed forces, their use of violence was of a more strategic kind—to provoke a disproportionate response from Belgrade that would compel the international community to intervene with military force. The suicide bombings of Palestinian extremists targeting Israeli civilians have an additional dimension that makes bargaining difficult, if not impossible: they are part of a quasi-religious mission to annihilate the state of Israel. This is, of course, a futile tactic because the suicide bombers hardly pose a threat to the survival of the state of Israel. However, it is also noteworthy that, while the non-recognition of Israel and desire to destroy this state had long been on the agendas of the PLO, Hamas, Hezbollah, and other such groups, suicide bombers are a far more recent phenomenon born out of a combination of the Palestinian desperation at confronting a far superior and at times brutal and cruel adversary and the growing influence of a radical, fundamentalist variety of Islam that thrives in such desperation and finds its willing recruits. This is particularly the case in the Middle East, but it is not a phenomenon exclusive to this region: while Russian tanks and artillery were pounding what is left of the Chechen capital of Grozny, Chechen rebels continued to plot their revenge attacks—kidnappings of soldiers and international observers, bombings in Moscow, and the large-scale hostage taking in the Bolshoy Theatre and a school in Beslan in North Ossetia.

At the same time, and even though ethnic conflicts are for the most part fought within the borders of existing states, the parties active in them are not only domestic agents. As a result of the threat to international security and stability, international organizations, neighbouring states, and regional and world powers may all have their own interests in particular conflicts: a potential nuclear confrontation between India and Pakistan over Kashmir is a global concern; violence in southern, eastern, and western Sudan remains a threat to the stability of the region; the wars in the former Yugoslavia were a serious source of concern for the EU and NATO as they occurred at their borders. But it is not only states and state organizations that become involved in ethnic conflicts. Stateless groups such as the Kurds or Tamils often have members of their own ethnic group living in neighbouring states or have a diaspora of economically better-off brethren elsewhere in the world willing and able to support their struggle with money, arms, and political lobbying.

Finally, inasmuch as ethnic conflicts create zones of instability and insecurity beyond the reach, and occasionally beyond the grasp, of law enforcement agencies, they are also a favourite 'playground' for common criminals and increasingly become operating bases for terrorists with an international agenda as well. This has been the case in Kashmir and the southern Philippines where Islamist extremists from the anti-Soviet war in Afghanistan grafted their own religious struggle on to pre-existing local conflicts and contributed significantly to their escalation in the 1990s. They achieved the same in Chechnya, but failed in Tajikistan, Bosnia and Herzegovina, and Kosovo.[5]

This mix of different domestic and international actors is another salient feature of many ethnic conflicts in today's world. Before we can understand more fully why and how some ethnic conflicts can be resolved whereas others seem to evade stable settlement for decades, it is necessary to explore the different kinds of agents that are active in ethnic conflicts, to analyze the strategies of various conflict parties, to examine their justifications for the use of violence and counter-violence, and to show what rationales they have in pursuing specific strategies. That is what this chapter sets out to do before we turn our attention to matters of conflict resolution in Chapter 5.

An easy way to begin addressing the various issues involved in coming to terms with understanding agents and their agendas and tactics in ethnic conflicts is to begin by mapping out different types of ethnic conflict according to which conflict parties are involved. A very simple distinction would be between inter-ethnic conflicts— that is, conflicts between different ethnic groups—and conflicts in which one or more ethnic groups are in conflict with the state in which they live. However, as we have seen earlier on, ethnic groups and the states in which they live are not the only agents involved in today's ethnic conflicts. Nevertheless, this distinction is a good starting point for further discussion, because we are concerned with ethnic conflicts in the sense that the ethnic dimension—at least one group defining the causes, fault lines, and potential solutions of the conflict along a real or perceived ethnic divide—is the predominant one in the conflict. In other words, purely or predominantly criminally motivated turf wars between gangs and insurrections caused by ideological or class differences are of lesser concern for the following examination of the parties to ethnic conflicts. On the other hand, however, ethnic conflicts at times overlap with other forms of violent conflict and some conflict parties occasionally even depend on their ability to continue the conflict by 'branching out' into other forms of violence, for example, to finance their war effort.

Let us begin our analysis from the perspective of individual groups. In their attempts to preserve, express, and develop their distinct identities, ethnic groups perceive threats and opportunities. The more deeply felt these perceptions are, the more they will be linked to the very survival of the group and the more intense will the conflict be that they can potentially generate. This is what we described earlier as the ethnic security dilemma. In a situation in which an ethnic group can rely only on itself to secure conditions in which its members can survive, it needs to acquire or retain sufficient power to fulfil this function—that is, to defeat the threats to, and seize the opportunities for, its survival. An ethnic group's desire to gain political power is, as we have seen in Chapter 2, expressed in the concept of ethnonationalism.

It is easy to see that different ethnic groups will have incompatible doctrines of ethnonationalism—manifest, for example, in claims to identical stretches of territory, attempts to eradicate other groups' cultural heritage, or the simple denial of their existence as distinct groups. Again, there is no automatism that leads from the existence of distinct groups in one state or region to intense violent conflict. It takes some people to lead and many to follow down a path at the end of which stands not peaceful accommodation, as in Switzerland or Belgium or many parts of India, but genocidal violence as in the Balkans or Rwanda.

In the relationship between different ethnic groups and between groups and the state in which they live, opportunities for, and threats to, group survival have various, yet concretely identifiable, meanings. For groups, these threats and opportunities relate, broadly speaking, to their secure survival as groups. For states, what is at stake is primarily their territorial integrity and their ability to enforce law and order. As we will see in Chapter 5, for ethnic groups, opportunities will manifest themselves, for example, in specific cultural rights or arrangements for self-government, realized in local, regional, or federal frameworks within the state in which they live. In the absence of these and similar forms of accommodation, the only real opportunities for ethnic groups to secure their survival may be secession followed either by independent statehood or by unification with another state. Threats to group survival generally occur when states or other ethnic groups deny an ethnic group access to the resources that the latter deems essential for its survival as a distinct group—for example, access to linguistic, educational, or religious facilities, and to positions of power in the institutions of the state. Threats can also become manifest in policies of forced assimilation, in discrimination, and in deprivation. At their most extreme, they take the form of ethnic cleansing and genocide.

It is in these most extreme cases that the distinction between inter-ethnic and group-state conflict becomes increasingly blurred—that is, one or more ethnic groups have monopolized the institutions of the state and now use them to commit gross human rights violations. The most obvious example of this kind is the Holocaust. In other recent cases of ethnic cleansing, such as in the Balkans and the Darfur region of western Sudan, and genocide, such as in Rwanda, states either partially relied on or backed allied ethnic groups to do their dirty work. Using irregular militias—the Janjaweed in western Sudan and Arkan's Tigers and Vojislav Seselj's Chetniks in Bosnia and Herzegovina spring to mind—states are, or at least think they are, able to keep their hands clean of war crimes while still achieving their aims in the conflict.

To be sure, genocide and large-scale ethnic cleansing are not the rule in most ethnic conflicts. Yet, even in its less extreme forms, the groups and gangs fighting in violent ethnic conflicts are responsible for the deaths of tens if not hundreds of thousands of people every year. In most cases, the overwhelming majority of these victims are civilians. At the dawn of the twentieth century, civilians accounted for about 10 per cent of war fatalities. By the Second World War, this figure had risen to about half of those killed in wars being civilians. In the Second World War, mostly as a consequence of Nazi Germany's total war strategy and its policy of extermination of 'inferior peoples', as well as to some extent the increased use of aerial bombardment by the Nazis and the Allies, civilian death tolls rose to about two-thirds of all people killed. By the beginning of the twenty-first century, more than 90 per cent of the victims of violent conflict were civilians. Apart from 'technological' reasons, such as the greater availability and use of airpower and missiles, the main reason for this staggering increase in civilian casualties is the changing nature of conflicts from battlefield wars between the regular armed forces of states to conflicts involving in part or wholly non-state actors, as is the case in all ethnic conflicts. These conflicts are fought among, and sometimes against, civilian populations. One reason for this is also that distinctions between combatants and non-combatants become difficult in the streets and squares of cities and villages where rival factions and insurgents do not always, if ever, identify themselves as fighters.

Another reason is that strategy and tactics in ethnic conflicts in many ways deliberately target civilians—to exact revenge, intimidate their opponents, and displace or destroy whole enemy populations defined on the basis of ethnic criteria. This means that civilians are increasingly no longer accidental victims caught in cross-fire.

The reasons why groups and states act in such a manner—that is, why they deny others the resources essential to their survival as a group, physically and/or culturally—differ. As we have seen, in some cases greed is the underlying motive; in others it is the perception of a threat aimed at one's own group that makes it seem rational to deprive another group of the means and opportunities to carry out this alleged threat. These are, of course, very general and unsatisfactory explanations. The underlying problem is that at this level of generalization—what explains the actions of all actors in all conflicts—explanations cannot but be highly general too. The alternative to this kind of generalization is to look at individual cases and perhaps small groups of cases and apply a more sophisticated analysis that involves several different levels.

Such a breakdown into different levels of analysis is useful, because it allows provision of a more systematic and accurate account of factors causing, or facilitating, the outbreak of ethnic conflict and their specific role. Such an understanding then enables the analyst to make more precise and potentially effective policy recommendations for the management, settlement, and prevention of ethnic conflicts. Taking us back to the analysis of causes of ethnic conflicts, it also allows us to be more specific about why people at times make particular decisions that have predictably grave consequences.

The different levels of analysis that should be considered when explaining ethnic conflicts are individuals (leaders and followers), groups (as direct and indirect factors: groups act on their own and influence the state's actions), the state (which can be a party to the conflict and/or a mediator between warring groups), the regional context (state and non-state actors interacting in processes of escalation and de-escalation), and the broader international setting in which a conflict originates and escalates (again, involving both state and non-state actors).

If we were to apply such an approach to analyzing the conflict in Kosovo as it headed towards escalation and international intervention in the second half of the 1990s, five levels of analysis are appropriate: Kosovo's inter-ethnic and intra-ethnic situations; involving individuals and groups; the situation in Serbia (the state level); the regional context (former Yugoslavia and its successor states); and the international setting of the post-Cold War era.

The inter-ethnic situation in Kosovo at the time was characterized by a curious numerical and power balance between the groups that saw the numerically largest group—Kosovo Albanians—deprived of political power by a local minority of Serbs backed by Belgrade. Splits between these two groups were ethnic, linguistic, and religious with virtually no overlap between them. Although the socio-demographic structure of Kosovo also included other small ethnic minorities such as Roma and Turks, the main line of confrontation existed between ethnic Albanians and ethnic Serbs, and the main bone of contention was over political power and the attendant privileges that it brought with it, such as access to education, healthcare, jobs, all of which had been largely denied to ethnic Albanians from the early 1990s onwards. Serb dominance in the 1990s, however, only reversed a pattern of discrimination experienced by Serbs themselves in the 1970s and 1980s when ethnic Albanians dominated the institutions of the province under the old Yugoslav constitution.

It would be misleading to assume that the two main groups in the conflicts—Serbs and Albanians—were homogeneous actors. Albanians were united by the common goal of achieving independence from Serbia, but agreed on little else. Some favoured violent rebellion, others argued for a campaign of civil disobedience. Some sought accommodation with local Serbs; for others every individual Serb was one too many in a territory in which Albanians claimed to have been the first settlers. Finally, some ethnic Albanians harboured a dream of a greater Albania uniting all Albanians in the Balkans in one state (and thus making territorial claims to

Macedonia, southern Serbia, and Montenegro as well), others 'merely' demanded a greater Kosovo bringing together all the Albanians from the former Yugoslavia, and others again were content with just an independent Kosovo.

Serbs in Kosovo were similarly divided over some crucial issues. Although some favoured accommodation with ethnic Albanians in order to preserve what was left of the former Yugoslavia, others took a more radical view. In particular, Serbian refugees from Croatia and Bosnia and Herzegovina who had been resettled in Kosovo after losing their homes as a result of the wars fought across the former Yugoslavia had no intention of living anywhere but in a Serb-dominated state, even if this meant large-scale killings and expulsions of ethnic Albanians. This war-hardened and highly radicalized faction was the one that received most support from Belgrade, similar to the increasing support that militant Albanians, soon to become the Kosovo Liberation Army (KLA), received from the Albanian diaspora in western Europe and the USA. Thus, intra-ethnic factionalization and inter-ethnic discontent mutually fed off each other and contributed to the violent turn that the conflict increasingly took after 1996.

Although the situation on the ground was where most of the dynamics of escalation played out, it is equally clear that developments at other levels contributed to this and interacted with factors in Kosovo. Not only did outside forces support different factions within Kosovo and thus help swing the pendulum away from the possibility of accommodation, but they also had agendas of their own in which Kosovo and the conflict there were merely one among many factors. For Serb President Milosevic, Kosovo was the last stand in his desperate attempt to cling on to power in Belgrade. Allowing Kosovo to break away from what by then had become the two-state Federal Republic of Yugoslavia, consisting of Serbia and Montenegro and the two provinces of Kosovo and Vojvodina within Serbia, was tantamount to conceding the end of even this much-reduced state. Having risen to power on the back of a rallying cry to defend Serbs wherever they lived and having lost this battle in Croatia and Bosnia and Herzegovina, Milosevic saw himself in no position to compromise; nor was any of the so-called democratic opposition in Serbia able or willing to challenge Milosevic over his Kosovo policy, because much of the Serbian public bought into the mythology over Kosovo—a historically significant, culturally important part of Serbia in which Serbs had been victimized by Albanians as much today as when they had been defeated in a fourteenth-century battle defending Christian Europe against the Ottoman Turks. Nor did Milosevic think that he needed to bow to international demands. Assuming Russia to be on his side and ready to stand up to Western powers, he was, however, sorely disappointed when this proved a miscalculation and NATO did launch air strikes against Serbia after the breakdown of negotiations in Rambouillet in March 1999.

For the international community, Kosovo was as important symbolically as it was for Milosevic. Having reacted too late and too indecisively, in Bosnia and Herzegovina, to prevent the war and ethnic cleansing there, Kosovo was meant to be a lesson learned from earlier failure. In addition, NATO was on the look-out for a new mission in the post-Cold War world, and humanitarian intervention seemed a worthwhile goal for which to employ its military capabilities. Finally, Milosevic was no longer seen as the guarantor of stability in the Balkans as he had portrayed himself during and after the Dayton negotiations that ended the war in Bosnia and Herzegovina. Rather, he had become something like public enemy number 1, and strategists in Western capitals were well aware that defeating him in Kosovo would deal him a significant blow. At the same time, Kosovo was in itself considered a major factor of instability with regard to neighbouring Macedonia. Here relations between ethnic Albanians—about a quarter of the population—and ethnic Macedonians had been uneasy and tense, but violent conflict had been avoided throughout the 1990s. With the deteriorating situation in Kosovo, however, a very grave risk of spill-over was perceived, which the international community was desperate to avoid. Thus, achieving a particular settlement for Kosovo became very important: independence would have sent the wrong signal to a similarly aggrieved Albanian minority in Macedonia, while standing by in the face of an increasingly brutal counter-insurgency campaign by Serbian security forces was equally counter-productive because this could have encouraged more radical elements among ethnic Macedonians to 'deal' with their particular situation in a similar way.

Thus, a multi-level analysis of the escalation of the Kosovo conflict reveals that grievances of ethnic groups, power struggles between and within them, personal agendas of power preservation, regional dynamics of past and present conflicts, and considerations of international security all interacted in a unique way that cannot be captured by broad generalizations about greed, creed, or grievances.

Another case that benefits from a more nuanced analysis at several levels is the Rwandan genocide, which is a particularly instructive example of why, by whom, and how an entire group can become the target of ethnic violence. Rwanda had a past history of inter-ethnic violence. Tutsi, a small minority of less than 20 per cent of the population, had ruled the country for a long period of time, backed by Belgium as the colonial power. They were ousted in 1959 when Rwanda became independent and held elections. The violence that accompanied and followed this 'revolution' until the late 1960s killed about 20,000 Tutsi and drove 10 to 15 times as many into exile. As discrimination continued in the years thereafter, the number of Tutsi in Rwanda decreased further. According to the 1991 census, the reliability of which is disputed, fewer than 10 per cent of Rwanda's population were Tutsi.

Decades of emigration and exile had radicalized many Tutsi in neighbouring Uganda from where they launched an attack on Rwanda in October 1990, spearheaded by the Rwandan Patriotic Front (RPF). Although initially not a serious military threat, Rwanda's Hutu president Juvenal Habyarimana saw the RPF as an opportunity to consolidate his power and suppress internal Hutu opposition to his nearly two-decade reign. In the course of the next three-and-a-half years, Habyarimana and his circle of advisers and allies managed to 're-align' Rwanda's population into true 'Rwandans'—those Hutu who supported the incumbent regime—and 'enemies'—the Tutsi in Rwanda and Hutu who opposed the president. Identifying Tutsi did not pose great logistical difficulties. Each citizen of Rwanda had had to register his or her ethnic identity since colonial times, and the physical appearances of Hutu and Tutsi are also different. However, despite a legacy of Tutsi domination, there was a relatively high degree of integration between the two groups. They spoke the same language, and had a shared history, similar customs, traditions, and religious beliefs. There were few signs of a cultural division of labour or of a segregated school system. In addition, divisions within each group were often more important than ethnic group membership: regional distinctions between the north-west and the rest of the country and between the poor and the better off were much more significant for most ordinary Rwandans, regardless of their ethnic background.

Yet, as the invasion of the RPF grew in pace and the government became militarily weakened and was eventually forced into signing a peace agreement that provided for Tutsi participation in the government, it became increasingly easy for Habyarimana and his supporters to create a situation in which perceptions of a security dilemma could take hold among large sections of the country's Hutu population. In parallel, Habyarimana and his allies began to train the youth wing of his party militarily, as did other Hutu parties. The spread of militias and the fact that most of their attacks on Tutsi and political opponents of the president were not prosecuted made violence more widely acceptable to many Rwandans. As the RPF grew politically and militarily more powerful, security concerns spread beyond supporters of the president to other Hutu who were easily susceptible to the political messages broadcast by the new pro-regime radio station Radio Télévision Libre des Mille Collines and joined the so-called Hutu Power movement, especially after Tutsi soldiers in neighbouring Burundi killed the country's first democratically elected Hutu president in October 1993. This easily confirmed anxieties among Rwandan Hutu about Tutsi intentions to restore the old regime of Tutsi-dominated government and made many of them fear for their status and security.

With increasing numbers of militarily trained young Hutu available, most of them armed with machetes specifically imported for subsequent use in the genocide, and all of them indoctrinated with fear and hatred of Tutsi, all that was needed for the mass killings of Tutsi and Hutu opponents to president Habyarimana and his regime to begin was a triggering event. This occurred when on 6 April 2004 a plane carrying Habyarimana was shot down. In a coup-like scenario, the Presidential Guard and other troops commanded by Habyarimana's closest associates initially turned against Hutu government officials and politicians opposed to the late president and his regime, thus establishing the political control of state institutions necessary to begin the systematic slaughter of almost one million Tutsi over the coming months. Virtually unopposed by a small UN force in the country and facing an international community unable and unwilling to intervene quickly and decisively, the genocide organizers gradually forced and gave incentives to ever greater numbers of Hutu to participate in the killing of their Tutsi neighbours.

Soldiers and policemen led the initial stages of the genocide in the capital and in major cities and towns. Their military training and technological advantages over unarmed Tutsi civilians made it possible for comparatively few of them to commit large-scale murder and prepare the ground for militias and civilians armed with machetes and other low-tech weaponry to finish what the military had begun with their machine guns.

By the time that the organizers of the genocide were weakened militarily by the advances of the RPF and threatened by an increasing determination in the organized international community to stop the genocide, they had murdered about three-quarters of the Tutsi population of Rwanda. Popular support for the genocide also waned, and ever-smaller numbers of civilians participated in it. Intra-Hutu rivalries began to resurface, further undermining the government, which was eventually defeated by the RPF in summer 2004, engaging in massive revenge killings that cost the lives of tens of thousands of Hutu by the end of August.

In almost all other ethnic conflicts in recent years, genocidal violence of the scale seen in Rwanda has been largely absent. Violence, rape, torture, and mass killings have, however, occurred, but their purpose has been to terrorize, intimidate, and expel members of other ethnic groups rather than to exterminate an entire group. Take the example of the conflict in Bosnia and Herzegovina. Even though the conflict in this successor state of the former Yugoslavia was not the first one in which mass rape was used as a weapon of war, it was the one that brought the issue to broad public attention. With tens of thousands of rape victims—a conservative estimate by the European Commission in 1993 already spoke of 20,000—Bosnia is among the largest documented cases of this kind in recent history. What distinguishes the use of rape as a weapon of war from instances where rape occurs in the course of conflict is that it is a deliberate, systematic, and well-organized strategy that serves purposes well beyond the sexual gratification of those who commit the crime. As a military strategy and an ethnonationalist 'policy', rape, often conducted in public, is used systematically to force communities to flee their villages in fear of further atrocities. This kind of rape-induced ethnic cleansing often acts in the fashion of the domino principle: the people fleeing one village will tell their stories to people in the next village who will then also try to escape. If used only in this way, rape as a military strategy aiming at ethnic cleansing would need only a small number of actual cases to terrorize an entire ethnic group into giving up their homeland. Yet rape as an ethnonationalist policy expresses deep inter-ethnic hatred and manifests itself in the kind of mass rape that happened in Bosnia and Herzegovina in the early 1990s. It is meant to humiliate, demoralize, and eventually destroy an ethnic group, not merely to force it to leave a piece of territory claimed by a different group. Rape as a war strategy and expression of extreme ethnonationalist hatred often goes hand in hand with torture and killing.[6] Many rape victims in Bosnia and Herzegovina were subjected to prolonged ordeals of rape and torture in prisons and camps, and some of the victims were later killed by their tormentors for fear of retribution.

Even though rape, torture, summary executions, and ethnic

cleansing were committed by all parties in the conflict in Bosnia and Herzegovina, the Serbs were infamous for the largest number of these gross human rights violations. Well-documented accounts of their victims allow the establishment of a pattern of modern ethnic warfare that, although often connected to the harrowing images of places like Srebrenica, has been commonplace in many other conflicts. Regular or irregular forces would arrive in villages and towns, often after prolonged bombardments and artillery fire, and concentrate the non-Serb population in public squares or buildings. Following the public execution of political and community leaders, women, children, and elderly people would be 'evacuated' while men of fighting age would be liquidated and their bodies buried in mass graves. What is particularly disturbing about many such cases is that local Serbs often aided paramilitaries in identifying, torturing, raping, and killing their non-Serb neighbours—out of fear of reprisals, and, as in Rwanda, out of a sense of misplaced loyalty to their own ethnic group, out of greed in the hope of sharing in the spoils of looting left properties, and often out of sheer lust in humiliating people of a different ethnic group.

The situation in Bosnia and Herzegovina is by no means unique. In many ways, it even pales when compared with other incidents of ethnic conflict, such as in the eastern part of the Democratic Republic of Congo (DRC), where civilians have borne the brunt of the humanitarian disaster unleashed by one of Africa's worst conflicts. Even since the official 'end' of the war, the area remains cut-off from government services and humanitarian aid by continuing insecurity and because of its geographical remoteness. Human suffering is additionally compounded by the plethora of human rights violations inflicted on the civilian population by as many as 10 different armed groups active in the area, including local gangs, government forces, and irregular and regular combatants based in neighbouring countries. Civilians also suffer disproportionately from the consequences of the material destruction afflicted on agricultural land, local hospitals, health centres, and schools. Sporadic and local violence has not only taken a devastating toll on civilians but has also threatened the resurgence of a wider war involving neighbouring Burundi, Rwanda, and Uganda. In early June 2004, Tutsi forces of the so-called RCD-Goma, who are opposed to the transitional government established as part of the peace agreement, attacked and took control of the capital of South Kivu province, Bukavu, close to the border with Rwanda. According to an Amnesty International report, more than 100 civilians were killed and many rapes committed in the few days before forces loyal to the transitional government recaptured the city.[7] The report also emphasises that the scale at which rape was committed in the DRC was unprecedented: some 40,000 cases have been reported in total for the eastern areas of the DRC, which is likely to be only the tip of the iceberg. Health problems, unwanted pregnancies, and being socially ostracized are the most common consequences that rape victims have to endure, in addition to the violence and humiliation committed against them during the actual rape or during their often weeks- and months-long enslavement in the camps of armed groups.

Impunity, 'reward', superstition, and fetishism are among the most common individual motivations to commit rape, according to Amnesty International. However, as sexual violence in the DRC, just as in Bosnia and Herzegovina, Bangladesh, Chechnya, and elsewhere, also has a clear ethnic dimension, individual motivation is not enough to account for its widespread occurrence. Rape remains a strategy of ethnic warfare to assert control, demoralize opponents, and force people to flee. One of Amnesty International's informants and her two sisters were gang raped in Bukavu in June 2004 while rebel Tutsi forces had control of the town. Her account is typical of the experiences of the countless victims of sexual violence in ethnic conflicts everywhere:

That evening, we could see them sitting with their vehicle in front of our house. The electricity in the town had been cut off and as soon as it got dark, they came in. They looted everything, and took it away in a truck. Then they asked us how old we all were. They only took the youngest—my mother and eldest sister were not touched. Jeanette was raped by seven soldiers in the storeroom, Francine by eight soldiers in the shop. They put me in the bathroom. I fought with five of the soldiers when they tried to make my brothers watch me being raped. But they beat me so hard. They tore off my clothes. It was the first time I'd had sexual relations. When I bled the soldier hit me in the face because he said I had 'dirtied' him. At some point my mother and brothers were brought in to watch. When one group had finished, another group came in. I just lay there, without moving. It lasted all night.

These and other cases also illustrate in dramatic fashion the inability and unwillingness of the organized international community to intervene decisively during the early stages of this and many similar conflicts. In Srebrenica, probably the best-documented case of this kind, 7,500 Bosnian Muslim men were killed in what was supposed to be a UN-designated safe haven, protected by some 800 poorly equipped Dutch soldiers with an ill-conceived mandate. By the time the Bosnian Serb army under the now indicted war criminal Ratko Mladić took Srebrenica, the UN peace keepers, morally and physically exhausted after a long siege, had little resistance to offer and received no back-up from international forces elsewhere in Bosnia and Herzegovina. Knowingly or unknowingly, they assisted Mladić and his troops by helping separate men from women and children, who were 'evacuated' from Srebrenica and negotiated their own free passage from the area while the remaining Muslim men were summarily executed.

More than a decade later, a similar scenario of ethnic cleansing, rape, torture, and mass killings unfolded in the Darfur region of western Sudan. In many ways, it bore all the hallmarks of the Bosnian experience: an ethnic conflict in which irregular forces fight each other, one side with the backing of the government, leading to massive displacement, a humanitarian crisis within Sudan and neighbouring Chad, and an international community that takes little if any action. Violence in the Darfur region in western Sudan erupted in February 2003 when an armed rebel group, calling itself the Sudan Liberation Movement/Army (SLM/A), began to launch attacks on government targets. Made up mainly of members of the Fur, Zaghawa, and Masalit ethnic groups of the region, it claimed underdevelopment as its main grievance. Two months later a second group, the so-called Justice and Equality

Movement (JEM), emerged, and the two groups continued their insurgency against the central government in Khartoum at a time when peace negotiations aimed at ending the decade-old conflict between the predominantly Arab Muslim north and the Christian black African south were headed towards conclusion, with a deal beginning to take shape according to which the south was to gain greater autonomy and a greater share in the oil revenue generated from its relatively rich natural resource base. Long a concern of the international community, the widespread, albeit fluctuating, attention that the north–south conflict had received was something that had eluded the western regions of Sudan thus far. The conflict between settled black African communities and nomadic Arabs and their Janjaweed militia had similarly been ongoing for some time, but the humanitarian disaster with which the international community was confronted in the summer of 2004 began to develop only as the government responded to the SLA and JEM insurgency. The main trigger for the government's counter-insurgency operation seems to have been an SLA attack on the airport of Al-Fashir, in which 70 members of the Sudanese army were killed. As in Kosovo some years earlier, insurgents used violence strategically to provoke a disproportionate government crackdown, in the hope of generating international attention and intervention. Their failure to achieve the latter has had tremendous consequences in terms of human suffering, borne, as always, by the civilian population of the region.[8]

During the conflict that developed, rebels as well as government-backed militias and government troops are said to have committed human rights abuses against civilians. Amnesty International reported in July 2004 that the SLA and JEM were implicated in a number of cases of deliberately targeting civilians, including torture and rape. There were also allegations of unlawful killings and hostage taking on the part of the insurgents, but few, if any, of them could be verified by the human rights organization as a result of the difficult situation on the ground.[9]

The government's main strategy so far has been to rely on irregular forces, the so-called Janjaweed, who are given free reign in their raids on villages of other ethnic groups thought to support the SLA and JEM. A young woman, interviewed by Amnesty International in a refugee camp in eastern Chad, described the tactics of the Janjaweed when attacking her village:

The attack took place at dawn in September 2003 when many Janjaweed arrived on camels, horses and by cars. Some Arab women, on donkeys and on camels, accompanied them. The women took part in the looting. I was sleeping when the attack took place. I was taken away by the attackers in khaki and in civilian clothes, along with dozens of other girls, and had to walk for three hours. During the day, we were beaten up and the Janjaweed they told us: 'you, the black women, we will exterminate you; you have no God.' We were taken to a place in the bush where the Janjaweed raped us several times at night. For three days, we did not receive food and almost no water. After three days, the Janjawid had to move to another place and set us free. They told us: 'next time we come, we will exterminate you all, we will not even leave a child alive'.[10]

There have also been reports of joint operations between government troops and militia. This is a 'tried and tested' approach that the government in Khartoum had also used in the civil war with the south, and its consequences are, if anything, even more devastating in the Darfur region. The scorched-earth tactics of the Janjaweed had, by early July 2004, resulted in 30,000 dead, 1.2 million people displaced within Sudan, and 130,000 refugees in neighbouring Chad. Using executions, rape, and torture, the aim of the government and its allied militias appears to be the systematic ethnic cleansing of the Darfur region in order to quell the rebellion, 'reward' its allies, and set an example for other potentially restive regions in the country that resent the exclusive nature of the north–south deal on power sharing and wealth sharing.

In the same way in which the international community remained restrained, if not silent, in relation to Kosovo until the Kosovo Liberation Army took up arms against Serbian government forces and Serb civilians because President Milosevic was thought to be an important guarantor of stability in Bosnia and Herzegovina, nothing was done over Darfur for nearly two years in order not to endanger the north–south peace negotiations. In both cases, the result of delayed action by the organized international community has contributed to the unfolding of major humanitarian crises. But there is another important point that arises from this discussion. American scholar Alan Kuperman has repeatedly made the point that international intervention creates a moral hazard. As the international community, spurred on by widespread news coverage, tends to intervene in cases of gross human rights violations, insurgent movements who are too weak to win their battles with the central government without external assistance have a clear incentive to provoke vastly disproportionate government crack-downs affecting significant numbers of civilians. There is certainly a lot of substance to this argument, especially if one considers Kosovo, Rwanda, and more recently Darfur. What it also highlights is that belated, if any, international intervention remains the predominant feature of the international community's approach to most conflicts, but also that rebel movements are prepared to sacrifice large numbers of innocent civilians in pursuit of their goals. This general acceptance of innocent victims, the consequential brutalization of all sides in ethnic conflicts, and the long-term traumatic effects on the societies in question are some of the most worrying features of this kind of 'new war'.[11]

Yet, not all the news is bad. Over the past several years, there have also been cases in which intervention occurred early on and prevented the massive escalation of conflicts into the genocidal violence that we have seen in Rwanda and to a lesser extent in Bosnia and Herzegovina in the mid-1990s, and in the Darfur region in western Sudan more recently. The best examples of relatively successful preventions of possibly major ethnic conflicts are Macedonia and Burundi. As we return to specific strategies of conflict resolution in Chapter 5, including the role of external actors, a brief account of these two cases focusing on the key strategies applied in both conflicts will suffice to examine this other dimension of the roles of international organizations in ethnic conflicts.

As part of the Balkan quagmire, Macedonia had been on the radar screen of international organizations since the early 1990s. The only one of the former Yugoslav republics to secede peacefully from the socialist federation, it has a significant minority of ethnic Albanians, comprising about 25 per cent of the country's total population and living mostly in the western part of the country bordering Kosovo and Albania. In the 1990s, small UN and NATO missions prevented a spill-over of the conflict from Kosovo to Macedonia. Yet, frustrated with a lack of recognition of their distinct identity, especially their language, in public life and education and supported, if not incited, by their ethnic brethren in Kosovo, ethnic Albanians in Macedonia formed their own National Liberation Army and began to attack government targets in 2000. Initially low level, the violence soon escalated with insurgents shelling the capital's airport and government forces retaliating against ethnic Albanian settlements suspected of sheltering the rebels. Intense pressure from the EU and NATO on both sides, as well as on Kosovo Albanian politicians, and mediation of negotiations between the Albanian political parties in Macedonia and the government in the summer of 2001 led to the conclusion of the so-called Ohrid Agreement in August, bringing a swift end to the violence. Subsequent cease-fire monitoring missions sponsored by the EU ensured that both sides stuck to their commitment to give up violence. Although the EU-led conflict prevention effort arguably failed to prevent all violence, it managed to stop hostilities before they escalated into a full-blown civil war. The two military operations by the EU—Concordia and Proxima—conducted to support the stabilization of the country, and thus to create conditions under which the Ohrid Agreement could be implemented, have arguably also been part of a larger strategy of efforts to prevent re-ignition of the conflict and towards eventual settlement.

In Burundi, the stakes were far higher, because here, as in neighbouring Rwanda, a potential genocide was on the cards. In Burundi, ethnicity began to dominate political and economic competition only after the country's independence in 1966. As in Rwanda, the minority Tutsi population—14 per cent—came to control the government and military, whereas the majority Hutu population—85 per cent—remained confined to providing labour for the large agricultural sector. Little wonder that the Hutu developed serious and legitimate grievances about their situation as well as a determination to change this. Equally unsurprisingly, however, the Tutsi had little interest in giving up their privileged status.

As a consequence, Burundi has seen inter-ethnic violence for almost four decades. In 1972, a failed Hutu rebellion led to 150,000 Hutu killed and tens of thousands displaced. Another 150,000 Hutu died in 1988 in the course of violent confrontations between the (Tutsi-dominated) armed forces of Burundi and the Hutu opposition movement. Again, there were tens of thousands of displaced people and large numbers of refugees fled to neighbouring countries, especially Tanzania. Here they formed their own militias and intensified their attacks against government targets and Tutsi civilians in Burundi. In turn, army reprisals killed further thousands of Hutu and forced many more out of the country. In 1993, under a new constitution, multiparty elections took place resulting in the leader of the (Hutu) Front pour la démocratie au Burundi, Melchio Ndadaye, winning the presidency. Four months later, in October 1993, Ndadaye was assassinated by radical Tutsi elements in the armed forces, triggering a fully fledged civil war in which, first, large numbers of Tutsi were massacred, and then several hundred thousand Hutu were killed in quasi-genocidal retaliation strikes by the Tutsi-dominated military mostly against civilians. In April 1994, the newly elected president of Burundi, Cyprien Ntayamira, together with his Rwandan counterpart Juvenal Habyarimana, died in a plane crash, which triggered the long-prepared Rwandan genocide. Hutu refugees from Rwanda further destabilized the situation in Burundi and heightened the acute perception of a serious security dilemma among all parties. A massacre of Hutu refugees in 1995 was followed by a successful Tutsi coup in 1996. A further coup attempt failed in 2001, and sporadic but intense violence continued until 2004, all of which begs the question how Burundi can be considered a successful case of conflict prevention.

Conflict prevention is a moving target. To the extent that we can say that fully fledged civil war in Macedonia was prevented, it is just as easy to condemn the failure to prevent the outbreak of violence between the ethnic Albanian National Liberation Army and government forces earlier on. In Burundi, the success–failure equation is similar: the international community failed to prevent all violence, but succeeded in averting genocide, the ingredients and example for which were all present. Similar to the situation in Macedonia, a sense of guilt and the lessons learned from failure elsewhere were the fundamental reason why extensive efforts to prevent genocidal conflict escalation in Burundi were made and eventually succeeded. The UN established a mission for Burundi immediately after the 1993 coup. Within a few years, and especially after the genocide in Rwanda and the escalating conflicts in the DRC, the UN changed from a country-specific approach to a regional one and appointed a Special Representative of the Secretary General for the entire Great Lakes Region. A proposal by the then UN Secretary General Boutros Boutros-Ghali to invoke Chapter VII of the UN Charter, which allows for peace enforcement without the consent of the warring parties, failed, mostly as a result of a lack of support from France and the USA, which wanted to avoid a repetition of other failed Chapter VII missions, such as in Somalia and in Bosnia and Herzegovina. The Organization for African Unity (OAU, later renamed African Union [AU]) also focused its attention on the ensuing crisis and crucially began to facilitate all-party peace talks under the leadership of former Tanzanian president Julius Nyerere. The OAU's basic goal was to engage Burundi in negotiations. Between the spring of 1996 and 1998 several unsuccessful rounds of on-and-off negotiations were held in Arusha, Tanzania. After Nyerere's death in 1998, the peace process regained momentum when Nelson Mandela was appointed chief mediator and managed to secure wider regional and international support for the Arusha process, resulting in a transitional power-sharing agreement, signed on 28 August 2000. Regional support was crucial in brokering this success. Rwanda, Tanzania, and the DRC were determined to end the conflict that destabilized the entire region and acted collectively and mostly within the framework of the OAU to achieve this.

The case of Burundi is also noteworthy for the involvement of non-governmental organizations (NGOs) as active players in an ethnic conflict rather than as merely delivery vehicles of humanitarian aid. After the 1996 coup in Burundi, the Rome-based Community of Sant'Egidio facilitated secret peace talks between the Tutsi government and the Conseil national pour la défense de la démocratie (CNDD)—together with its military wing, the Forces pour la défense de la démocratie (FDD), one of the main armed Hutu opposition groups. Four rounds of meetings in Rome in 1996 and 1997 did not, however, end in a political settlement, because the parties could not agree on a new constitution. Only after the EU and the USA, which backed these efforts by the Community of Sant'Egidio, had had to acknowledge the failure of the talks, and the government and CNDD re-engaged in the Arusha process, which was backed by the UN and OAU and by 1998 mediated by Nelson Mandela, did the process move towards an inclusive settlement, even though the FDD and another Hutu rebel group initially refused to participate in it. Although there has been significant and legitimate criticism of Sant'Egidio's secret negotiation efforts and failure to involve other Hutu guerilla groups, it did, however, manage to engage representatives of the government and the CNDD/FDD into negotiations for a political solution, thus breaking down barriers between two of the major conflict parties.

The most important lesson that can be learned about conflict prevention, or more precisely the prevention of genocidal conflict escalation, from Burundi and Macedonia is that there must be an engagement of all conflict parties in conflict settlement. The early failure of Nyerere's efforts to broker a breakthrough in Arusha in 1996 and 1997 was the result of the parallel, but equally non-inclusive, negotiations in Rome. Thus, if the international community is partial towards talks with moderates only and lacks comprehensive coordination of all external efforts, it is bound to fail in conflict prevention. This, of course, must not be taken as blueprint prescription for successful conflict prevention as such: even well-coordinated, sustained, and inclusive outside efforts will always be limited to the extent that domestic actors have, or lack, a genuine interest in peace. They can be given incentives, and sometimes pressured to develop such an interest, but in the end external mediation is unlikely to overcome a domestic determination to fight a specific conflict to the bitter end.

Benign and constructive intervention by international organizations or coalitions of states is not, however, the only form of external influence on ethnic conflicts. The other two major external actors that we need to consider in our treatment of who participates in ethnic conflicts, and how, are diasporas and neighbouring states. To begin with the latter, neighbouring states, broadly defined as states of the same region even if they do not have a common border with the state in which the ethnic conflict takes place, often become willingly or unwillingly involved in such conflicts. We can distinguish between two different ways in which other states may be drawn into an ongoing conflict—diffusion and escalation.[12] Diffusion means that because of an ongoing conflict in one state conflict also occurs, or is at least more likely, in another. Both of the examples discussed earlier in this chapter fall into this category. The tensions in Rwanda and Burundi mutually heightened perceptions of a security dilemma among Tutsi and Hutu in both countries, and the 1993 coup in Burundi and the violence that followed it were, arguably, one of the factors that led radical Hutu elites in Rwanda to intensify their preparations for genocide.

In Macedonia, the conflict in neighbouring Kosovo had a similar effect. Radicalized and well-armed elements among the ethnic Albanian population in Kosovo lent their active support to their cousins in neighbouring Macedonia in the increasingly bitter struggle for more rights and recognition in which they were involved. The other way in which ethnic conflict in one country can 'spread' is through outside states intervening in an ongoing conflict elsewhere. Such escalation has occurred, for example, in the case of the DRC where several neighbouring states have intervened by supporting or harbouring militants, sending their own troops in to 'pacify' border regions, but also in order to share in the spoils of exploiting the DRC's rich mineral resource base. If we look at the Balkan wars in the 1990s, Serbia's involvement in Bosnia and Herzegovina and in Croatia could also be seen as a case of escalation. The rationale behind Serbian strategy was, however, different. It was a mission of territorial aggrandizement seeking to create a Greater Serbia, and it had a clear domestic purpose—helping Milosevic tighten his grip on power in what was left of the former Yugoslavia. Finally, the example of Russia's role in the south Caucasus, especially in Georgia, is typical of the behaviour of a regional hegemon trying to assert and maintain a position of power and influence in neighbouring states. The presence of Russian 'peacekeeping' troops in Georgia's two break-away regions of Abkhazia and South Ossetia ensures the continued separation of both territories from the rest of Georgia and keeps them beyond the control of the central government in Tbilisi. At the same time, Russia justifies its presence there both with an existing mandate of the Organization for Security and Cooperation in Europe (OSCE), which authorized Russian peacekeepers in South Ossetia, and with the need to fight Chechen terrorism, which is said to have bases in Abkhazia as well as in other regions of Georgia bordering Chechnya. Thus, the motivations that draw neighbouring states into ethnic conflicts elsewhere range from local and regional stability to serving national security interests to pursuing a specific domestic agenda to seeking economic gain. The two predominant modalities of their involvement are either direct military intervention or the covert or not so covert support for militant groups. In other words, states fight in ethnic conflicts elsewhere either themselves or by proxy. As we have seen in the preceding section, and will see again in Chapter 5, not all intervention by neighbouring states is malign. Often intervention is driven by humanitarian concern rather than narrowly defined self-interest. From this perspective, a temporary escalation of an ethnic conflict through the active military involvement of one or more neighbouring states may be a legitimate step towards an eventual peace settlement that brings the conflict to an end.

As with states, the role of diaspora communities can be both positive and negative. Diasporas can support moderates in their search for peace, but they have also been known to provide the funding for militants who pursue an otherwise legitimate agenda by means of violence. In many cases, the two even go hand in hand, because splits within a community on the ground about how best to promote its interests are often reflected in the diaspora as well. Take the examples of Northern Ireland and Kosovo. The Irish diaspora in the USA, for many years, was a major fundraising source for the IRA, but from the mid-1990s, and especially after the terrorist attacks on the USA on 11 September 2001 (9/11), it became instrumental in securing and maintaining two IRA ceasefires and pushing the paramilitary organization towards its first-ever act of decommissioning some of its weapons. In Kosovo, the Albanian diaspora communities in western Europe and the USA for many years provided financial assistance to Ibrahim Rugova's Democratic League of Kosovo (LDK) which peacefully pursued the goal of Kosovo independence and funded the Kosovo Albanian shadow state after 1991. However, a large portion of the funds that helped the Kosovo Liberation Army (KLA) establish itself in the mid-1990s also came from diaspora circles.

Another example of the destabilizing influence of diaspora groups is illustrated by recent developments in Macedonia. As part of the August 2001 Ohrid Agreement that ended the ethnic Albanian insurgency for greater rights and recognition in Macedonia, the country had to implement a controversial decentralization law that was to give greater autonomy to local governments, but also meant redrawing local administrative boundaries and reducing the number of local districts, leading to ethnic Macedonians losing their majority position to ethnic Albanians in a number of the new districts. While the inter-ethnic coalition government haggled in secret for weeks if not months over the precise details of the reform, unofficial local referenda were already taking place against any proposed boundary changes among ethnic Macedonians. The government, with a secure parliamentary majority, chose to ignore these referenda rather than engage with the population and address their concerns. This provided an opportunity for the World Congress of Macedonians to enter the debate. This international diaspora organization advocates 'Macedonia for the Macedonians' and casts its territorial net suitably wide to include not only the current Republic of Macedonia but also Aegean Macedonia, 'presently' within the borders of Greece, Pirin Macedonia 'at the moment' within the borders of Bulgaria, and two 'currently' Albanian regions, Mala Prespa and Golo Brdo.[13] It launched and funded an initiative for a referendum in Macedonia against the decentralization law and gathered 180,000 signatures in a six-month campaign—30,000 more than needed to force the government to hold a referendum on the decentralization law. Even though the referendum failed, because of deliberately low turn-out on the part of ethnic Albanians and pro-accommodation ethnic Macedonians, the issue has created new security concerns in Macedonia and throughout the wider region, contributed to renewed polarization in the country, and cast at least some doubt on the long-term future of inter-ethnic relations which had stabilized after the brief spell of violent conflict in 2001.

Although the impact of states, diaspora groups, and international governmental organizations and NGOs on ethnic conflicts can be both positive and negative as we have seen, that of criminal and terrorist networks is exclusively negative. The main reason for this is that criminal and terrorist networks benefit from the instability and insecurity created by ethnic conflicts. In turn, political leaders in conflict situations often depend on resources and revenues generated by organized criminal activity. As a consequence, criminal and political objectives become ever more closely intertwined the longer a conflict lasts, and the conflict becomes more protracted because its continuation serves the interests of key players.

Links between ethnic conflicts and organized crime, and more recently also between ethnic conflicts and international terrorism, are very real and add another dimension to the complexity that these conflicts already pose. In Afghanistan, continued inter-ethnic tensions and violence facilitate, and are sustained by the country's vast opium growth and trade. Drug trafficking also provides much-needed resources to buy weapons and reward followers in Chechnya and in the various Uighur separatist conflicts involving China, Kazakhstan, and Kyrgystan. Narcotics trafficking is also rampant in the instability created by ethnic conflicts in Burma, Kosovo, Kenya, Laos, Malaysia, Lebanon, Nigeria, Pakistan, Somalia, and the ethnic Albanian areas of southern Serbia bordering Kosovo. Drug-related organized crime may be the most common and most profitable activity that flourishes in the context of many ethnic conflicts, but it is not the only one. Human trafficking in its various forms—from the smuggling of illegal immigrants to that of prostitutes—is happening, for example, in Bangladesh, Chechnya, Kosovo, and Macedonia. Weapons are illegally traded and smuggled both for local 'consumption' and as a source of financing ongoing ethnic conflicts in Georgia, Ghana, Kazakhstan, Kosovo, the Solomon Islands, and Somalia. Kidnapping for ransom is common in Chechnya, Georgia, Kyrgystan, the Philippines, and Somalia, whilst in Mauritania and Sudan it has also been associated with modern forms of slavery. Diamond smuggling has sustained several parties in the civil war in the DRC, as well as in a number of non-ethnic conflicts elsewhere in Africa. That the connections between ethnic conflict and organized crime are not simply a phenomenon in developing countries is evident from Northern Ireland. Here paramilitary groups on both sides have financed their terrorist activities through a wide-ranging portfolio of criminal activities from extortion rackets to drug trading to the cross-border smuggling of petrol and diesel. On occasion, such as in the summer of 2001, turf wars between rival Loyalist gangs—otherwise claiming to defend the rights of Protestants—have exposed paramilitary activity as greed rather than grievance driven. This, however, does not mean that such conflicts are exclusively greed motivated. In many cases agendas of greed and grievance coexist in the same conflict, and not always in an uneasy way.[14]

Social, political, and economic instability, ethnic conflict, and organized crime often become so closely linked, and mutually reinforce each other to such an extent, that, over time, it becomes increasingly difficult to establish any clear causal relationships. In other words, in many cases it is impossible to determine whether criminal agendas drive ethno-political agendas or vice versa, whether instability is a cause or consequence of conflict and crime, and it is often difficult to distinguish politicians from criminals, warlords from community leaders, and paramilitaries from businessmen. We have already seen how, in relation to the DRC, ethnic, political, economic, and security concerns became intertwined in such a way that the 'civil' war there eventually involved regular and irregular armed forces based in several different countries across the region. Links between organized crime and ethnically based politicians in the former Yugoslavia are equally strong, yet on occasion the business interests of criminal gangs trump the political and ethnic rivalries of nations and national minorities. Ethnic Albanian and ethnic Serb gangs have allegedly struck deals with each other in carving up the 'market' for the sex trade and illegal migration, and during the siege of Sarajevo, local crime networks used their pre-war links with criminals among Serbian paramilitaries to supply the city with food, petrol, weapons, and ammunition.

In some of the successor states of the former Soviet Union, crime has also flourished, in particular in those regions where ethnic conflicts have occurred. Take the example of Transdniestria, a region in Moldova that has had quasi-state status for more than 10 years now. Here, the complete absence of any recognizable system of accountable and transparent government has created and sustained a continued market for illegal weapons, a flourishing drugs trade and transnational drug trafficking, automobile theft, the smuggling of various types of goods across borders, and a sizeable contribution to illegal migration and the sex trade. The situation in Transdniestria is in many ways similar to that in the southern Caucasus and central Asia. Politics, business, and crime have become indistinguishable in Georgia's separatist regions of Abkhazia and South Ossetia, in Nagorno-Karabakh, a territory disputed between Armenia and Azerbaijan for more than a decade, and in parts of Kazakhstan, Kyrgyzstan, and Uzbekistan.

Increasingly over the past 10 years, in many of the cases where a link between ethnic conflict and organized crime has emerged, a triadic relationship has subsequently become dominant, incorporating international terrorist networks or their local offspring. This relationship is predominantly one of convenience and necessity rather than one that has its basis in a common political agenda. Nevertheless, it contributes to perpetuating ethnic conflicts, delegitimizes often justified grievances of ethno-political movements, and presents governments with an opportunity to crack down on opponents without significant outside criticism, which in turn contributes to increasing polarization and intractability of ethnic conflicts.

The primary link between ethnic conflicts and local, regional, and international terrorist networks remains, however, the instability created by ethnic conflicts that seriously limits central government control over portions of states' territories, which can then become safe havens for terrorists to establish the bases from which they can plan operations and create the training camps in which they can 'educate' local and foreign recruits. Take the example of Somalia. The almost complete lack of anything resembling, even remotely, a functioning central government means that it is an ideal location for international terrorist networks offering easy access to Asia Minor and presenting a potential transit route from and to the Arab world. A domestic fundamentalist Islamic group, Al-Ittihad al-Islami, has over the past few years carried out attacks in Ethiopia, targeted Western interests in the Horn of Africa, and maintained links with al-Qaeda and provided local assistance to its members.

Similar cases in which social, political, and economic instability, causing and resulting from ethnic conflicts, provides the conditions in which terrorists can operate exist in Asia. Despite a large international troop presence, continuing lawlessness in Afghanistan and the rivalries between local warlords, who often have their support bases in specific clans and ethnic groups, still create the conditions in which remnants of the Taliban and significant numbers of al-Qaeda members can operate with impunity in the Afghan–Pakistan border regions. Further to the east in Asia, Kashmir remains a terrorist flashpoint providing a focus of activity for Islamist terror groups infiltrating from Pakistan and Pakistan-controlled Kashmir and attacking Indian government targets in the region as well as in India proper. In south-east Asia, the Philippines are another terrorist hotspot. Separatist Muslim forces in Mindanao have been 'credited' with a number of domestic terrorist attacks, whilst regional terrorist groups, such as Jemaah Islamiya, have used the Philippines as a basis for operations in the wider Asia–Pacific region. Other separatist groups in south-east Asia, such as in Indonesia, Malaysia, and Thailand, have, similar to those in the southern Philippines and in contrast to Jemaah Islamiya, a primarily domestic agenda in their struggle. However, their background in the Afghan Jihad in the 1980s fighting Soviet forces that had invaded the country in 1979 still provides regional links among them and between local groups and wider international terrorist networks such as al-Qaeda.

In the Middle East, Israel, the Gaza Strip, and the West Bank remained the main focus of terrorist activity, even though terrorist organizations, such as Hamas, the Palestine Islamic Jihad, the al-Aqsa Martyrs Brigade, and Hizbollah, received support from and shelter in other states in the region, including Lebanon, Syria, and Jordan. Suicide bombings, rocket attacks, and car bombs remain the preferred tactic of these organizations, who focus their activities predominantly on Israel, but who have occasionally also attacked Western targets in the region.

Links between terrorists and the parties fighting in ethnic conflicts are not a unique feature of the Middle East, Asia, and parts of Africa. In Europe, Georgia remains a crucial terrorist 'hub' for Chechen terrorists and their foreign partners. Bosnia and Herzegovina, too, continues to struggle to combat terrorism in the form of foreign Islamic extremists who provided support to Bosnian Muslim forces during the war in the early 1990s, and have subsequently used their local contacts to build a network of Islamic organizations, such as the Benevolence International Foundation, the Al-Haramain Islamic Foundation, and the Global Relief Fund, all of which reportedly have direct links to al-Qaeda.

In many parts of the world in which ethnic conflicts are ongoing we are thus faced with an increasing complexity of involved actors and a concurrent overlapping and interlocked interest structure. This may not necessarily be a novel feature of ethnic conflicts, but it is one that has become more and more 'routine'. There are fewer and fewer 'traditional' ethnic conflicts in which an aggrieved minority fights for greater recognition and more rights. As Chapters 3 and 4 have demonstrated the stakes in contemporary ethnic conflicts are high and diverse for a range of different actors, who include political leaders of states and rebel movements, as well as ordinary criminals and international terrorists who all fight fierce and ruthless campaigns, predominantly against civilians. This has important implications for the management and settlement of ethnic conflicts—the issue that we turn to in Chapter 5.

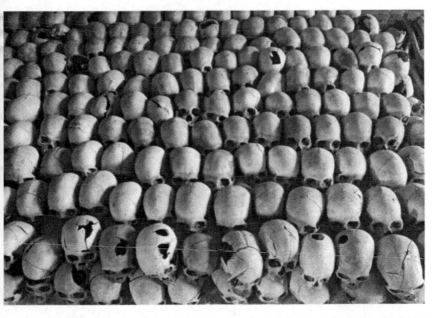

1. Skulls of the victims of the Ntarama massacre in Rwanda during the 1994 genocide, Nyamata, February 2004. © Gianluigi Guercia/AFP/Getty Images

2. MILF Parade in Mindanao, June 2005. © Mark Navales/AFP/Getty Images

3. Kashmiri women arguing with an Indian soldier in Srinagar, December 2001
© Stringer/India/Reuters

4. Women grieving at the burial of relatives in Ramallah, Palestinian territories, April 2002. © Laszlo Balogh/ Reuters

5. Israeli ambulance worker helping a woman away from the scene of suicide bomb, 21 March 2002. © Laszlo Balogh/Reuters

6. Arkan's Tigers, a notorious Serb paramilitary gang, posing for photographs in Croatia. © Rex Features/Sipa Press

7. Dubrovnik burning during the war in Croatia, 1991. © Jon Jones/Corbis Sygma

8. Young woman training to be a soldier for the Free Aceh Movement, November 2000. © Jacqueline M. Koch/Corbis

9. Nigerian woman standing outside her burnt-out home in Yelwa Town, Central Nigeria, May 2004. © George Esiri/Reuters

10. Displaced children, Darfur. © Islamic Relief

11. A former child soldier handing over a revolver to a UN peacekeeper in Liberia, December 2003. © Sven Torfinn/Panos Pictures

12. Child at a candlelight vigil for the victims of the Omagh bomb in Northern Ireland, August 1998. © Pacemaker Press International

5

Managing and settling ethnic conflicts

In 1998, Ulster Unionist leader David Trimble and the leader of the Social Democratic and Labour Party (SDLP) in Northern Ireland, John Hume, were jointly awarded the Nobel Peace Prize for their ultimately successful efforts to find a peaceful settlement to the conflict in Northern Ireland. Upon hearing news of the award, Trimble noted that he hoped this was not a premature decision. To many this may have seemed a surprising, and somewhat ungrateful, response, but in the light of Northern Ireland's history, in which peace deals had been made before and broken down, a more generous interpretation of his comments would be that Trimble was merely cautious about the long-term prospects of peace in the region. Despite this, international enthusiasm was unanimous when after 30 years and the death of more than 3,000 people, representatives of political parties from both communities in Northern Ireland and the governments of the UK and the Republic of Ireland agreed a comprehensive peace deal in the early hours of 11 April 1998 just after the deadline set by the US mediator George Mitchell had officially expired. Variously named after the venue of negotiations—Northern Ireland's capital Belfast—or the date on which agreement was reached—Good Friday—the Agreement, brokered after intense negotiations under international mediation, was hailed as a breakthrough to permanent peace in the troubled region. Subsequently, separate referenda in Northern Ireland and the Republic of Ireland endorsed the agreement, and elections to the new Northern Ireland Assembly returned a majority of pro-agreement politicians.

Was Trimble's scepticism mere political rhetoric? Hardly. The strains that the Agreement has had to endure so far have been enormous. Among them were the Omagh bombing of August 1998: the single worst atrocity committed in over 30 years of conflict, costing the lives of almost 30 people in a single incident. The annual marching season in Northern Ireland, in which primarily Protestants celebrate events in the region's history that are seen by many Catholics as reminders of centuries of oppression and second-class status, has led to regular stand-offs of police, Protestant marchers, and Catholic protesters, and on occasion sparked serious riots across Northern Ireland. More directly related to the deal concluded in 1998, the institutions agreed among the parties were set up only after a long delay—the Executive for Northern Ireland, for example, was formally established only in December 1999, more than a year and a half after the original agreement. Problems were also encountered in implementing police reform. Most critical of all, thus far, the question of the decommissioning of paramilitary weapons has led to serious impasses in the so-called political process: on several occasions, Trimble's Ulster Unionists threatened to walk out of the Executive, prompting the British government to suspend the very institutions meant to bring peace to Northern Ireland and to resume direct rule over the region. Nevertheless, the agreement appeared to hold and, in October 2001, Trimble greeted the beginning of arms decommissioning by the IRA, the main Republican terrorist group who had maintained a ceasefire since 1997, as finally seeing 'the day they said would never come'. A year later, in autumn 2002, allegations over continued intelligence gathering by the IRA prompted another resignation threat by Trimble followed by yet another suspension. Any attempt to restore the institutions has since failed, and elections in November 2003 returned the hard-line Unionists of Ian Paisley's Democratic Unionist Party and Sinn Féin, the Republican party, which, for many years, was considered by many as nothing but the political front of the IRA, as the two strongest political parties in Northern Ireland's assembly. No deal to restore self-government to Northern Ireland has been reached since then.

Despite .this rather gloomy picture, the situation in Northern Ireland in the aftermath of the 1998 Agreement compares favourably to what happened after earlier 'settlements' had been reached, most notably in 1973–74 and 1985, in that none of these political and institutional problems has led to a resumption of violence. In order to understand and appreciate this, it is useful to consider in some more detail the ups and downs of conflict management and settlement in Northern Ireland in the quarter century before the historic 1998 deal.

With the Northern Ireland conflict at its early climax in 1972 and 1973, the British government published a paper on 'The future of Northern Ireland'.[1] This followed the first suspension of government institutions in the region after the civil war-like escalation of violence since the late 1960s and the introduction of direct rule over Northern Ireland administered by a government department in London, with offices in Belfast, rather than by locally elected politicians. After a consultation process in Northern Ireland, new constitutional proposals for the region were introduced in the parliament in Westminster, which foresaw a power-sharing executive and closer, formal links between Northern Ireland and the Republic of Ireland. After their approval, elections to a Northern Ireland assembly were held on 28 June 1973, which returned 78 representatives of 8 parties to the new assembly. The predominantly Protestant so-called Official Unionists won 29.3 per cent of the vote and sent 24 members to the assembly, followed by the mainly Catholic SDLP with 22.1 per cent and 19 successful candidates. Together with the cross-communal Alliance Party, which won 9.2 per cent of the vote and 8 seats, they formed a coalition government, initially supported by 52 of the 78 members of the assembly.

Between 6 and 9 December 1973, representatives of the British and Irish governments and of the three parties involved in the designated executive met at Sunningdale and discussed and agreed the setting up of the Council of Ireland, a body meant to address the demand of Catholics for closer and more formal links with the

Republic of Ireland. The conference also agreed on closer cooperation in security-related matters, on inviting the Council of Ireland to draft a human rights bill, and on the possibility of a future devolution of further powers from Westminster to the Northern Ireland assembly and the institutions of the Council of Ireland.

The initially favourable situation of seemingly widespread support for these arrangements began to change dramatically early in 1974. In Northern Ireland, the general elections to be held across the UK on 28 February had been turned into a referendum on the new constitutional status of the region. Opponents of any change in the status quo united in a coalition called the United Ulster Unionist Council and won 51 per cent of the vote, which enabled them to take 11 of the 12 seats in Northern Ireland, with the remaining seat going to the SDLP. Riding high on the apparent widespread popular support among a vast majority of Protestants, the newly established Ulster Workers' Council called for new elections to the Northern Ireland assembly. When a motion against power sharing and the Council of Ireland was defeated in the assembly by 44 to 28 votes on 14 May 1974, the Ulster Workers' Council called for a general strike. The following two weeks of the strike brought Northern Ireland to an almost complete standstill. The British government failed to break up the strike and was unwilling to negotiate with the strike leaders. This led to the resignation of the Northern Ireland executive on 28 May 1974. The assembly was prorogued two days later, and direct rule was resumed.

Why had what seemed such a promising opportunity initially failed to bring peace to Northern Ireland? The reasons for this are manifold and must be sought in Northern Ireland itself, as well as in London and Dublin. Even though the initial elections to the Northern Ireland assembly in 1973 seemed to be a clear vote in favour of the new constitutional status, the reality of the situation in the region betrayed this superficial impression. The cooperating elites had a rather secure two-thirds majority inside the assembly, but their influence and control over their (former) electorate outside were far less permanent and stable. To complicate the situation even further, Harold Wilson, the Labour Prime Minister, condemned the strike called by the Ulster Workers' Council in 1974 in a TV broadcast as a 'deliberate and calculated attempt to use every undemocratic and unparliamentary means for the purpose of bringing down the whole constitution of Northern Ireland'. He also accused the strikers of 'sponging on Westminster and British democracy', a remark that both broadened and deepened the alienation of the Unionist community and strengthened their resolve to undo the recent changes.

The situation in the Republic of Ireland, too, did little to help ensure the success of Sunningdale. Not only was the Sunningdale Communiqué vague in its wording but it also lacked a guarantee by the Irish Government concerning the continued status of Northern Ireland as part of the UK. This was further aggravated by a ruling of the Irish Constitutional Court on 16 January 1974 on the compatibility of the Sunningdale Communiqué with Articles 2 and 3 of the Irish Constitution, which had established, as far back as 1937, a constitutional imperative for all Irish governments to seek unification with Northern Ireland. Although the Irish Prime Minister at the time, Liam Cosgrave, gave assurances to Unionists in Northern Ireland, stating that 'the factual position of Northern Ireland is that it is within the United Kingdom' and that his 'government accepts this as a fact', this was too little, too late. As the British government also did little to assure Unionists, and fears among them about the future of Northern Ireland were further compounded, their enthusiasm about the new arrangements, if it had ever been strong at all, now evaporated into thin air.

Ten years of fruitless attempts to settle the conflict in Northern Ireland passed, years in which the British government treated the conflict primarily as a security problem. As a consequence of this approach, the government in London increasingly sought to involve the Republic of Ireland in sharing the responsibility of managing the continuously serious security situation in the region. This coincided with a growing Irish interest in stabilizing the situation in Northern Ireland and preventing a spill-over of violence. Thus, both governments decided to enter into negotiations, which resulted in the Anglo-Irish Agreement of 1985.

The agreement dealt with a variety of issues, including an Intergovernmental Conference, a human rights bill for Northern Ireland, security and judicial policies, and cross-border cooperation on economic, social, and cultural matters. The British attempt to address concerns of Catholics was apparent and put off many Unionists. However, as the implementation of the agreement did not produce any dramatic or even particularly noticeable results for Catholics, the reward for London was not forthcoming as expected. Although the influence of Sinn Féin decreased towards the end of the 1980s, the activities of the IRA increased. However, the declining electoral appeal of Sinn Féin in the mid- to end-1980s set in motion a rethinking process among the leadership of the party. Eventually, the party moved away from its unqualified support for, or at least tolerance of, violence to become one of the participants in the peace process(es) of the 1990s that finally brought about the Agreement in 1998. However, strong Unionist opposition to what was perceived by many as a sell-out of their interests by the British government prevented a strengthening of moderate Protestant leaders, seen as more likely to be willing to attempt striking another deal with Catholics.

Popular attitudes towards the Anglo-Irish Agreement revealed the persistently deep divisions within Northern Irish society. In a survey of January 1988, 55.1 per cent of those who declared themselves as Protestants voiced their opposition to the Anglo-Irish Agreement, compared with 7.9 per cent of those describing themselves as Catholics. Only 8.7 per cent of Protestants opted more or less in favour of the agreement, as compared with 31.8 per cent of Catholics who did so. Asked in the same survey about the biggest problem in Northern Ireland, only 8.6 per cent of Catholics, but 29.5 per cent of Protestants, pointed to the Anglo-Irish Agreement.[2]

Although the Anglo-Irish Agreement had by no means failed as badly as Sunningdale, it also did not produce a significant breakthrough in the political stalemate in Northern Ireland. In some respects, such as the increasing alienation of parts of the Unionist community, it even worsened the situation and prevented major progress for years to come. Although the stalemate continued, it did so on a different level. The agreement had shown that solutions were possible to which the two governments and a significant number of Catholics could agree. This had a positive long-term effect on the opportunities to reduce the level of violent conflict and to increase the chances to achieve an inclusive agreement for the future of Northern Ireland, because it made uncompromising, hard-line approaches by Protestant politicians less credible as a strategy to preserve Northern Ireland's link with Great Britain, and indicated that there was overwhelming support for constitutional, non-violent politics among Catholics.

By 1994, the situation in Northern Ireland had changed significantly. Following a 'Joint Declaration' by the British and Irish prime ministers in 1993, a number of confidence-building measures were introduced, leading to ceasefires by the major paramilitary organizations on both sides. In addition, the British government had entered into official and formal talks with representatives of these paramilitary organizations, and Sinn Féin was heading back into the political process, being recognized as a necessary partner by both governments. However, both governments also realized that the causes of conflict in Northern Ireland had not been removed. Thus, they developed 'A New Framework for Agreement', which proposed structures for north–south (or, Northern Ireland–Republic of Ireland) and east–west (British–Irish) institutions and sought to integrate these with new negotiations on the institutions in Northern Ireland, which were subsequently outlined by the British government in a document called *A Framework for Accountable Government in Northern Ireland*.[3]

Throughout 1995, contacts continued between the British government and Sinn Féin, but no major progress was achieved. The end of the IRA ceasefire in February 1996 and the resumption of violence throughout the region and in England proved to be a major setback. Nevertheless, the British and Irish governments announced the beginning of all-party talks involving specifically elected representatives for June 1996. Although Sinn Féin polled a record 15.5 per cent of the vote in these elections, the party was not allowed to take its seats at the negotiation table, because IRA violence continued. The multi-party talks commenced as planned but did not bring about any significant results in their first year.

With the election of a Labour government in the general elections in the UK in May 1997, the emphasis Labour put on reaching a settlement in Northern Ireland, and the perception, primarily among Catholics, that there was a new policy approach in London offered new opportunities. In July 1997, the IRA renewed its ceasefire and Sinn Féin was allowed to take its place at the negotiation table, which, however, resulted in Ian Paisley's Democratic Unionists and another minor Unionist party walking out. After more than half a year of intensive negotiations with several setbacks, eight political parties in Northern Ireland and the British and Irish governments concluded negotiations on what has become known as the Belfast or Good Friday Agreement.

What distinguishes the 1998 agreement from previous conflict settlement attempts in 1973–74 and 1985 is the comprehensiveness and detail of the arrangements made. It was also significant that this agreement was the only one approved in separate referenda in the Republic of Ireland and Northern Ireland, rather than being imposed on the people of Northern Ireland by government decree. The majorities endorsing the agreement north and south of the border and across the communities in Northern Ireland was, at the time, unprecedented in the history of the conflict. It also helped, of course, that all the major paramilitary organizations on both sides upheld their ceasefires. A further critical factor was significant international support: the skilful mediation by former US Senator George Mitchell in brokering the agreement in 1998, the pressure by Irish Americans on the IRA to commit to peace, the personal interest taken by President Bill Clinton in the peace process, and the funds provided by the EU since 1996 for peace-building initiatives must not be underestimated in their importance.

What this brief overview of the Northern Ireland conflict illustrates is that the complexity of the causes of ethnic conflict, the variety of parties involved in them, and their multiple and conflicting interests mean that once such conflicts have escalated into violence their resolution cannot simply be willed into being. Often years pass by before a settlement can be agreed upon by all the relevant parties, years that are often characterized by ups and downs in the level of violence and failed and partially successful attempts to settle a given conflict. It also indicates that there are only very few cases of ethnic conflict that permanently elude any even temporary resolution. The Middle East and Kashmir might be among them, but even the conflict in Cyprus, after decades of failed negotiations and collapsed peace plans, seems to be nearing its conclusion.

In the Solomon Islands, it took at least nine different peace deals and ceasefire agreements between June 1999 and February 2001, involving various conflict parties, including the central government, the provincial authorities of Guadalcanal and Malaita, leaders of Guadalcanal insurgents, and Malaitan militias and their allies in the security forces. Two of them came about under international mediation—the Honiara Peace Accord of 28 June 1999 (facilitated by Commonwealth envoys) and the Townsville Peace Agreement of 15 October 2000 (facilitated by diplomats from Australia and New Zealand). Yet, it took the decisive Australian-led intervention by the Pacific Islands Forum, a regional inter-governmental organization, before peace and stability could be established. Some conflicts, such as those in the Middle East and Burundi, at times get tantalizingly close to a permanent settlement, but peace agreements nevertheless are not signed because the parties are either not willing or not able to make a last necessary compromise. Sometimes agreements do get signed for only tactical reasons—to allow the parties to regroup on the battlefield, to procure new arms, or to shore up internal and external support. Once they have accomplished this, the peace agreement collapses. As one person familiar with the conflict in the Democratic Republic of Congo (DRC) once observed ironically, 'The peace agreement was signed on Tuesday. Just in time for the massacre on Thursday'.

Why is it that resolving ethnic conflicts is such a complicated process, fraught with difficulty and often frustration for those offering their good offices in support? Is it the unreasonable intransigence of individual agents, more interested in their aggrandizement than in peace and prosperity for their followers? Is it the lack of attention of the international community to conflicts where the parties are entrapped in a vicious cycle of violence from which they cannot break free without outside help? Is it the lack of resources and skills to find and implement solutions that satisfy all parties? These are the questions on which we focus in this chapter. Examining a number of successful and failed cases of ethnic conflict resolution, we explore different approaches to how best to settle ethnic conflicts, show their strength and weaknesses, and above all their dependence upon the concrete situation to which they are to be applied.

Yet there is one more fundamental issue that needs investigating before we can turn to strategies aimed at settling ethnic conflicts, and this is the question of what can be done in cases where conflict resolution is, for one reason or another, at least temporarily impossible. This is the question of how ethnic conflicts are managed, rather than resolved, the policies and objectives involved in conflict management, and the consequences for conflict settlement.

The distinction between conflict management and conflict settlement is necessary in order to understand properly the particular choice of policy that any of the conflict parties and other actors involved in a given conflict can make. It is also important to do this in order to be able to assess whether such a policy choice will be effective in achieving a desired outcome and why it can, or cannot, be attained. For example, the introduction of a UN peace-keeping force in Cyprus in 1974 was effective in providing a buffer zone between two hostile population groups that had just experienced a military coup attempt, a foreign invasion, and a very comprehensive case of what was euphemistically called a population exchange, rendering the Greek and Turkish parts of the divided island 99 per cent ethnically homogeneous. UN troops prevented any further fighting, yet they did not resolve the ethnic conflict between Greek and Turkish Cypriots, nor were they meant to do so. The Anglo-Irish Agreement of 1985, providing, among other things, a framework for security cooperation between the UK and the Republic of Ireland in relation to the Northern Ireland conflict, or the 1999 Lusaka Agreement, signed by the state parties involved in the war in the DRC, are similar examples of conflict management. On the other hand, if we look at the negotiations that led to the 1998 Agreement in Northern Ireland, the 2001 Ohrid Agreement between the government of Macedonia and ethnic Albanian parties in the country, or the Dayton Peace Accords that brought an end to the war in Bosnia and Herzegovina in 1995, these are different from any of the above-mentioned policies in that they tried to settle actual disputes or provide conditions in which the conflict parties themselves could address their issues in non-violent ways. The same holds true for the so-called Arusha Accords, signed in August 1993 by the Rwandan Patriotic Front, the Tutsi-led rebel movement that had invaded Rwanda from Uganda, and the Hutu government under Rwandan president Juvenal Habyarimana. Meant to establish a transitional government including Hutu and Tutsi, several key players in Rwandan politics obstructed the implementation of the Accords and, following the assassination of President Habyarimana, the peace process soon collapsed into the Rwandan genocide.

These few examples reveal a number of interesting aspects that will help us further distinguish between conflict management and conflict settlement. First of all, to classify a policy as aimed at the management or settlement of an ethnic conflict does not say anything about its actual success. The 1985 Anglo-Irish Agreement was only a partial success and the 1999 Lusaka Agreement was barely remembered a few years later when several states were once again militarily involved in the DRC. The establishment, in 1974, of a UN-led peacekeeping mission in Cyprus, however, put a permanent end to the inter-communal fighting on the island. Yet, despite this success, it has made little, if any, contribution to the settlement of the actual conflict between the two communities. The Anglo-Irish Agreement, on the other hand, although far less successful in achieving its aims of improving the security situation in Northern Ireland, can be seen as a first in a number of steps that led to the conclusion of the Agreement in 1998. This Agreement, in turn, has been very difficult to implement, as has been the Ohrid Agreement in Macedonia, but both have been comparatively much more successful than the Arusha Accords on Rwanda.

The second aspect of conflict management and settlement that these examples shed light on is this: conflict management is an attempt to contain or limit the effects of an ongoing ethnic conflict. This can mean the provision of humanitarian aid to civilians in conflict zones or in refugee camps outside an actual conflict area, as in western Sudan and neighbouring Chad during the Darfur crisis or in Kosovo, Macedonia, Albania, and Montenegro during the Kosovo conflict in the spring of 1999. It can also mean the provision of troops to keep conflict parties apart—the case of Cyprus springs to mind again—or to monitor ceasefire agreements, as, for example, in the case of the UN Operation in Burundi. Conflict management as containment can also imply preventing the spillover of a conflict across international borders, something that was successfully achieved in Macedonia throughout most of the 1990s. Thus, conflict management is primarily a strategy that is chosen when the settlement of a conflict is impossible. As we have seen in previous chapters, the continuation of an ethnic conflict may be seen as desirable by some of those involved because it creates conditions in which they can preserve or increase the amount of political power that they already have or in which they make economic gains. In other words, the actual conflict then becomes instrumental for some actors to achieve other goals that are at best loosely connected to the conflict. Unfortunately, it requires comparatively few resources on the part of such parties to prevent, or at least delay, an actual settlement of the conflict, and a much longer, more sustained, and better resourced effort to overcome their resistance to settle the conflict.

A third aspect in the relationship between conflict management and conflict settlement, which becomes clearer on the back of these observations, is that conflict settlement aims at establishing an institutional framework in which the conflicting interests of the different principal conflict parties—ethnic groups or the states with which they are in dispute—can be accommodated to such an extent that incentives for cooperation and the non-violent pursuit of conflicts of interest through compromise outweigh any benefits that might be expected from violent confrontation. As such, using the term 'conflict resolution' is in fact not always completely accurate: in many cases, the conflict itself may continue to exist for a shorter or longer period of time after a peace agreement has been reached, or at least some of its underlying aspects will, but the conflict parties have found non-violent, sometimes even democratic, ways in which they can address their differences. To achieve this is obviously difficult as so many different ethnic conflicts around the world—from the Middle East to Kashmir and from Sri Lanka to the Darfur region in western Sudan—prove. Other cases, like Northern Ireland, Bosnia and Herzegovina, or Bougainville in Papua New Guinea show, however, that resolving ethnic conflicts is not impossible either, but rather that it depends on the timing of initiatives and the skill and determination with which they are pursued.

Finally what becomes clear from these initial observations is that conflict management and conflict settlement are essentially tasks that require an often significant contribution from the organized international community—in the form of the UN or regional organizations such as the Organization for Security and Cooperation in Europe (OSCE), the EU, or the Africa Union (AU)—or individual states or non-governmental organizations (NGOs). Regardless of the actual end-result, the 1998 Agreement on Northern Ireland would not have been possible without American facilitation; the Oslo Accords between Israel and the PLO, although signed in Washington, were the result of many years of Norwegian efforts to build confidence between the two sides; Burundi may have experienced a similar genocide to neighbouring Rwanda had it not been for the involvement of the AU; and without the role played by NATO and the EU, civil war in Macedonia could well have been the inevitable endpoint of the escalating tensions between ethnic Albanians and ethnic Macedonians. This is not to say that local conflict parties are marginal to the success of conflict management and settlement—on the contrary. As we concluded in Chapter 4, even well-coordinated, sustained, and inclusive outside efforts will always be limited to the extent that domestic actors have, or lack, a genuine interest in peace. What it means, however, is that an analysis of conflict management and conflict settlement has to focus to a significant extent on the role of international efforts.

The case of the policies employed so far in the management and settlement of the conflict in Macedonia is a very instructive example for the importance of international assistance to local conflict parties. Operation Concordia, the first EU-led military crisis management effort, is a follow-on mission from NATO's operation Allied Harmony. The background of both missions was to ensure sufficient levels of security and stability in Macedonia in order to enable the implementation of the 2001 Ohrid Agreement, which had been brokered by the EU, between the Macedonian government and representatives of the Albanian minority in the country after a brief spell of violence in the spring and summer of that year following a long period of inter-ethnic tension. With both the late Macedonian president Boris Trajkowski requesting EU assistance and the UN Security Council passing a resolution authorizing the operation, there can be very little doubt about its legitimacy before international law and in the eyes of the conflict parties.

The importance of Operation Concordia lies in its contribution to the stabilization of the entire western Balkan region. Following the collapse of communism in central and eastern Europe in the late 1980s and early 1990s, what used to be called Yugoslavia gained notoriety as one of the most intensely violent incidents of state disintegration in recent European history. The wars of Yugoslav secession throughout the 1990s—from the brief skirmishes in Slovenia to the NATO air campaign against Serbia in the context of the Kosovo conflict—left tens of thousands dead and hundreds of thousands displaced. The legacy of communism, ethnonationalist mobilization, and war left their unmistakable marks on the region, creating a very complex situation that forms the background of this EU crisis management operation. First of all, there are overlapping, multiple, unresolved ethnic conflicts in Bosnia and Herzegovina, Kosovo, Macedonia, and Serbia and Montenegro, all of which have increased the requirements for managing the individual yet inseparable conflicts and crises emerging from them. This is further complicated by a generally high level of economic and political instability in the region as a whole, resulting from, among other things, the incomplete, or only partial, implementation of reforms of the economic system on the way to a market economy; the incomplete process of democratization where institutions function only to a limited degree; the lack of sufficiently well-trained and motivated civil servants and other state employees caused by a skills and brain drain to the West and the private sector; the high degree of (transnational) organized crime and corruption; and an insufficiently developed and independent cross-community civil society. By the same token, the heavy involvement of the international community, and especially the EU, has increased the dependence of local actors on the international community. This reduces local political capacity to address existing problems and creates solutions in which the local population has a sense of ownership and an interest in implementing them. In addition, the institutions established with international mediation, and occasionally with significant international pressure, as was evident in the Dayton negotiations, generally lack flexibility, democratic legitimacy, and output efficiency and therefore enjoy little, if any, local support.

Given this explosive mix of factors that, under 'normal' circumstances, would surely have led to widespread domestic and regional conflict, it is surprising that, since the end of NATO's air campaign against Serbia in 1999, violence has either been prevented or locally contained. In the case of Macedonia, this can in significant part be attributed to much improved EU crisis management capabilities, including the swift and decisive deployment of diplomats and troops, and the use of incentives and pressures, primarily related to Macedonia's desire to join NATO and the EU. Despite the fact that Macedonia's path to greater stability since 2001 has not been without some setbacks, the example of this case also highlights the importance of combining, wherever possible, conflict management with conflict settlement. Containing the violence of spring and summer 2001 was, from this perspective, only one element in a longer-term engagement of the international community in the country and the region before and after violence occurred. What we discussed in Chapter 4 as successful conflict prevention thus appears as one specific policy of conflict management and as preparing the ground for a successful conflict settlement.

This link of prevention, management, and settlement is part of the reason why the international community has, since the end of the Kosovo conflict, been more successful in the western Balkans, and it contains important lessons. Success crucially depended on a number of factors—a developed institutional framework and a set of policies that enable decisions to be made quickly, to provide adequate funds and personnel, and to cooperate and coordinate activities are some of them. Another factor is the effectiveness of the policies employed: in the western Balkans, for example, EU-imposed conditionality is so much more effective vis-à-vis countries where the promise of closer association with, and potential accession to, the EU is credible and where both political elites and the general public are ready to make compromises in order to attain what many believe to be a panacea for all their problems. This leverage often does not exist elsewhere because there is no clear long-term commitment to a particular country or region, but rather an ad hoc and often belated response to an emerging crisis, a lack familiarity with, and sensitivity towards, the situation on the ground and no credible intelligence sources. Comparing the situation in Macedonia with that in Bosnia and Herzegovina or Rwanda in the early 1990s illustrates this point.

At this stage, it is useful to return briefly to some of the more theoretical observations on the causes of ethnic conflicts that we made earlier on in Chapter 2. With reference to the distinction between proximate and underlying causes of conflicts, it appears that conflict management is primarily aimed at preventing proximate causes from facilitating the violent escalation of ethnic conflicts. For example, the UN-led and later the NATO-led spill-over mission in Macedonia was to minimize the impact of a bad neighbourhood on the volatile situation in the country. Providing humanitarian aid in cases of natural disasters or other sudden crises, man-made or otherwise, addresses serious domestic problems that can easily escalate into deadly violence when scapegoats are needed. Exercising pressure on, or offering incentives to, political leaders in the country itself or in neighbouring states—for example through sanctions, travel bans, and freezing their accounts abroad—can compel them in the short term to diffuse a particular crisis or at least not contribute to its further escalation. US pressure on Pakistani leaders, for example, has been instrumental in achieving a decrease in the overt and covert support that they have lent to Muslim radicals fighting the Indian government and attacking civilians in Kashmir.

However, what is important to bear in mind is that none of these policies directly addresses the underlying causes of ethnic conflicts —policies that do this fall into the realm of conflict settlement. Ideally, they successfully tackle structural, political, social and economic, and cultural and perceptual factors and defuse the security dilemmas arising from them. The 1998 Agreement on Northern Ireland, for example, created institutions in which political discrimination could be ended and fair power sharing be enabled. The 2004 agreement between the Sudanese government and the rebels in the south of the country included an arrangement on wealth sharing between Khartoum and the south, aiming to stop economic discrimination. The 2001 Ohrid Agreement on Macedonia sought to guarantee equal rights for the Albanian minority in the country and included measures aimed at protecting its cultural identity and enhancing the status of the Albanian language in public life. These and various other settlement agreements, such as in Moldova in relation to Gagauzia, in Papua New Guinea in relation to Bougainville, or in the Philippines in relation to Mindanao, also attempt to diffuse intra-state security concerns that arise from problematic ethnic geographies by granting autonomy to minority groups in exchange for them abandoning or postponing demands for independence, and by protecting individuals and their rights more generally and regardless of in which part of the state's territory they live.

To be sure, there are many other ways in which conflicts can be managed and resolved, including acceptable 'solutions', such as federalization, integration, and arbitration, as well as unacceptable ones, such as genocide, ethnic cleansing, and control regimes. How can we best systematize this wide variety of conflict resolution approaches? A very simple and useful distinction can be made between methods that aim at eliminating differences between conflict parties and methods that try to manage them.[4] Elimination of differences can be achieved through genocide, ethnic cleansing, partition or secession, and integration or assimilation. Differences are managed through control regimes, third-party arbitration, federalism, and other forms of territorial organization, giving conflict parties greater autonomy over their own affairs, and through various forms of power sharing. A slightly more refined classification would distinguish methods of elimination, control, and recognition.[5] Although operating with a similar set of conflict resolution methods, this approach is more clearly driven by normative judgements—that is, by a distinction between acceptable and unacceptable policies aimed at resolving ethnic conflicts. Thus, elimination strategies comprise genocide, ethnic cleansing, and forced assimilation, whereas control regimes include coercive domination, co-opted rule, and limited self-rule. In contrast to these two categories of unacceptable approaches to conflict management and resolution, so-called policies of recognition, which are seen as morally superior and ultimately more effective, include minority rights, power sharing, territorial solutions, and bi- and multilateral regimes.

Putting different ways of classifying the wide range of existing approaches to conflict management and resolution approaches to one side, between them the two classifications above cover all known and applied policies. Rather than debating the merits of one or other classification, we shall now illustrate how different policies of conflict management and resolution have been applied in practice before turning to an assessment of why some policies fail in some cases and succeed in others.

To begin with, elimination strategies, such as ethnic cleansing and genocide, have been widely tried and tested. Apart from being morally unacceptable, genocide is always likely to fail for two reasons—the magnitude of the task and, more recently, the determination of the international community to prevent it. Rwanda and Burundi, Darfur in western Sudan, as well as the Nazi Holocaust against the Jews and the attempted extermination of Roma are cases in point. Ethnic cleansing, on the other hand, has a different track record. First of all, only in the post-Cold War period has there been universal condemnation of this practice. For almost 100 years prior, many states in their search for internal stability and external security have sought to minimize the political impact of ethnic minorities with an affiliation to other, often neighbouring, states or parts of their population by expelling them or exchanging them for ethnic kin of their own. Such forced population transfers are not an exclusively European phenomenon, but they were particularly common there and are primarily linked with two phenomena, which in themselves are interrelated: the collapse of (multinational) states and the redrawing of state boundaries. From the First and Second Balkan Wars, to the First and Second World Wars, and finally to the violent break-up of Yugoslavia, Europe has seen numerous expulsions and exchanges of populations that were seen as actual and potential threats to domestic and international peace. Today's most ardent advocates of preventing or reversing ethnic cleansing—the USA and the EU—were, in different constellations, yesterday's advocates of this policy, endorsing, legitimizing, and facilitating, for example, the Greco-Turkish population exchange of the 1920s and the post-1945 expulsions of millions of ethnic Germans from central and eastern Europe. Outside Europe, the practice is most commonly associated with the Middle East—the expulsion and flight of Palestinians from what is now Israel and what are or were Israeli-occupied territories since 1948 as well as from Jordan, amounting to a total of 4.1 million refugees currently registered with the UN Relief and Works Agency for Palestine Refugees in the Near East—but also with the displacement of Hutu and Tutsi in post-colonial Rwanda and Burundi, and with the ethnic cleansing of Christians from southern Sudan and black Africans from the country's western Darfur region.

A third method of eliminating differences is forced assimilation, which manifests itself in policies intended to force members of one or more particular ethnic groups to abandon their own distinct identity, or some of their cultural, linguistic, or religious components, in favour of a dominant identity and culture. The imposition of an official or state language, school curricula that ignore a country's multi-cultural past and present, and legislation that prevents even private initiatives from preserving distinct cultural traditions are some examples of how a strategy of forced assimilation can be implemented. It has occurred in many cases in Europe—from France to the UK, from Italy to Russia, and later the Soviet Union, and from Spain to Romania and Bulgaria, in all cases affecting ethnic minorities and for the most part with only limited success. There is an abundance of similar examples elsewhere in the world. Australian attempts to assimilate Aborigines included the forced adoption of their children in white families, in South Africa black Africans were forced to learn Afrikaans, and various assimilation policies directed at First Nations people in Canada have included required attendance at residential schools and forced adoption of young children. These are but a few examples of this particular practice, the success of which at best is limited and at worst has contributed to heightened inter-ethnic tension and violence.

If we now look at control regimes, the related policies are examples of managing differences rather than eliminating them, and we distinguish three different types of such regimes—coercive domination, co-opted rule, and limited self-rule. What they have in common is that they are applied by political leaders of dominant groups to maintain that group's privileged status and, by implication, to secure the power base of its elites. Institutional structures of control regimes vary from case to case, as does the degree of force that elites are willing to use in order to sustain them. Coercive domination is the most repressive form of control regimes and the one that involves a significant degree of violence. Israeli policy in the occupied territories, the Apartheid system in South Africa, and Serb policy vis-à-vis Kosovo throughout most of the 1990s are examples of this kind of control regime, as was until recently Indonesian policy in Aceh and Sri Lankan policy vis-à-vis the Tamil minority. In all these cases, conflicts are addressed by military means. Unless one side achieves a decisive military victory or both sides step back and re-assess their strategies, this approach is most likely to keep the conflict in a perpetual limbo with occasional serious violent escalation.

Co-opted rule, on the other hand, relies on a limited degree of participation in political decision-making by non-dominant groups. Also referred to as *divide et impera* (divide and rule), it is typical of colonial regimes but has also been used by dominant groups in multi-national empires to secure their power in ways that are less costly than the kind of permanent repression required for the maintenance of regimes of coercive domination. The Russian, Habsburg, and Ottoman empires of past centuries are an example of this kind of conflict resolution strategy, and the colonial empires of the British and French in Africa and Asia are another case in point. That there are often severe, negative repercussions of the application of such strategies has already become evident from our discussion of Rwanda and Burundi, as well as Sri Lanka where the colonial powers co-opted local minorities into positions of power and failed to make adequate arrangements for post-colonial transitions.

The exercise of control by a dominant ethnic group can also be achieved by permitting limited self-rule for non-dominant groups, while excluding them simultaneously from senior central government positions. This policy manifests itself in various systems of segregation. This can take the form of social separation, as under the Ottoman millet system which provided three non-Muslim groups (Greek Orthodox, Armenian, and Jewish) with a degree of autonomy in cultural and other matters. It can also be applied according to territorial principles, such as the ghettos established by the Nazis for Jews, the so-called homelands created by white South Africans for the country's black majority, or the reservations to which Native Americans were sent in the USA.

As the above examples indicate, control strategies are more common in non-democratic states, but, at least temporarily, democratic states are no strangers to them either. Apart from the example of the treatment of Native Americans in the USA in the nineteenth century, African–Americans, too, experienced control well into the twentieth century, especially in the south. There are other examples as well. The UK allowed a control regime, disguised as a (majoritarian) democracy, to exist in Northern Ireland for five decades. Based on a plurality electoral system and the occasional 'creative' delineation of electoral constituencies, otherwise know as gerrymandering, Protestants permanently held the absolute majority of seats in the regional assembly and were constantly able to exclude the Catholic minority from power. As we have seen above, Israel is another example. On the one hand, a democracy in which secular and religious parties share power, the country also has a long history of using coercive domination as a strategy to manage its conflict with the Palestinians.

Strategies of recognition incorporate both methods of eliminating differences and of managing them. Minority rights regimes and power-sharing mechanisms clearly fall into the category of difference management, as do bilateral and multilateral regimes. Territorial solutions can be both. Federal solutions or the granting of territorial autonomy is an example of managing differences, whereas secession and partition eliminate existing differences. Importantly, their inclusion into the category of recognition strategies implies that these types of territorial solutions have to be arrived at consensually—that is, the seceding entity does so with the permission of the entity from which it separates—and in the case of partition there needs to be consensus among those affected about how the line of partition is to be drawn.

As the organized international community, as well as individual members, have played an increasingly important role over the past 15 years in attempting to bring about solutions to new and old ethnic conflicts, it hardly comes as a surprise that strategies based on the recognition of existing differences and the need to manage them peacefully have been prominent among mechanisms proposed to, and imposed on, conflict parties. Minority and more generally human rights legislation is almost by default part of any policy package aimed at resolving ethnic conflicts: from Northern Ireland to Macedonia, from South Africa to Sudan, from the Kurdish conflict in Turkey to that in Muslim Mindanao in the Philippines. Yet in many cases of ethnic conflict, merely offering long-aggrieved minority groups non-discrimination legislation and rights to use their native language and practise their religion freely and without fear of repercussions is unlikely to be enough to address their concerns and demands. Conflict parties often require far more serious concessions and guarantees from their opponents before they are willing to give up their reliance on guns. Most commonly, compromises that are arrived at include power-sharing regimes at the centre and increased levels of self-governance on a territorial basis for different groups. Take the example of the arrangements made between the Sudanese government in Khartoum and the rebel movement in the south of the country. Several protocols signed by the government and the main rebel group in the south (the Sudan People's Liberation Movement/Army [SPLM/A]) guarantee the right of the south to control and govern affairs in their region; full and equal participation in the central government; the sharing of the wealth derived from the exploitation of natural resources; and non-discrimination on the basis of religion. Power sharing, territorial autonomy, and human and minority rights are all part of a comprehensive attempt to resolve this decade-old conflict between north and south. Similarly complex arrangements have been agreed for the province of Bougainville and its relationship with the central government in Papua New Guinea. As in Northern Ireland, this agreement also provides for power sharing at the regional level—autonomy is not meant to be abused by new majorities created as a result of a partly territorial solution for an ethnic conflict. What these three conflict settlements also have in common is that they include future options of referenda to change the international status of these regions. The people in Northern Ireland will have opportunities in the future to pronounce themselves on the question of (re)unification with the Republic of Ireland, and the populations of Bougainville and the southern provinces covered by the peace agreement in Sudan will be able to decide at some point whether they want to remain part of their current states or seek independence.

This recent trend, which also applies to other cases, such as Kosovo, and Serbia and Montenegro, has been described by international legal scholar and practitioner Marc Weller as the emerging practice of interim settlements.[6] As the examples of Bougainville, southern Sudan, Northern Ireland, Kosovo, and Serbia and Montenegro show, such interim settlements normally involve a period of self-governance during which the territory in question remains part of its current state before a referendum on independence is carried out. During this period, the secessionists 'suspend' their claim for independence without renouncing it. The objective behind this strategy is, of course, to demonstrate to the secessionist movement and its followers that the 'interim' settlement agreed in fact addresses all their claims and resolves the security dilemmas emerging from them so that it can be made permanent—that is, the hope is that, rather than insisting on independence, the compromise achieved in the interim settlement will be approved by the population of the potentially independent new state as a permanent solution to their grievances.

From a conflict resolution perspective, there are a number of advantages and disadvantages to this practice. On the positive side, it enables the conflict parties to address the resolvable issues sooner rather than later. Violence will stop and civilians will no longer be targeted. Giving secessionists the option of achieving independence without violence removes the incentive to fight, whilst the central government simultaneously has a strong incentive to implement the agreement reached fully, fairly, and quickly to convince the secessionist party and its followers that independence is not necessary, but that all other of their demands can be just as effectively addressed within the framework of the negotiated interim agreement. Yet, at the same time there are significant disadvantages to such an approach as well. To begin with, given the fact that a referendum on independence will take place and that its result will be recognized by the state and the international community, there is little pressure on the secessionist party to work in good faith towards implementing the interim settlement. In fact, if its leaders think that they will gain more from independence than from remaining in their current state, they have all the reason in the world to sabotage the interim agreement, thus proving to their constituents that independence is the only viable 'solution'.

In addition, even with safeguards in place, such as a commitment to a referendum and to the recognition of its outcome by the conflict parties and the international community, the resurgence of violence cannot be ruled out. East Timor saw significant levels of post-referendum violence once an overwhelming majority of its population had expressed a wish to secede from Indonesia. In other cases, violence may be prevented through the presence of large numbers of international peacekeepers, such as in Kosovo. Even if there is no immediate outburst of violence, protracted 'technical' negotiations on how to administer secession and the difficult compromises that they may involve could well lead to such levels of frustration among followers of either conflict party that violence might be inevitable. Lastly, even where consensus is achieved, post-independence problems are likely—Ethiopia and Eritrea, after a peaceful partition, have gone to war over the demarcation of their common boundaries. None of this is to deny the need for interim settlements or their advantages, but to counsel against too much, and possibly unfounded, optimism. Interim settlements occupy a grey area between conflict management and conflict resolution policies, and they are too novel a strategy to determine precisely when they will succeed or fail to break the cycle of violence. In the end, however, they are no different from other strategies of dealing with ethnic conflict in that individual leaders, and their followers, have to make choices—to implement or to sabotage them—and that these choices in many ways are more important as factors in deciding about success and failure than either the content or the context of any given interim settlement.

This brings us to the last issue of conflict settlement policies to consider in this chapter. In order to assess the reasons of why some policies fail in some cases but succeed in others, it is useful to return to some of the observations made in Chapters 2 and 3 about ethnic and territorial claims that are made in ethnic conflicts and the security dilemmas to which they give rise. This means looking at the issue of conflict settlement from the perspective of accommodating all the ethnic and territorial claims that conflict parties make in an ethnic conflict. In reality, total accommodation of these claims is close to impossible. Rather, for many of the claims, a compromise will have to be reached between the conflict parties and occasionally, some claims may have to be withdrawn, perhaps on a reciprocal basis, in order to make a settlement possible and sustainable. In the same way that the combination of ethnic and territorial claims and the intensity with which they are pursued often account for the degree and duration of violence in an ethnic conflict, different combinations of ethnic and territorial claims can also explain which kind of conflict settlement will be possible and its long-term prospects of success. Broadly speaking, there are only four combinations of ethnic and territorial claims that offer the chance to achieve and sustain settlements for ethnic conflicts.

Imagine a situation in which an ethnic conflict is primarily about control over a particular territory and in which the stretch of land is disputed between two or more ethnic groups and two or more states. If none of the parties is prepared to give up its claims completely but is willing to share control of the territory, a condominium-style arrangement is the most likely outcome. Much like its residential equivalent, the conflict parties would all 'own' a share in the territory, but, rather than exercising their rights sequentially, they would do so simultaneously. This is not just an exercise in creative application of conflict resolution theory—condominia are real but rare in international politics. Two of them, Andorra and the New Hebrides (now the Republic of Vanuatu), came into existence in an attempt not to settle an ethnic conflict in a disputed territory, but to accommodate conflicting territorial claims by regional powers (in the case of Andorra, a French Prince and a Spanish Bishop) or by colonial rivals (in the case of the New Hebrides, France and Britain). There are plenty of other cases to which such a settlement could be applied: Kashmir, Cyprus, Nagorno-Karabakh, and Jerusalem are all cases of ethnic conflicts in which groups allied with states claim identical stretches of territory. However, not only would this require innovative constitutional design, but more importantly it would necessitate compromises that the political leaders in these conflicts seem not yet willing or able to make.

More frequently domestic conflict parties reach a compromise over their respective territorial claims either in the absence, or after the withdrawal, of any external territorial claims and are at the same time able to accommodate their ethnic claims to cultural and other rights. This has been the case, for example, in Quebec, Northern Ireland, Catalonia, Bosnia and Herzegovina, Serbia and Montenegro, Crimea, Gagauzia, southern Sudan, Bougainville, and Muslim Mindanao. Territorial autonomy and enhanced rights of self-governance go hand in hand with human and minority rights legislation and regional or central power-sharing arrangements, giving conflict parties assurances that their grievances will be addressed and their security guaranteed. If both parties remain committed to the implementation and operation of the agreement that they concluded and do not undermine it, the chances of success are reasonably good. However, other factors, often beyond the control of the conflict parties, may still throw the settlement into doubt and reignite security dilemmas. The consequences of the conflict in Darfur for the north–south conflict settlement in Sudan remain to be seen, as do those of the potential solution of the Transdniestrian conflict in Moldova for the settlement achieved with Gagauzia. Shifts in the balance of power in Northern Ireland from moderates to hardliners cast doubt on the future of the political process there, and changes in government from more compromising to more confrontational parties or coalitions may destabilize arrangements in Bougainville and Muslim Mindanao.

The conflict between Israelis and Palestinians also illustrates these dynamics very well. The inability of Palestinian leaders to accept what was on offer during the Wye River and Taba negotiations—interim autonomy and the clear prospect of statehood on over 90 per cent of currently Israeli-occupied territories—and the unwillingness of the Israeli side to offer a genuine compromise on refugee return and the status of Jerusalem led to further entrenchment of positions on both sides, and the marginalization of moderates in Israel. This is not to deny that the issue of a right to return to their former settlements in Israel for millions of Palestinian refugees is a highly complex and difficult issue, as much as the status of Jerusalem. These issues had, over decades of conflict, become central to the identities of both parties to the conflict and the elites in both saw compromises as the equivalent of political suicide. Yet, without leaders willing to take risks, intractable conflicts will remain exactly that—quagmires without any realistic hope of resolution. This is not to say that acceptance by the Palestinians of the terms offered by Israel would have led to an end of the conflict, or that more compromises would have allowed for a deal. Rather the point is that, especially over the issue of refugees, a backward-looking agenda dominated the negotiations. Palestinian refugees, their miserable living conditions undeniable, had been used as pawns in the wider Arab–Israeli conflict for a long time, and this pattern did not change during the Arafat–Barak negotiations. Rather than stubbornly insisting on the right to return for by now several generations of refugees, it might have been better to think about how the still existing refugee camps can be improved to offer their residents better life prospects. This may be seen as cynically advocating the recognition of unjust acts of ethnic cleansing, and there is no denying that such a policy would accept the status quo rather than working towards the recreation of the status quo ante. Yet historical comparison, as flawed as it may be, indicates that integration rather than return offers much better prospects of peace and stability. Between 1945 and 1950, over 10 million Germans were expelled from central and eastern Europe to German territories under allied occupation. Coming primarily from today's Poland and the Czech Republic, German and allied policies worked towards their social, political, and economic integration into what by 1949 had become two German states. This process was largely completed by the end of the 1950s, and putting to one side the occasionally heated public debates in Germany, Poland, and the Czech Republic, instigated by a small and politically insignificant minority, the post-war expulsions no longer constitute a matter of any political significance in the relations of the three countries.[7] The question that political leaders have to ask themselves then is: 'Which approach will benefit the people who we claim to represent most?' Translated into the dynamics of the Israeli–Palestinian conflict, this means thinking about what contribution to peace can possibly be expected from a strategy that keeps alive the unrealistic hope of return to Israel for several million Palestinians. From my experience, the answer is none. On the contrary, the focus on the refugee issue locked Palestinian negotiators into an impossible situation and distracted seriously from how to achieve a Palestinian state, which, by the 1990s, had been widely recognized and endorsed as the only viable solution to the Israeli–Palestinian conflict and an essential building block for peace and stability in the Middle East more generally.

The Israeli–Palestinian conflict is, therefore, no longer primarily about whether there should be a Palestinian state, but where and how big it should be. The conflict parties, as well as the international community, have for the most part recognized that an autonomy solution, as illustrated in the examples in the previous paragraphs, is unacceptable. However, one should bear in mind that significant elements on both sides deny their opponent the right to a state. Extremist Israelis advocate mass expulsion of Palestinians to Jordan, whilst the radicals of Hamas and Hizbollah openly demand the destruction of the Israeli state. Even less 'controversial' cases, such as Eritrea and East Timor, demonstrate that, even if secession or partition is the only alternative to perpetual violent conflict, it is hardly ever a process that occurs smoothly—a banal, but nevertheless true, observation to which the disintegration of the former Yugoslavia testifies as well. On the other hand, the 'velvet divorce' of the Czech Republic and Slovakia, as well as the dissolution of the Soviet Union, despite the subsequent more or less violent conflicts triggered in successor states such as Azerbaijan, Georgia, Moldova, Ukraine, and Russia itself, demonstrate that independent statehood is a potentially viable solution provided that it is consensual and well managed by the parties involved, including the international community.

As not all ethnic conflicts are about control over territory, so not all solutions need to have a territorial dimension. Where no territorial claims are made or where they are withdrawn by conflict parties, integration of different ethnic groups into mainstream social, political, and economic processes offers the best way forward. Minority rights systems that enable equal opportunities, and in some cases specifically promote affirmative action on behalf of ethnic minorities to overcome the consequences of past disadvantage and leave sufficient room, and funding, for ethnic groups to preserve, express, and develop their distinct identities have been applied with more or less success in many central and eastern European states. Not always perfect in letter or spirit, they have nevertheless defused many potentially dangerous conflict situations and contributed to preventing prolonged violent conflict, for example, between ethnic Russians and ethnic Estonians and Latvians, between ethnic Hungarians and Slovaks and Romanians, or between ethnic Germans and Poles.

Consequently, we can identify a number of general conditions that are necessary to make a settlement of an ethnic conflict possible. The government of the state in which the conflict occurs, if it is one of the immediate conflict parties, needs to be willing to accommodate key interests of its opponents and be ready to cooperate and compromise, where necessary, with an existing kin or patron state, including over issues relating to territory. The same goes for ethnic groups in conflict with each other or the government of the state in which they live: unless there is a degree of realism and pragmatism involved in their approach, including an ability to accept that their opponents have legitimate concerns as well, conflict settlement is unlikely. Once again, this underlines the importance of political leaders in the process of conflict settlement, and the responsibility that they individually and collectively have to achieve a sustainable settlement. Yet, as we have also seen, local leaders cannot be left alone in this process. The organized international community needs to provide incentives where possible and exercise pressure where necessary to bring the conflict parties together and enable them to come to a settlement. Political leaders in individual states, be they kin or patron states of an aggrieved minority, neighbouring states, or regional powers with an agenda of their own, need to balance their own interests against those of the conflict parties and those of other actors in a responsible way. This is a tall but not impossible order. Conflicts that were apparently beyond resolution for decades, such as Northern Ireland, were settled once leaders had emerged or reinvented themselves as peacemakers. In other cases, political leaders stepped back from the abyss of civil war or genocide, or allowed themselves to be guided back by external mediators, such as in Burundi or Macedonia. In other cases again, responsible leadership can be credited with coming tantalizingly close to a settlement, as in the Israeli–Palestinian conflict or in Sri Lanka, before being overtaken by events beyond their control and being marginalized by hardliners and extremists within their own communities.

This also highlights another dimension of the importance of leaders, domestic and international, for the successful resolution of ethnic conflicts. The presence of the conditions that make a settlement possible means nothing except that an opportunity exists for decision-makers to achieve a settlement. It does not say anything about whether this opportunity will be taken, what kind of settlement will be agreed, or whether an adopted settlement will be stable; it merely points to the fact that the strategies of the conflict parties towards the conflict are no longer incompatible. Once this has been realized, and there is no guarantee that every such opportunity will indeed be recognized, the overall success of the settlement process depends upon the flexibility, determination, and skill of those involved to design an institutional framework that fits the variety of contextual circumstances of their particular conflict situation, so as to provide for opportunities to resolve differences by peaceful and democratic means. Thus, success in many ways crucially depends on the coming together of skilled and determined leaders with a vision of peace and the authority to lead their communities towards this vision despite the significant risks that this might often entail. In Northern Ireland, Gerry Adams and Martin McGuiness have done this for Republicans and the IRA;

David Ervine has accomplished the same for one section of the Loyalist community. In South Africa, Frederick de Klerk and Nelson Mandela were instrumental in negotiating and seeing through a peaceful end to the Apartheid system. In Israel, Yitzak Rabin and Shimon Peres, and later on Ehud Barak, presented a similar opportunity but had no equal counterpart on the Palestinian side, a situation that may have changed now with the death of Yasser Arafat and the ascent of Mahmoud Abbas to the Palestinian presidency. In other conflicts around the world, responsible, far-sighted, and skilled leaders have been absent altogether, and petty rivalries, paranoia, and particularist agendas dominate relations within and between political elites of the various conflict parties.

Although clearly the most desirable strategy to be pursued from the perspective of peace and security, settling ethnic conflicts will not always be possible, and some conflicts may require rather long periods of international conflict management to contain and minimize their worst consequences before any settlement may become viable. By the same token, settlements may fail if they prove too inflexible to cope with changed situations or if they were negotiated or implemented under false assumptions or in bad faith. We must not underestimate the importance of individual choice, especially by political leaders, yet leaders can choose only among options realistically available to them (that is, pursue policies based on thorough and objective analysis of the conflict at hand and for the implementation of which proper resources exist). In order to make the right choices—choices that minimize human suffering, rather than aggrandize or enrich an individual leader and his or her inner circle—leaders are needed who are willing and able to take risks. In the final analysis, then, the success of conflict management and resolution depends on the proper analysis of the conflict situation, the willingness and ability to employ well-resourced policies, and the skill to maximize their impact—an impossible task to accomplish without able, determined, and visionary leadership.

6

Post-conflict reconstruction

Once a peace agreement has been signed, interrelationships of conflict parties, their domestic supporters and external sponsors, as well as international mediators, move into a qualitatively new stage. This is usually described as post-conflict reconstruction or post-conflict peace building. Despite its widespread use, the label 'post-conflict' is in many ways misleading. As we have seen in Chapter 5, peace agreements do not resolve conflicts—at best they provide a framework in which conflicting goals can be accommodated and pursued by means other than political violence, and in which compromises are negotiated and become acceptable because bargaining becomes part of a mutually beneficial political process. Take the example of the Northern Ireland conflict. The fundamental conflict between the proponents of two competing visions of national belonging—Irish unification or remaining in the UK—is far from over; (some of) the conflict parties merely agreed on a new framework in 1998 in which they want to pursue these distinct visions. A similar case can be made for Bosnia and Herzegovina. In 1995, at the Dayton Air Force Base in Columbus, Ohio, representatives of the Bosnian Muslims did not even negotiate directly with Bosnian Croats and Bosnian Serbs, but with their external sponsors in Zagreb and Belgrade, and the agreement that was brokered under heavy US pressure signalled anything but an end to the conflict, which lingers on to the present day. What both the Agreement on Northern Ireland and the Dayton Accords for

Bosnia did achieve, however, was a permanent end to large-scale inter-communal violence, in Bosnia additionally guaranteed by the presence of international peacekeeping forces.

In many other cases, agreements have not even been able to prevent the resurgence of violence in the conflicts that they were meant to resolve. The 1994 agreement between Hutu and Tutsi political parties in Burundi was never fully implemented and did not contribute to preventing the inter-ethnic violence that the country has seen over the past 10 years. A peace deal and subsequent agreement reached between Russia and Chechnya in 1996 and 1997 collapsed after initial progress. In the Middle East, the Oslo Accords, also known as the Declaration of Principles on Interim Self-Government Arrangements, were assumed to be a promising start to resolving the Israeli–Palestinian conflict, when they were signed on the White House lawn in 1993. Although many of the provisions of this declaration, and of two subsequent agreements initialled by late PLO chairman Arafat and Israeli foreign minister Shimon Peres in Cairo five months later, were implemented, these initial gains were not built upon successfully. No agreement has been reached between the two sides to date on the status of Jerusalem, borders, and refugees. The escalation of violence since the beginning of the second Palestinian Intifada in 2000 and the radicalization and polarization of both conflict parties made such agreement even less likely before the death of Yasser Arafat and the election of Mahmoud Abbas; the latter seems to have injected new life into the Middle East peace process. In many other cases elsewhere the 'settlement' achieved was only a temporary reprieve before violence escalated anew.

Reconstruction is also, in fact, misleading because post-conflict reconstruction is aimed at establishing institutions that are superior to those that existed before the violent escalation of the conflict and do not contain the same failures that led to the conflict in the first place. Unless post-conflict reconstruction succeeds in addressing the underlying causes of the ethnic conflict, it will amount to little more than permanent crisis management, trying to prevent violence or contain its spread beyond local flash points and international borders. Such policies can be successful over long periods of time, but, as the case of Macedonia highlights, they are bound to fail at some point unless a more comprehensive settlement is achieved that provides a framework in which the underlying causes of an ethnic conflict can be tackled. Filling the bold, and often vague, pronouncements of peace settlements with substance is the unique contribution that post-conflict reconstruction makes to conflict settlement, and in doing so it is, indeed, a fundamental and necessary element of the conflict settlement process.

As a consequence, there is now an increasing realization that ethnic conflicts do not simply end whenever a peace agreement has been concluded, and that it takes sustained international and local efforts to build a stable peace. As the international community has been confronted by complex post-agreement scenarios in the Balkans, the Middle East, Northern Ireland, Africa, and southeast Asia, success in sustaining peace has often eluded those who managed to forge the original agreement. Increasingly, therefore, post-conflict reconstruction, to stick with this commonly used term, is seen as an integral part of the conflict settlement process. Once an agreement has been signed, especially if it was reached with international mediation, programmes and projects are launched to aid the transition from war to peace, to democracy, and to a market economy that offers equal opportunities for everyone to prosper. This involves building acceptable, accountable, and transparent institutions, to generate self-sustaining economic growth, and to create a civil society with free and independent media, civic organizations, and a general climate in which people once again begin to trust each other, and are reconciled with their troubled past and willing to live together peacefully. Looking at how some countries have recovered from ethnic conflict, or are on the way to doing so, such as in Northern Ireland, the Balkans, or East Timor, this penultimate chapter looks at how politics and economics can and must combine to bring a successful conclusion to peace processes in ethnic conflicts.

Protracted ethnic conflicts shape the societies in which they occur in many different, yet almost always exclusively negative, ways, resulting in a lack of functioning or legitimate political institutions, weak economic performance, non-existent or polarized structures of civil society, and antagonized elites. Post-conflict reconstruction has therefore to address the legacy of ethnic conflicts by building political institutions, kick-starting economic development, and supporting social reconstruction. This is a tremendous task, posing a significant challenge even to powerful external actors and well-resourced international organizations, and testing their commitment and stamina in more than one way. At the same time, the setting in which post-conflict reconstruction is to begin is often unfavourable in the extreme for the task to be accomplished.

Take the example of East Timor. A Portuguese colony since the sixteenth century, the eastern part of the island of Timor had a separate existence from the western part, which was under Dutch control for centuries. Occupied by Japan during the Second World War, Dutch and Portuguese rule were restored after the defeat of Japan. As the Netherlands withdrew from its colonial overseas possessions, western Timor became part of the newly founded state of Indonesia in 1949. Portugal, ruled by an authoritarian regime at the time, held on to its colony until the country's transition to democracy began in 1974. Power in East Timor was then transferred to a left-wing political party in 1975, but factional fighting among the East Timorese political parties and their armed supporters threw the area into chaos. Exploiting internal instability in East Timor, Indonesia invaded the country and had taken control of it by 1976, subsequently incorporating the largely Catholic region into the predominantly Muslim country as its twenty-seventh province. Although the invasion was widely denounced by the international community, Australia recognized Indonesia's sovereignty over East Timor in 1985, despite a resolution of the UN Human Rights Commission two years earlier affirming East Timor's right to independence and despite gross human rights violations committed by the government in Jakarta in its attempt to quell all resistance against Indonesian rule. With almost one third of East Timor's population of about 750,000 killed in the fighting between rebels and the Indonesian army, the worst single atrocity occurred on 12 November 1991 when Indonesian armed forces massacred approximately 200 unarmed civilians at a cemetery in East Timor's capital Dili. The award of the 1996 Nobel Peace Prize to two East Timor peace and democracy activists—exiled resistance leader Jose Ramos Horta and East Timorese Catholic bishop Carlos Belo—put East Timor back up high on the international agenda, but it was not until 1998 that, as a result of political instability in the aftermath of the Asian financial crisis, changes in Indonesia itself were started that created the conditions under which progress in East Timor could be achieved.

After 32 years, President Suharto, the country's military dictator, stepped down and thus created an opportunity for his successor, Bacharuddin Jusuf Habibie, to revisit Indonesia's traditional hardline stance on the possibility of East Timor's independence. Allowing a referendum on the issue to be held in East Timor, Habibie made it possible for the people of East Timor to exercise their right to self-determination in 1999. Yet independence came at the price of serious human rights abuses suffered by the East Timorese before and after the referendum held on 30 August 1999. Although armed gangs had tried to intimidate the population to vote one way or another in the run-up to the vote, the referendum itself passed off mostly peacefully, allowing some 99 per cent of the electorate to participate. When the predictable result of an overwhelming vote in favour of independence from Indonesia (almost 75 per cent of the votes cast) was announced on 4 September 1999, pro-Indonesian militias unleashed a campaign of killings, beatings, random shootings, forced displacement, looting, and almost unprecedented material destruction, in which they were significantly aided by Indonesian security forces. All this happened under the helpless eyes of the UN Assistance Mission to East Timor, which had conducted the referendum. Eventually, an Australian-led UN peacekeeping force was despatched and order restored. The trauma of the violence in the summer of 1999, however, added to the decades of human rights violations previously endured by the East Timorese and to the difficulties faced by East Timor and the UN

Transitional Administration set up to assist the new country in the process of implementing its independence. An Amnesty International Report of 1999 highlights that 'divided and grieving families, uncertain futures, and . . . the physical and psychological scars'[1] inflicted upon the population of East Timor in the aftermath of the referendum added significantly to the difficulties of the post-conflict reconstruction process. One of Amnesty International's informants described her experiences as follows:

We were very frightened because we did not know if the military would keep to their agreement not to kill us. . . . The TNI [Indonesian National Army] were all around us on the truck. We were told to lie down in the bottom of the truck. . . . On the way to the airport, the [TNI] officer shouted out to some militia, 'Look at the dogs and monkeys we have here'.[2]

As for what happened next, she continued:

The truck slowed right down as we went round the bend. The abusive TNI officer addressed my father: 'You only make us busy. We should cut off all of your heads like this one.' My father does not understand Javanese dialect but I did because I had been studying in Java, so I sat up and looked through the slats of the truck. I saw the most terrible thing that will stay in my memory forever. I saw a man being executed. He was a Timorese man. . . . His back was facing me and I could see that his hands were tied. He was naked and being pulled backwards by a piece of wire towards a flagpole. When he arrived at the flagpole, I saw his head being cut off with a machete or a sword. I saw his head fall off onto the ground. I could not see the person who cut off his head because my vision was obstructed by one of the TNI's legs in the truck. It was outside the front of the Aitarak militia headquarters. I saw the machete and then I saw the man's head fall off. I did not see any other adults. I only saw children with the Indonesian flag tied onto their heads. When I saw this I screamed to my mother, 'Mummy! Mummy! They cut off his head!' The military in the truck did not react in any way.[3]

Another informant interviewed by Amnesty International also corroborated the direct and indirect involvement of Indonesian security forces in the violence:

The moment they saw the Kopassus [Special Forces Command troops], the refugees panicked and started running. The Kopassus troops ran into the trees, fanned out and then started shooting at us. I was running away when I saw an older woman hit by a bullet in her head. She was standing next to her husband who cannot walk and was in a wheel chair. She was looking after him as she always did. When the bullet hit her she fell and her head fell directly into her husband's lap. It was very sad and he was so shocked. She died instantly. She was the mother of five. She was known as Lita and her husband was known as Tilo. They originally lived in Bemori but had fled to Dare when the situation became too bad. There was another elderly lady who was so shocked by the shooting that she fell onto a rock and suffered a head wound. I do not know if any others were injured.[4]

According to the World Bank, as a consequence of this reign of terror, approximately 75 per cent of the population was displaced and almost 70 per cent of all buildings, homes, schools, etc., were destroyed. In economic terms, East Timor's GDP dropped from $US375 million in 1998 to $US228 million in 1999, a decline of almost 40 per cent, while inflation grew from 10 per cent in 1997 to 140 per cent in 1999.[5]

Against this background, the UN embarked on a massive post-conflict reconstruction mission. The UN Transitional Administration in East Timor—deployed in October 1999—remains the most comprehensive of all the UN's peacekeeping operations concluded to date. An initial Security Council Resolution in September 1999, on the deployment of an Australian-led military force to provide security in East Timor in response to the intense violence after the referendum on East Timor's independence, was followed by a second resolution in October 1999 which established a UN government of East Timor for a transitional period of three years to prepare the territory for full independence by exercising all functions of government. This included the tasks of providing security and maintaining law and order, carrying out all functions in relation to the administration of East Timor, helping to build local capacity in the provision of modern civil and social services, providing humanitarian assistance, and beginning to create conditions for self-sustaining economic development. This meant that the UN mission had three personnel components: public administration, civilian police, and an armed peacekeeping force. Under the skilful and committed leadership of Sergio Vieira de Mello—later tragically killed in the attack on the local UN headquarters in Iraq—the UN successfully prepared East Timor for independence by May 2002, accomplishing two key tasks: building legitimate, stable, and effective political institutions, and creating conditions for economic sustainability.

As in most other cases of international intervention, those intervening had to tread a careful line between accomplishing their mission and not falling into the trap of doing so by essentially authoritarian means. In other words, the dilemma that internationalized post-conflict reconstruction efforts often face is that they would be most effective in the short term by bringing in outside expertise and running everything themselves, but this would be detrimental to the long-term success of the post-conflict reconstruction process because it fails to create local capacity to take over from the international mission. In addition to this, trying to build democratic societies is difficult if it is done by authoritarian means, just as it is close to impossible to create the conditions of sustainable economic growth on the basis of humanitarian aid alone. The example of Bosnia and Herzegovina with its continued aid dependency and a High Representative with quasi-dictatorial powers is an indication of these problems: in the presence of international peacekeepers and continuing economic aid, the country is reasonably stable and secure, but one can only guess what would have happened if either or both had been suddenly withdrawn in the first few years after the conclusion of the Dayton Accords.

The UN mission in East Timor followed a dual approach to avoid falling into the trap of creating an overly dependent territory that would have little chance of success as an independent state. After consolidating its own power and control within the first months of the mission, during which there was little if any local input, de Mello created a so-called National Consultative Council in 2000. This was meant to be both part of the creation of local government institutions and a way in which the East Timorese population could gradually have a greater say in the direction of their country's future development. In addition, and even though missions like the one in East Timor derive their legitimacy from Security Council Resolutions and are therefore accountable only to the UN, in an effort to increase local support for the UN mission an Ombudsperson Office was established, providing a mechanism through which decisions of the UN mission could be challenged. Such an office, also established in Kosovo, is extremely important in the sense that it makes sure that UN staff can be held accountable for their actions and are not perceived as acting with impunity.

Given the complexity of the task faced by such UN missions that take over all government functions, it is barely surprising that they are few and far between. In relation to ethnic conflicts, there are only two other similar UN operations: Eastern Slavonia, a relatively short-lived mission between 1996 and 1998, and Kosovo, an ongoing mission since 1999. In Eastern Slavonia, the task of the UN mission was to reintegrate three Serb-dominated regions that had 'seceded' during the war in Croatia into the country. The UN's role in Kosovo has been to perform basic civilian administrative functions; to promote the establishment of substantial autonomy and self-government in Kosovo; to facilitate a political process to determine Kosovo's future status; to coordinate the humanitarian and disaster relief efforts sponsored by all international agencies; to support the reconstruction of key infrastructure; to maintain law and order; to promote human rights; and to assure the safe and unimpeded return of all refugees and displaced people. However, more than in East Timor, post-conflict reconstruction in Kosovo has been a multi-agency effort: NATO provides security, the EU has the task of developing the economy, and the Organization for Security and Cooperation in Europe (OSCE) has a wide range of responsibilities related to democratization and governance, election organization and supervision, media affairs, human rights monitoring, the rule of law, and police education and development.

What East Timor and Kosovo, as well as a variety of other post-conflict situations, thus illustrate is that the essential aim of post-conflict reconstruction is to create a set of political, economic, and social structures in accordance with an agreed conflict settlement that allows the conduct of a non-violent, just, and democratic political process in which incentives for peaceful political strategies outweigh any potential benefits to be gained from a return to violence. This can be achieved only through a comprehensive and multi-dimensional approach to post-conflict reconstruction and by taking a holistic and long-term view of transforming conflicts. Ceasefire agreements that stop the fighting between conflict parties are a necessary first step in this process, but hardly ever its endpoint. Building on the end of violence achieved with ceasefires and confirmed in peace agreements, the foremost task of any post-conflict reconstruction operation is to establish and maintain basic security. Recent experience from a variety of post-conflict situations underlines the importance of achieving security for a range of follow-on tasks. This has become particularly apparent in Iraq and Afghanistan. Although not ethnic conflicts in the strict sense, the challenges of post-conflict reconstruction in these two cases are not dissimilar to situations observed in ethnic conflicts. In fact, the extreme conditions in the two countries bring the significance of providing basic security as a pre-condition for further post-conflict reconstruction efforts into sharp focus. In Iraq, only a fraction of international private and public donor funds could be disbursed because a constantly deteriorating security situation prevented large-scale infrastructure reconstruction projects. In Afghanistan, the limited reach of control that the interim government under Hamid Karzai and its international backers exercised meant that campaigning during the October 2004 presidential elections was often restricted to the use of media, and Karzai himself barely survived an assassination attempt on one of his few campaign trips outside the capital.

Of course, not everywhere are the challenges and dangers as grave. Levels of violence in Northern Ireland were much lower, and state institutions, infrastructure, a functioning economy and elements of civil society were all in place and did not have to be constructed from scratch, even though serious and far-reaching reforms were envisaged in the 1998 Agreement. In Kosovo and East

Timor, on the other hand, the situation was more complicated. Not only were legitimate institutions missing, but there were also hardly any institutions present and the economies in both conflict zones were far from functioning and guaranteeing revenue streams on which new political institutions could rely in providing basic services to citizens. Post-conflict reconstruction efforts in Kosovo, East Timor, and Bosnia and Herzegovina were further complicated by hundreds of thousands of displaced people who required short-term humanitarian assistance and long-term perspectives of return and reintegration. In these and other conflicts, an additional problem is the disarmament, demobilization, and reintegration into society and regular labour markets of partisan armies of the former conflict parties. And, as we have seen in Chapter 4, there are often also other 'interest groups' whose agendas need to be addressed if post-conflict reconstruction is to succeed, most prominently among them criminal gangs driven by greed rather than grievance, but generally benefiting from the lawlessness created by ethnic conflict.

Thus, the provision of security extends not only to ensuring that all hostilities between the former conflict parties cease but also that no other forms of violence persist or emerge. As it is often difficult to distinguish clearly between politically and criminally motivated conflict parties, traditional post-conflict reconstruction policies fail because they start from the assumption that, apart from anything else, the local actors involved in the process are in one way or another politically legitimate representatives of their communities and of civil society. Yet, in Bosnia and Herzegovina, Serbia, Afghanistan, Iraq, the Democratic Republic of Congo (DRC), and elsewhere this assumption no longer holds true. 'Political' elites rely on criminal networks to finance their wars, whilst criminal gangs benefit from the lack of law and order, accountability, and transparency that sustains their 'business' and keeps these elites in power. Serious efforts to break this deadly alliance often lead to renewed violence. When Zoran Djindjic, the first post-Milosevic Prime Minister of Serbia, tried to take on the criminal underworld on which his predecessor had, in part, relied to maintain his grip of power, he was assassinated. Hamid Karzai, now the popularly elected President of Afghanistan, faces severe challenges in eradicating his country's opium economy. Criminal hostage taking and extortion in Iraq have long surpassed the kidnapping of the few international contractors and other foreigners who remain in the country, and is one source of financing terrorist insurgency. The unchallenged control that ethno-nationalist parties exercise in their enclaves in Bosnia and Herzegovina has enabled them to establish a system of clientelism, which privileges few in the privatization process but exposes many to the consequences of corruption in an economic system in which private and public sectors are hard to distinguish, enabling transnational criminal networks to operate virtually unchecked. This suggests the need for a two-pronged approach. On the one hand, credible and legitimate political institutions have to be built to confront criminals and tackle corruption and, on the other, economic incentives are needed that will provide a viable alternative for many who turn to criminal activity to sustain themselves and their families.

At the level of political institutions, therefore, one of the foremost tasks is the restoration of law and order and an effective judicial system. Equally important is the setting-up of a system for accountable government bound by the rule of law. Although accountability is important in the long run and from the perspective of consolidating an inclusive and democratic political process after conflict, it is critical to realize that elections alone are insufficient to guarantee this particular outcome. In most cases of agreed settlements, elections figure prominently as part of the rebuilding of political institutions, yet at the wrong time and based on the 'wrong' electoral system they can just as easily destroy a beginning post-conflict reconstruction process by giving opponents of an agreement an opportunity to polarize public opinion, to encourage 'ethnic' voting, and to limit the room for manoeuvre and compromise for moderate political leaders. Thus, institution building needs to focus on the establishment of a system of governance that is appropriate for the particular conflict and that is created in a way and by people most suitable for the particular conflict situation.

This can mean both immediate elections and elections after a transition period. The primary task of the institutions set up in accordance with an agreed settlement is to create conditions that are conducive to the success of a comprehensive programme of post-conflict reconstruction. This means that the way in which the agreement is implemented, and thus how leaders act during the process of implementation, is a major factor that has bearing on the eventual success or failure of post-conflict reconstruction.

What is most crucial in this respect is that leaders can make a transition from leading their community during conflict to leading them to and in peace. This is a challenging task, and for many a leader it has proved one too difficult to accomplish. Take the example of some of the long-term leaders in Northern Ireland. At the age of 25, Ian Paisley founded the Free Presbyterian Church in 1951 and was soon to become its Moderator and to assume a growing role in public life in Northern Ireland. It was his fierce opposition to the Catholic Church that combined with his absolute rejection of Irish nationalism and increased his popularity among the largely Protestant Unionists and Loyalists in the 1960s. In opposition to more reform-minded Unionists he founded the Democratic Unionist Party in 1971, thus creating a second power base for himself and his beliefs from which he has, so far successfully, resisted any compromise that could have weakened Northern Ireland's position within the UK. His political appeal has always been based on symbolic yet highly effective campaigns. In 1963, he organized a march protesting the lowering of the British flag at Belfast City Hall, marking the death of Pope John. Only one year later, he announced another march—to the Belfast Sinn Féin office where he intended to take down the Irish Tricolour displayed there. Authorities in Northern Ireland bowed to his demand and removed the flag, thus preventing his march but sparking a vicious riot in the city. Another 10 years later, in 1974, he was instrumental in bringing down the Sunningdale Agreement, an early attempt to resolve the Northern Ireland conflict by establishing a power-sharing government and closer links between the region and the Republic of Ireland. Charismatic, outspoken to the extent that he becomes offensive to opponents within and outside Unionism, Paisley has a clear, unchanging, and almost single-issue personal agenda that has made him an icon of resistance to any 'sell-out' of Northern Ireland. His most 'famous' public insult, however, occurred when he verbally assaulted Pope John Paul II during the latter's visit to the European Parliament in 1988, yelling several times 'I denounce you, Anti-Christ!'. Following a predominantly go-it-alone strategy, and reluctant, if not unable, to look for allies, Paisley has also, however, a reputation for protecting the rights of his constituents regardless of their religious or political convictions—he attracts a large number of Catholic votes in his electoral district, including once and famously all the votes from an entirely Catholic off-shore island. Most famously associated with the 'Ulster says No!' slogan, he has nevertheless occasionally moderated his stance—assuming, for example, the chairmanship of the Agriculture Committee of the Northern Ireland Assembly in 1999, where he was respected for his effective coordination of its work and famously argued that Northern Ireland should not be considered part of the UK when it came to exporting livestock and beef products at the height of the BSE crisis. Yet events such as these have remained episodic and Paisley continues to be a stern defender of Northern Ireland's status as part of the UK. This, clearly, is his right, but in his uncompromising attitude towards Nationalists and Republicans he remains the icon of Loyalist and Unionist resistance to change. His almost unchallenged status, however, also means that he has a unique responsibility and opportunity as a leader of his community to bring about a permanent end to the Northern Ireland conflict acceptable to the vast majority of people in his own community and beyond.

This is not dissimilar to the task ahead of another of Northern Ireland's political heavyweights. Gerry Adams gradually moved Sinn Féin from a political support base of IRA terrorism to a professional political party after he became its president in 1983. Although he, too, has a very clear political vision for Northern Ireland—unification with the Republic—he takes a flexible approach towards reaching this goal. He explored alliances and commonalities of interest with other political leaders in Northern Ireland, most notably John Hume of the Social Democrat and Labour Party (SDLP), as well as with the British and Irish governments. Adams played a key role in moving the IRA towards its first ceasefire in 1994 and towards decommissioning in October 2001. Aware of his controversial past as an IRA member, he did not take a seat on the Northern Ireland executive in 1999. Also in contrast to Paisley, he surrounded himself with several capable and charismatic other leaders, thus not leaving succession a hostage to fortune. The dominance that Gerry Adams has achieved within the Republican movement has enabled him to bring Sinn Féin and, some would observe with a certain unease, the IRA into the political mainstream. Favoured by an electoral system in Northern Ireland that rewards moderation, Sinn Féin has moved from the margins of politics to centre stage and is now regarded among Nationalists and Republicans more generally as a 'champion of a peace process and a negotiated settlement'.[6] Adams called on the IRA in public to abandon their armed struggle in early 2005, and the organization followed suit at the end of July 2005, formally ordering an end to its armed struggle.[7]

With Adams and Paisley now the leaders of the two strongest political parties in Northern Ireland, it is hardly surprising that the political process in the region has stalled since the elections in November 2003. Yet Paisley's and Adams's acceptance of non-violent and democratic politics as the only way to achieve their ultimate goal has left the peace process in Northern Ireland largely intact, and the likelihood of a return to large-scale violence is very slim, despite the political stalemate. This is in sharp contrast to the situation in the Israeli–Palestinian conflict, where, between 2001 and 2004, two uncompromising political leaders were at loggerheads—the late Yasser Arafat, the long-time chairman of the Palestinian Liberation Organization (PLO), and Ariel Sharon, the then newly elected right-wing Israeli prime minister. Any hope that there might still have been to bring to a successful conclusion negotiations on yet unresolved issues following the 1993 Oslo Accords was destroyed within a fortnight in the autumn of 2000. On 28

September, Ariel Sharon, then leader of the opposition Likud party, visited the Temple Mount in Jerusalem, a site of equal significance for Jews, Muslims, and Christians. Despite protests from moderates on both the Israeli and the Palestinian side, Sharon insisted on his right to visit the site with his over 1,000-strong, armed bodyguard, saying that he intended to deliver a message of peace, not confrontation. However, in response to his proclamation of the site as eternal Israeli territory, serious riots broke out in Palestinian-populated Old Jerusalem the following day, killing several Palestinians, including a 12-year-old boy caught in crossfire between Israeli soldiers and Palestinian militants. As images of this tragic death were widely broadcast around the world, Palestinians became further radicalized and started their second Intifada. When, on 12 October, two Israeli reservists were arrested by the security forces of the Palestinian Authority and subsequently lynched by a Palestinian mob, again in front of running cameras, Israeli public opinion became equally radicalized. Amid a worsening security situation and failing negotiations shared by outgoing US President Bill Clinton in early 2001, Ariel Sharon mounted a successful bid for the premiership. Seen by many as a war hero and strong leader in securing Israel's future, his premiership underlined his reputation for tough talk and equally tough action. Since then, what appeared as a promising post-conflict phase in the 1990s apparently succumbed to renewed conflict with no end in sight until Mahmoud Abbas succeeded Yasser Arafat as President of the Palestinian Authority and Chairman of the PLO, creating a new opportunity for constructive negotiation with Israel.

Yet, not all post-conflict reconstruction efforts falter or break down in renewed violence. There are examples of success, too, yet virtually none in which success has been unqualified. In South Africa, stable political institutions have been built in a now democratic and inclusive state, but economic problems and rampant crime, along with an AIDS epidemic left unchecked by the government for too long, have created serious difficulties in the country. In Bosnia and Herzegovina, political stalemate and economic crisis dominated the first years after the conclusion of the Dayton

Agreement. The country grew increasingly dependent on international aid and inter-ethnic peace seemed to be guaranteed only by the presence of a large peacekeeping force. More recently, however, and although economic problems remain and corruption and organized crime continue to hinder progress in many areas, the political stalemate has begun to dissolve gradually and a more pragmatic sense of at least punctual cooperation between the (former) conflict parties has established itself. The problems in Kosovo are very similar: an aid-dependent economy, high unemployment, political frustration, and deep inter-ethnic divisions. This explosive mix briefly erupted in March 2004 into violence of a so far unprecedented scale and intensity since the UN Interim Administration Mission in Kosovo (UNMIK) established itself in the province in 1999 in the aftermath of NATO's bombing campaign. Following the death of three Albanian children, allegedly driven into a river by a Serb mob, an organized, widespread, and targeted campaign led by Kosovo Albanian extremists against the Serb, Roma, and Ashkali communities of Kosovo left 19 people dead, while 3,000 mostly Serbs were driven from their homes. However, elections in October 2004, which passed by peacefully and with high turnout among ethnic Albanians, underlined that a political process has been started in Kosovo to which all key parties among the majority community have committed. By the same token, however, low turnout among Serbs and other minorities condemns this political process to suffer from a degree of ethnic exclusiveness that merely reverses the situation from a decade ago.

Despite high-level international involvement—in terms of both financial and personnel support—most post-conflict reconstruction processes seem, at best, to lead to a precarious peace sustained by international troops, to economies that remain dependent on foreign aid, and to societies in which former conflict parties are not reconciled. Is internationally driven post-conflict reconstruction, peace-building, nation-building, or state-building, or however this process may be described, therefore a resounding failure, an impossible task to master? The answer to this is yes and no: sustainable success in post-conflict reconstruction depends primarily on building stable and effective institutions before liberalizing political competition and economic activity.[8]

The choice of appropriate democratic institutions—forms of devolution or autonomy, *electoral system design*, legislative bodies, judicial structures, and so on—designed and developed through fair and honest negotiation processes, are vital ingredients in building an enduring and peaceful settlement to even the most intractable conflict.[9]

The holding of elections is often considered as a key criterion for democracy and democratization and as such is seen as synonymous with political liberalization. However, after an ethnic conflict, elections often take on added significance because they lay the foundations of the new post-conflict political order. This has been the case in Bosnia and Herzegovina, Kosovo, and Northern Ireland, to name just a few recent European examples.

Apart from ending a conflict, peace agreements aim to establish democratic forms of governance and/or to improve existing political systems, with a view towards both greater stability and inclusiveness. There are two major challenges in relation to these closely connected objectives. The first one is how to encourage elites of conflict groups to give up violence as a means of pursuing political power and to rely instead on exclusively democratic means (including elections). The second one is how to deal with the wider legacy of a conflict in terms of its effects on political culture, the structures of civil society (or lack thereof), and a range of other factors normally influential in sustaining democratic political processes. From a broader perspective, the issue is simply this: at a time when demands and expectations are high, the capacity of institutions and individuals to deliver is limited at best. Consequently, those elected into office in the first post-conflict elections are likely to be held to standards and expectations that are impossible to fulfil. As a result, they will either blame (former) opponents or fall victim to more radical elements within their own ethnic group, who present themselves as more reliable defenders of the interests of the group in question. Although international assistance can go some way to address capacity issues, implementation (in the sense of translating a peace agreement into long-term practice) is essentially a task that can be performed only with the support of the society in question. Yet this is at best difficult to achieve when political calculations are in part based on re-election: toughness plays better than giving former opponents the benefit of the doubt and working jointly towards achieving common goals.

The ideal scenario for a post-conflict election is to move straight from a situation of instability and exclusion of some ethnic groups from the political process to one of stability and inclusion, addressing issues of uncertainty, mistrust, and fear, and overcoming the social and institutional legacies of the conflict. This is most often reflected in complex electoral formulas and institutional structures to assure all former conflict parties that they have a fair chance of seeing their interests represented and their concerns addressed in the new democratic power structures. Credible commitment is meant to be aided by institutional design. However, evidence from Bosnia and Herzegovina, Kosovo, and Northern Ireland, among others, suggests that inclusiveness and instability or exclusion and stability are far more likely interim, if not long-term, outcomes. In other words, political liberalization early on in the post-conflict reconstruction process is unlikely to achieve both an inclusive and a stable political process. The reasons for this are, for the most part, the unwillingness or inability of elites to cooperate within the new democratic structures and/or the mismatch between political institutions and communal aspirations (ill-suited electoral systems, institutions favouring genuine power sharing versus a desire of communities to separate, etc.). The consequences of the failure of elections to facilitate the transition from conflict to stable and inclusive democracy are obvious: a political system is 'established' that is unsatisfactory for at least one conflict group, thus making a relapse into violence or the need for a sustained international peace-keeping presence more likely.

This is not to say that post-conflict reconstruction should not aim at genuine political participation of all relevant actors concerned or that there should be no democratic process or no transparency in, or accountability of, government. However, what is important to realize is that post-conflict reconstruction may involve elements of democratization processes—as in central and eastern Europe after the collapse of communism, or in southern Europe, Latin America, and parts of Asia at the end of military dictatorships or authoritarian rule—but it is not the same. Post-conflict reconstruction is more and less at the same time. It is more in the sense that it needs to address a great many more and often far more complex issues than 'ordinary' transitions to democracy, as will become clear below. For that reason, it is also less: democratization (in the sense of political liberalization and the holding of elections) is not always the most pressing issue in post-conflict reconstruction processes and may well have to be postponed in the interest of the long-term success of rebuilding state and society after prolonged violent conflict.

Democratization in post-conflict situations is difficult and perilous for a number of reasons.[10] First among them is a lack of trust between the former conflict parties—can the former battlefield opponent be trusted not to abuse power gained in elections? Why lose something that had not been lost during an often decade-long civil war? Another key problem is that, with the end of violence, the underlying political, social, and economic divisions between the former opponents do not vanish—they persist and are likely to dominate politics, making it difficult for political elites to reach compromises in a situation in which their own (political) survival depends on support gathered at the ballot box. As the new dynamics of elections and political processes begin to take hold, divisions within communities begin to matter as much as, if not more than, those between them. Where voters are likely to vote along ethnic lines, vote pools are limited and appeals most probably made to an audience that consists primarily of one's own ethnic group. Then the issue arises of who is best suited to represent, pursue, and defend group interests, and political competition becomes an intra-group rather than a society-wide phenomenon. As a consequence, divisions between groups are reinforced and society remains polarized rather than coming together. As intra-group political competition rises and group interests rather than common interests shape and dominate political agendas, trust decreases further and former opponents begin to doubt each other's credible commitment to a peace deal once negotiated, supposedly in good faith. Without credible security guarantees by third parties, as provided, for example, in Macedonia and Bosnia and Herzegovina by the EU, in Kosovo by NATO, as well as more recently in Sudan by the UN, new/old security dilemmas are likely to emerge and conflict to reignite.

This is not to argue against the need for and importance of political liberalization. In the long run, democracy is likely to be a much more effective guard against violent ethnic conflict than an enduring foreign troop presence. The point is that democracy requires viable, efficient, and legitimate institutions, a strong civil society and civic political culture underpinning them, and economic conditions in which both institutions and civil society can be sustained. In post-conflict situations these conditions are not easy or quick to achieve. Therefore, in order for the entire post-conflict reconstruction project to succeed, political liberalization and full-scale democratization may have to take second place behind institution building for some time.

The success of post-conflict reconstruction is, first of all, predicated upon the suitability of the agreement negotiated to end the particular conflict as a framework for sustainable peace. The second critical factor of success is the willingness and ability of political leaders to work in good faith towards its implementation. This means that agreements need to be specific enough to allow all the conflict parties a realistic assessment of their consequences and prevent the emergence, or deliberate creation, of unrealistic expectations about the post-conflict process on the part of some of the conflict parties. The 1998 Agreement in Northern Ireland, for example, was seen by one community as a guarantee for the end of all paramilitary violence, whereas the other interpreted it as ensuring that it would be able to participate in a power-sharing political process. Delays in the decommissioning of paramilitary weapons and in creating and sustaining the political institutions foreseen in the Agreement disillusioned many on both sides of the traditional divide in the region. This combined with the often less than optimal degree of responsibility displayed by leaders of all communities in overcoming their differences, and has created a political stalemate, not dissimilar to the pre-1998 period in which the British government in London had to resume responsibility for most functions of government in Northern Ireland. Elsewhere, it is the lack of sufficient resources provided by the international community in assisting local parties to implement peace agreements that leads to their breakdown—a better equipped and more sizeable peacekeeping force in Rwanda, and more generally an international community able and willing to react to early warnings of an impending collapse of the 1993 Arusha Accords, could have easily prevented the genocide that engulfed the country, the consequences of which have destabilized the entire region till today.

In many of the most devastating ethnic conflicts, once a peace agreement has been signed, or at least once a ceasefire has been agreed, the international community is called upon to provide humanitarian assistance to the civilian population. This is often the first step in beginning a broader reconstruction process. Yet, although addressing people's basic needs for food, shelter, medical care, and the like are very important, the key challenge for local and international actors is not to fall into the trap of making people dependent on aid in the long term. This means that, as soon as it is feasible, international assistance has to be channelled into programmes that enable economic recovery. To put it simply, post-conflict societies generally benefit more from fishing rods than fish. The intuitive logic of such an approach is often, however, complicated by the difficulty of dealing quickly and satisfactorily with a number of issues that have become 'standard' in most ethnic conflicts of today. These include the return of displaced people and the demobilization and reintegration of ex-combatants. Refugees often become dependent on aid when they cannot return to their places of origin out of fear, as in many places across the Balkans or the Great Lakes Region in central Africa, or as a matter of policy, as in the Israeli–Palestinian conflict or in the Darfur region of western Sudan. At the same time, their permanent settlement in the areas to

which they fled or were expelled is often impossible, thus condemn-
ing them permanently to the status of aid recipients. With conditions in the camps often devastating, it is not surprising that they
become bases of unrest and recruiting grounds for militants. The
Tutsi invasion of Rwanda in 1993, which was one of the triggering
factors for the 1994 genocide, was launched from refugee camps in
neighbouring countries. Palestinian attacks against Israel have been
launched from refugee camps in the West Bank and the Gaza Strip.

Another major problem of aid dependency is that it fosters
corruption and organized crime. Without proper control, which
is often missing, international aid facilitates the creation of systems
of cronyism, can lead to situations in which criminal gangs target aid as a valuable commodity, and contributes to misuse and
misappropriation. Take the example of Operation Lifeline Sudan,
launched in 1989 as the then largest international humanitarian
relief operation in response to a famine caused to a large extent by
decades of civil war. In order to administer the programme in
Sudan, international relief agencies required agreement from the
two main conflict parties—the Sudanese government in Khartoum
and one of the main southern rebel groups, the Sudanese People's
Liberation Army (SPLA). Food supplies often had to be channelled
through these two conflict parties, who, instead of distributing
them to the civilian populations in areas under their control, used
them for their own soldiers. The control exercised by the conflict
parties over the distribution of food aid intended for the starving
civilian population of Sudan allowed them to use it as a weapon
instead—to force civilians to take sides in the war, to extend their
control over more territory, and to resell it to generate income for
the acquisition of arms. Thus, international aid can easily become
an integral element of war and post-war economies, in which
soldiers, politicians, and organized criminals benefit the most. This
creates conditions in which the international community finds
it increasingly difficult to build self-sustaining economies in
post-conflict zones that are, after all, an essential feature of successful post-conflict reconstruction. Thus, the task of economic
reconstruction is one of transforming a conflict-driven economy

177

into a robust peace economy with sustainable levels of growth, benefiting all.

This also includes the reintegration of former combatants and refugees into the economic process, as well as in some cases addressing additional economic problems that are directly related to the consequences of the conflict. In Northern Ireland, for example, the most obvious effect of the conflict on the economy, apart from overall economic decline and high unemployment rates, has been the disproportionately strongly developed security sector, providing employment almost exclusively to Protestants as a result of discrimination against Catholics within the police service and the army, as well as of peer pressure in the Nationalist/Republican community not to join security forces. Downsizing the security sector will therefore also primarily affect Protestants, thus potentially contributing to disaffection and resentment. The other major economic problem in Northern Ireland during the years of conflict (and before) has been the decline in its traditional industries (mainly linen and ship building), also affecting suppliers and service industries, which combined with low levels of inward and foreign direct investment. This resulted in high levels of unemployment throughout the period from the late 1960s onwards. The worst affected population group has been that of Catholic males, who, at persistently high levels of unemployment, were on average more than twice as likely not to have a job as Protestant males. The challenge for post-conflict reconstruction in the area of the economy, therefore, then becomes not merely one of creating new jobs but also one of addressing long-standing and potential new inequalities in the labour market.

Another set of challenges exists in situations where ethnic conflict has created conditions in which large parts of the population have become dependent for their own survival on cooperation with transnational criminal networks. This is particularly obvious in relation to drugs production and trafficking. In Afghanistan, for example, a large part of the country's population in the north-east and -west has its only source of income in the growing and processing of poppies for heroin production. Simple eradication programmes, as advocated by the USA, are unlikely to be either popular or effective. What is needed instead is a more comprehensive approach offering farmers and others credible alternatives to sustain themselves and their families. This is also crucially linked to weakening the influence of local lords and crime lords, and extending the control of the central government to some of the more remote regions of the country.[11]

Although there is no straightforward connection between economic recovery and political stability in post-conflict zones, it is easy to see how economic recovery must be an essential element of any overall post-conflict reconstruction effort: if people feel that they were economically better off in times of conflict, incentives to support leaders advocating change rather than the status quo are few and far between, whereas opportunities to mobilize support for a return to the status quo ante are strong. Thus, although establishing security may be the foremost task in any post-conflict reconstruction programme, (re)building an economy suitable for peace times and increasingly less dependent on foreign aid is an equally important objective that cannot simply be postponed for too long.

Providing security, building legitimate political institutions, and reviving the economy are important and necessary steps in facilitating a successful process of post-conflict reconstruction. Yet they alone cannot guarantee that the end result will be a stable, prosperous, and democratic society. The reason for this is that much of the damage caused by ethnic conflicts cannot be repaired by giving people security, jobs, and a greater say in how their lives are run. The physical and emotional injuries inflicted on civilians during a conflict not only serve to polarize and radicalize societies during conflict, but they also often prevent reconciliation afterwards and contribute to continued tensions between the (former) conflict parties and their supporters, regardless of any deals that leaders may have struck. And this cannot be surprising if we consider the 'tactics' used by many of the combatant factions. The Bangladeshi Army, for example, has consistently targeted civilians alongside militants, committing rape, forced religious conversion, and torture against non-combatants. In the DRC, civilians have been victims of torture, mutilation, and random acts of brutality, often following rape. Just as in the conflicts in many parts of former Yugoslavia, women are frequently enslaved for months by their rapists who force them to provide sexual as well as labour services. The case of the DRC also shows that usually none of the combatant factions is free from blame: rebel forces in the DRC, armed Rwandan Hutu and Burundian rebels, as well as DRC government forces have been involved in human rights abuses. The Osh region of Kyrgyzstan, an ethnically mixed area with a majority of Kyrgyz and significant numbers of Uzbeks, Russians, Tajiks, Ukrainians, and many others, experienced serious ethnic rioting in June 1990. All sides burnt, killed, looted, beat, tortured, and raped members of other communities. Adding insult to injury, many of the victims, especially women, were paraded naked on the streets.

Victims need to be helped to cope with the trauma of their experiences on an individual basis, but successful post-conflict reconstruction often also requires that communities and their members see that justice is being done to their tormentors. The question of how to deal with past human rights abuses, to prevent victors' justice and to maintain a careful balance between reconciliation and retribution has occupied many post-conflict societies, often without satisfactory results. In order to achieve justice in post-conflict situations, a number of options are available. These range from truth and reconciliation commissions to the creation of ad hoc local or international tribunals. In some cases, a mixture of domestic and international tribunals has been created to deal with the past human rights violations committed or ordered during a conflict. All of these institutions serve different purposes.

Truth and Reconciliation Commissions often involve the granting of amnesty to those who committed human rights abuses because their aim is not to deal with any specific event in its own right, but to use individual instances of human rights violations to come to terms with a conflict as a whole in order to achieve reconciliation and peace. In South Africa, the Truth and Reconciliation Commission offered amnesty in exchange for a full account of abuses. Although not always satisfactory in its individual outcomes, it has enabled many victims and relatives of those killed during the Apartheid regime to achieve some form of closure and to move on. In contrast, the Commission for Reception, Truth and Reconciliation in East Timor does not have the power to grant amnesty, but has nevertheless been charged with establishing the truth about human rights violations there during the period of Indonesian occupation from 1974 to 1999, and thus to enable reconciliation within East Timor.

Ad hoc tribunals derive their legitimacy from UN decisions. Thus, the UN Security Council established the International Criminal Tribunal for the Former Yugoslavia in 1993 to deal with war crimes and crimes against humanity committed by any of the parties during the wars following the disintegration of Yugoslavia. One year later, in 1994, an ad hoc tribunal was also created to deal with the genocide in Rwanda. Such a judicial approach, which has its earliest example in the Nuremberg tribunal established after the Second World War to prosecute German war criminals, has some very clear advantages over Truth and Reconciliation Commissions. Tribunals enjoy primacy over the national courts in the country in which the conflict occurred and, according to their UN-approved statutes, all states are required to assist them in apprehending indicted war criminals and transfer them into the custody of the relevant tribunals. In determining individual guilt, which can normally be found on all sides of a previous conflict, they are less likely to reinforce notions of collective blame or victimhood, which are common in conflict and post-conflict zones. As a result of their independence from national judicial institutions and because they are staffed with international judges and prosecutors, they are more likely to administer justice impartially and enable all conflict parties to come to terms with the complexities of guilt and victimization in ethnic conflicts. Yet ad hoc tribunals are not simply the ideal institutions which some of their advocates would like them to be seen as. First of all, they normally depend heavily on the cooperation of local law enforcement agencies. In Bosnia and Herzegovina and in Kosovo, this happens to be, to some extent, a significant international peacekeeping presence on the ground; in Serbia and Croatia it is a national police service often less than enthusiastic about arresting national heroes of past wars won or lost. The case of the International Criminal Tribunal for the Former Yugoslavia raises another shortcoming—international tribunals are often seen as partial to the victorious side in an ethnic conflict if the ending of the conflict involved an international military intervention.

With blame less clearly attributable than at Nuremberg in 1945, the International Criminal Tribunal for the Former Yugoslavia has tried to be even-handed in its indictments and has prosecuted Serbs, Croats, and Bosnian Muslims alike, depending on their individual degree of guilt. Sitting in The Hague in the Netherlands, the court has underlined its independence and its judicial approach to dealing with war crimes. This has not, however, stopped its proceedings from being instrumentalized domestically. Each indictment and arrest of a non-Serb defendant increases the sense of injustice among Croats or Bosnian Muslims, who feel that their actions served to defend their nations and should not be judged on a par with the actions of those whom they see as Serb aggressors. Serbs, on the other hand, feel victimized and humiliated as the main targets of international 'persecution'. None of the ethnic groups, however, has so far managed to address and deal with the underlying issues—there is little evidence that any of them accept responsibility and admit guilt for what happened during several years of inter-ethnic warfare. Thus, in the eyes of many people across the Balkans, there are only two categories of people—the victims of your own group and the perpetrators elsewhere. In such a climate, there is little hope of finding truth, let alone justice. Even more importantly, it prevents people from achieving some sort of closure, and finding out about what happened to their family, friends, and neighbours, and thus makes it impossible for them to move on, as this Bosnian Muslim describes:

For the people of Podrinja, for the women of Podrinja, the war isn't over yet. In our hearts there is still war. Because until we know the fate of the last of our disappeared from all of the Podrinja, from the exodus of

Srebrenica, until we all go back to our own homes, something the Dayton Agreements enabled and promised, until that is carried out, in our hearts it is still war.[12]

East Timor, on the other hand, seems to provide a more promising approach to deliver justice in post-conflict societies, in a way that is less divisive and can also potentially contribute to peace and reconciliation in war-torn societies elsewhere. The court in East Timor's capital, Dili District Court, was given exclusive jurisdiction over genocide, war crimes, crimes against humanity, murder, sexual offences, and torture. With prosecution and investigation services staffed only with international personnel, and so-called Special Panels made up of one East Timorese judge and two international judges of other nationalities, there is more pronounced local involvement while the entire process remains under international control. Judgements passed by the Special Panels can be appealed in the Court of Appeal, which also has a majority of International judges serving, thus providing an additional layer of security against biased, retaliatory justice. With all of its budget funded by outside donors, such a system of international-cum-domestic judicial proceedings dealing with conflict-related human rights violations has the additional advantage of contributing to building and improving local judicial capacity.

In Rwanda, another feature of post-conflict justice has been tried. So-called gacaca courts, relying mostly on traditional tribal methods of dispute resolution, have been established to speed up the judicial process in post-genocide Rwanda, thus far conducted by domestic courts and the International Criminal Tribunal for Rwanda. However, despite the multi-pronged approach of combining domestic, international, and traditional forms of administering justice, revenge, rather than reconciliation, dominates most of the procedures, especially where Tutsi, the victims of the 1994 genocide, control the judicial institutions. It is not difficult to understand why this is the case, but it does not bode well for future inter-ethnic relations between Rwandan Hutu and Tutsi.[13]

In Northern Ireland, where international involvement in the

post-conflict reconstruction effort has been relatively marginal, public enquiries have been the chosen route for some of the most symbolic events in the region's three-decade-long conflict. High-profile murder cases, such as those of Catholic lawyers Rosemary Nelson and Pat Finucane, the killing of 14 unarmed civil rights protesters in January 1972 in Derry/Londonderry—to become infamously known as Bloody Sunday—and other such events with victims and perpetrators on both sides have been the subject of public hearings and investigations. In some cases, prosecutions have followed; in others no charges were brought. In all cases, however, investigations have been marred by revelations of half-truths and have left victims no closer to having 'their' truth confirmed, while many of the alleged perpetrators feel victimized.

Between the extremes of East Timor and the Balkans, on the one hand, where international involvement occurred at the highest level of the UN, and Northern Ireland, on the other, where international involvement was marginal compared with local efforts, regional initiatives have come to play an increasingly important part in helping countries rebuild after ethnic conflicts. An example of how successful regional efforts in assisting local post-conflict reconstruction can be is the Regional Assistance Mission to the Solomon Islands, led and mainly sponsored by Australia, but also involving personnel from New Zealand, Fiji, Tonga, Papua New Guinea, Cook Islands, Kiribati, Samoa, Vanuatu, and Nauru. After years of unsuccessful international mediation by Commonwealth, Australian, and New Zealand diplomats, and in the face of continuing violence in the Solomon Islands, the Pacific Islands Forum invoked its crisis response mechanism to send a fact-finding mission to the Solomon Islands in 2002. Almost a year after the report of the mission had been received, the foreign ministers of Pacific Islands Forum member states decided in June 2003 to deploy a joint police and military force, assisted by civilian experts and under civilian command to the Solomon Islands, a move that was generally welcomed in light of the worsening situation there, and received official UN approval in a statement by the president of the UN Security Council in August 2003.

As in other similar cases, the challenges were complex: restoring law and order, disarming rebel fighters, tackling corruption in government and public services, creating professional security forces, rebuilding the economy, and facilitating national reconciliation. Backed by laws passed by the parliament of the Solomon Islands, military and civilian mission personnel had an extensive mandate to end the fighting, actively pursue and arrest suspected perpetrators of crimes committed during the conflict, and, if necessary, to use lethal force in doing so.

According to a report by the Australian Foreign Ministry, the mission's police officers have arrested over 4,000 people and charged them with over 6,000 offences.[14] Further investigations led to over 500 arrests on more than 900 serious charges, including official corruption, murder, assault, intimidation, inappropriate use of firearms, and robbery. The mission also took control of almost 4,000 guns and more than 300,000 rounds of ammunition. A comprehensive programme of police reform was brought on the way with the aim to 'identify sustainable strategies to enable the [police service] to operate as an effective and trustworthy service'. As part of this, 30 new police personnel from all provinces in the Solomon Islands were recruited in June 2004.

Much of this was carried out in a very public fashion. Weapons were decommissioned in public disarmament events and reports on arrests, trials, and charges of those who committed crimes during the five-year conflict were covered in the press and electronic media—not with the aim of retribution, but in order to restore the faith of ordinary Solomon Islanders in their government, and in an accountable and transparent political and judicial process that offers better ways to resolve disputes than the violence that engulfed the islands between 1998 and 2003.

Although it might be too early to draw any conclusions as to which approach is the most useful in dealing with the abuses and violations of the past, there can be little doubt that they must be dealt with as part of any post-conflict reconstruction programme that aspires to long-term success. It also appears that, rather than exclusively focusing on a judicial approach, reconciliation is at least equally important. The handshakes between Israeli and Palestinian leaders on the White House lawn in 1993 may have been symbolically important, but they were not sufficient as the strong foundations that the Israeli–Palestinian peace process required. Although reconciliation, too, requires visionary leadership, it is foremost a task for civil society to accomplish. By way of analogy, take the example of German–French reconciliation after the Second World War. Konrad Adenauer and Charles de Gaulle, the two countries' leaders at the time, provided the symbolism and created the institutions of rapprochement, but it took decades of school exchanges, cultural programmes, tourism, and cross-border cooperation to come to a situation in which clear majorities in both countries recognize the other as their most important partner, and in which the French president and German chancellor represent each other at European summits.

The importance of civil society in the reconciliation process in conflict-torn societies must not be underestimated in its complexity because such societies are characterized either by a complete lack of any civil society or by a strongly polarized one—in other words, the existence of two (or more) separate civil societies strongly aligned with different ethnic groups. After often decades of violent conflict with countless victims on both sides, the trust and reconciliation required from antagonized communities to build a vibrant civil society underpinning democratic institutions may take years to establish. In Northern Ireland, for example, levels of social and political participation, cooperation, and trust within each community are much higher compared with those across the communities. With only one significant political party that presents itself as cross-communal and hardly any opportunities for children to receive education in so-called integrated schools, in which they attend classes with their peers from the other community, prospects for a renewal of civil society are slim. If not even in a situation like Northern Ireland, with a relatively prosperous economy and 'only' some 3,000 people killed over a 30-year conflict, efforts at building a common civil society succeed, how much slimmer must be the prospects in the Balkans, Rwanda, the Middle East, or

Sri Lanka. Of course, (re)building civil society takes time, and real reconciliation can begin only once civil society re-emerges from the ruins of a conflict-torn society.

This point about the length of time it takes to embed reconciliation firmly in war-torn societies also underlines the limits of internationally driven post-conflict reconstruction, especially in its now fashionable disguise as nation-building. The international community by now has significant experience and even a partially positive track record in re-building state institutions after ethnic conflicts and reviving economic activity. It has been far less successful in promoting reconciliation, a process that requires people's heart and minds and cannot be resolved by the presence of large numbers of peacekeepers or by the funding of economic recovery programmes. These and other measures of international assistance are necessary as part of post-conflict reconstruction, but without domestic input they will not succeed in the long term. In other words, just as ethnic conflicts can be settled only if the groups' leaderships are willing to do so and only if they are able to bring their followers along on the path to peace, so it is unlikely that conflict-torn societies can be truly rebuilt without the people living there buying into this process with their hearts and minds.

7

The future of ethnic conflict

Possibilities and probabilities

Ethnic conflict is not a recent phenomenon and has regional and global implications beyond the countries in which it originates. There is no evidence that this will change in the foreseeable future. Nor is there any evidence that the ethnic conflicts that will undoubtedly occur in the future will be less devastating than those of the past, or that they will be prevented. Forecasting future trends with any reasonable degree of precision seems a futile exercise. So should we just accept that, with regard to ethnic conflict, everything is possible? Renewed violence in Northern Ireland, a continuation of the stand-off in Cyprus, Nagorno-Karabakh, and Kashmir, another genocide in Rwanda or one in neighbouring Burundi, a perpetuation of violence in Sri Lanka and Aceh, more ethnic cleansing and border changes in the Balkans? Doomsday scenarios of this kind exist for other conflicts as well, but nothing is gained from them. Rather than developing an indefinite number of worst-case scenarios, a realistic assessment of what is probable—not just possible—will provide useful guidance about future threats and challenges and allow states, international governmental organizations, and non-governmental organizations (NGOs) to decide how and where to concentrate resources in order to reduce threats and master the challenges ahead. This means considering carefully the local, national, regional, and global dynamics of ethnic conflicts, drawing lessons from the past, and examining recent and long-term trends.

A 2000 report of the US Central Intelligence Agency (CIA) estimated that many 'internal conflicts, particularly those arising from communal disputes, will continue to be vicious, long-lasting and difficult to terminate—leaving bitter legacies in their wake'.[1] The report went on to say that these conflicts most likely to be prevalent in sub-Saharan Africa, the Caucasus and central Asia, and parts of south and south-east Asia:

... frequently will spawn internal displacements, refugee flows, humanitarian emergencies, and other regionally destabilizing dislocations. If left to fester, internal conflicts will trigger spill-over into inter-state conflicts as neighbouring states move to exploit opportunities for gain or to limit the possibilities of damage to their national interests. Weak states will spawn recurrent internal conflicts, threatening the stability of a globalizing international system.

Perhaps most importantly in this assessment is the emphasis of the continuing regional and international importance of ethnic conflicts. Notably, the report was published before the events of 11 September 2001 (9/11), when the terrorist attacks on the USA occurred, which are rightly considered a major juncture in world politics, comparable in its significance to the beginning of the 'nuclear age' and the end of the Cold War. Regardless of what motives al-Qaeda had, Afghanistan and its two decades of conflict provided the environment in, and from which, al-Qaeda could grow into an international terrorist network of yet unknown, but almost certainly unprecedented, proportions, reach, and capabilities. Although terrorist organizations remain in need of operational bases, ethnic conflicts have acquired a new dimension because they can potentially create conditions in which central governments are unable or unwilling to enforce law and order and in which terrorist organizations find the freedom and infrastructure to mount their local, national, regional, and global challenges. The significance of ethnic conflicts has therefore increased because, in our interdependent world, states that are failing or collapsing in the face of challenges mounted against them by ethnic or religious self-determination movements pose major regional and global threats as breeding grounds and safe havens for international terrorist networks and their local off-shoots and allies, and as sources of complex humanitarian emergencies. Rather than being merely a local human tragedy, ethnic conflicts now have the potential, more than ever before since the end of the Second World War, to become a major international security problem, capable of creating humanitarian disasters of varying scales on a global basis.

This realization has, however, also triggered more assertive policy proposals in response to the continued gravity of ethnic conflicts as a factor in international politics. The National Security Strategy of the USA, published in 2002, emphasizes that:

... concerned nations must remain actively engaged in critical regional disputes to avoid explosive escalation and minimize human suffering. In an increasingly interconnected world, regional crisis can strain our alliances, rekindle rivalries among the major powers, and create horrifying affronts to human dignity.[2]

Three particular regions are singled out in this section of the National Security Strategy to illustrate key dynamics of concern to the USA: the Israeli–Palestinian conflict, south Asia (in particular India and Pakistan, and Indonesia), and Africa, highlighting the importance of 'constructive conflict mediation and successful peace operations', of 'tolerating ethnic minorities', and of 'just and comprehensive' conflict settlements.

The EU's Security Strategy, published just over a year after that of the USA, takes a similar perspective:

Problems such as those in Kashmir, the Great Lakes Region ... impact on European interests directly and indirectly, as do conflicts nearer to home, above all in the Middle East. Violent or frozen conflicts, which also persist on our borders, threaten regional stability. They destroy human lives and social and physical infrastructures; they threaten minorities, fundamental freedoms and human rights. Conflict can lead to extremism, terrorism and state failure; it provides opportunities for organised crime.[3]

As a remedy, it suggests that the 'most practical way to tackle the often elusive new threats will sometimes be to deal with the older problems of regional conflict'.

Despite recent disagreements between the USA and a number of influential member states of the EU, and within the UN more widely, there seems to be a relatively similar assessment of the nature of the threats posed by ethnic conflicts and the need to tackle them. Agreement also seems to prevail in terms of specific regional hotspots—the Middle East, sub-Saharan Africa, the Caucasus and central Asia, and south and south-east Asia. Not all threats in these regions emanate from ethnic conflicts, yet there is a significant concentration of actual and potential trouble spots in these areas with very clear ethnic dimensions to them. A recent UN report on international security broadly concurs with American and European threat assessments and emphasises the importance of the peacekeeping and peacebuilding support that the UN can provide.[4]

The 'Minorities at Risk' project, based at the University of Maryland, College Park, just outside Washington DC, currently monitors the situation of 284 minority groups in 116 countries worldwide. Most importantly for ethnic conflicts, the project includes among the groups monitored, 'culturally distinct peoples, tribes, or clans in heterogeneous societies who hold or seek a share in state power', such as Hutu and Tutsi in Rwanda and Burundi; 'regionally concentrated peoples with a history of organized political autonomy', such as Abkhazians and South Ossetians in Georgia; and 'segments of a trans-state people with a history of organized political autonomy whose kindred control an adjacent state, but who now constitute a minority in the state in which they reside', such as Turks in Cyprus and Albanians in Kosovo.[5] In the post-communist states of eastern Europe and the former Soviet Union, there are over 40 such groups in 23 countries. In Asia, more than 30 groups are monitored in 20 countries, and in sub-Saharan Africa more than 50 groups in 29 countries. This, however, does not mean that all these countries are experiencing serious ethnic conflict at the moment or are on the brink of collapse into civil war. For many of the groups included in the survey, the risk of violent conflict is assessed as relatively low, and it would be wrong to conclude that all-out ethnic warfare is on the agenda in even a majority of cases.

Take the example of Europe. Here ethnic tensions arose in many countries following the collapse of communism in 1989–90. Issues of ethnic identity and minority rights came to dominate the political agenda in a number of states: Poland, Hungary, Slovakia, Romania, the then newly independent Baltic republics, the former Yugoslavia, and virtually all of the successor states of the Soviet Union. Many ethnic groups in these countries were 'at risk' in the sense of being marginalized in the political process, excluded from new social and economic opportunities, or forcibly assimilated to conform to a new national ideal shaped in the image of a majority population liberated from communist domination. Yet, only in a few cases was the result violent ethnic conflict. Tensions were high in Slovakia and Romania, in Estonia and Latvia, and in Ukraine, yet, apart from some occasional riots, no organized campaign of violence took place. The bloodshed that happened elsewhere was, however, significant: the conflicts in former Yugoslavia, Georgia, Moldova, and Azerbaijan killed tens of thousands and displaced several times as many people. Instability remains the name of the game in all four areas. Bosnia and Herzegovina and Macedonia may be on the way to closer integration with the EU, but the question mark that still hangs over the future of Kosovo could, once again, unsettle the entire region. In Georgia, Moldova, and Azerbaijan, quasi-states have emerged that are beyond the control of the central governments in each country and enjoy the backing of powerful external actors whose interests are better served by a lack of resolution of these conflicts. Russia plays that role in relation to the Georgian provinces of South Ossetia and Abkhazia, Russia and Ukraine have supported, to varying degrees, the Transdniestrian region of Moldova, and Armenia has sustained the status of Nagorno-Karabakh. Over time, powerful interest groups have emerged in these statelets that also have a strong interest in the preservation of the status quo—criminal gangs that profit from smuggling and trafficking and political elites that rely on them to sustain their grip on power. Renewed major violent conflict seems unlikely at the moment in any of these cases, but it cannot be ruled out for the future, especially if these now frozen conflicts edge closer to a resolution that those who have a big stake in the status quo might resist and undermine.

Although the situation in the Balkans has benefited very significantly from the persistent and increasingly consistent engagement of the EU, Russian influence in the so-called 'near abroad' has been less beneficial and must be seen as part of the problems plaguing, in particular, the Caucasus region. On the other hand, Russia also has a reasonable track record in resolving some conflicts constructively—fears that the status of Crimea could become a major factor of instability between Russia and Ukraine, potentially a cause of war, have not materialized. By the same token, Russia has encouraged a peaceful resolution of the various issues relating to the situation of the often very large Russian minorities in most of the successor states of the Soviet Union. Despised as agents of Soviet domination, ethnic Russians suffered significant disadvantages in many former union republics after the dissolution of the USSR—ranging from the denial of citizenship and pension entitlements to cultural and linguistic discrimination. Yet, with the exception of Transdniestria, acceptable solutions have been found to all these potentially explosive situations.

Another European 'trend' emerges from this discussion and allows some predictions for the future. Power struggles between ethnic groups combined with territorial challenges—in the form of secessionist demands or irredentist claims by another state—are most likely to lead to violent confrontations, but they are, fortunately very rare. On the other hand, states and ethnic groups, often with the help of outside mediators, have proven themselves highly able to reach negotiated solutions in cases where ethnic minorities have demanded some kind of special status, be it cultural rights, enhanced political participation, or territorial autonomy. This trend holds across Europe and is not specific to its eastern part. Peace in Northern Ireland has held for almost a decade amid difficult negotiations, because a widely acceptable formula was found accommodating political and postponing territorial claims. This has, so far, not been possible in relation to the conflict in Spain's Basque country, where a renewed campaign of violence in

December 2004 cast its shadow on the elections in spring 2005, or in Cyprus, where a 30-year stand-off between Greek and Turkish Cypriots continues. Back in the 1970s solutions were found for the conflicts involving the German-speaking community in South Tyrol in Italy and the French speakers in the Swiss Jura.

In addition, where this combination of power struggles and territorial demands occurs in a context of political instability, as was the case in the former Yugoslavia and the successor states of the Soviet Union, the consequences of ethnic strife are even more grave, including massive ethnic cleansing and mass killings. With political instability prolonged, conflicts become protracted and their just and fair settlement only a dim prospect. Although it is possible to contain such conflicts effectively—there has been little serious violence in any of the cases mentioned since the mid-1990s, with the exception of Kosovo—the lack of a permanent and broadly acceptable resolution means that there is a continuing potential for conflict if the status quo, or changes to it, are unacceptable for significant players in the conflict. In these situations of political instability and economic crisis, political leaders have ample opportunity to exploit ethnic differences for their own purposes, aggravate persistent inter-ethnic tensions, and hype up emotions among their followers, so that violence might become, once again, an acceptable strategy to achieve a 'solution' that protects one's own ethnic group.

The cold peace that has prevailed in most of Europe's ethnic conflict hotspots stands in sharp contrast to the situation in Africa where inter-ethnic violence has continued to fester and devastate the lives of millions of Africans. The Darfur region in western Sudan may be the latest major humanitarian crisis with tens of thousands killed and, in some estimates, more than a million people driven from their homes, as well as an increasingly destabilizing influence on neighbouring Chad and the Central African Republic, but it is part of a long and unfortunate tradition of violent conflicts. In the last few years, a number of conflicts have escalated into open violence, adding to the already significant number of cases of ethnic strife on the continent. In the south-western state of Gambella in Ethiopia, tensions between ethnic Nuer and Anuak have existed for decades, with members of the two groups staking rival claims to scarce land and water resources. Exacerbated by famine, the influx of Nuer refugees from Sudan and the availability of arms following the collapse of the communist regime in Ethiopia in the 1990s and a limited spill-over from the conflict in Sudan, these tensions erupted leading to some 2,000 people being killed and tens of thousands displaced. Inter-communal violence in Kenya, on the other hand, has been ongoing for more than a decade, especially in the north-western parts of the country, where an ethnic mosaic of tribal groups exists that links Kenya, Sudan, Somalia, and Uganda. The conflict has so far cost an estimated 5,000 lives and involved several episodes of ethnic cleansing amid signs that civilians have increasingly become the deliberate targets of organized mob violence.

The pattern of inter-ethnic violence in Nigeria is also driven by various political, economic, and religious factors. It involves state security forces, no strangers to heavy-handed tactics, seeking to maintain order across the vast and relatively resource-rich country, numerous ethnic groups who fight the state for more rights and a greater share in political power and economic wealth, as well as each other over resources and the preservation of their distinct lifestyles. Some of the conflicts in contemporary Nigeria are linked over the issues at stake, some through kinship among the groups fighting, and others just occur at the same time in different parts of the country without any clear connections. Thus, there were several simultaneous inter-ethnic conflicts in Nigeria in 2004: between Ijaws and Itsekiris in the Niger Delta, between Ilajes and Ijaws, Yorubas and Ijaws, and Yorubas and Hausas in the south-west, between Yorubas and Hausas in the north, between Tivs and Jukuns, and Fulani and Kutebs in the centre of the country, and between Fulani and Berom in the Plateau State. Added to these eight ethnic conflicts, vicious fighting between Muslim and Christian groups broke out following the introduction of Sharia law in the northern states. In total, it is estimated that, since 1999, more than 10,000 people have been killed as a result of this violence.

These and other similar conflicts such as in Senegal or Somalia pale in comparison to the situation in the Great Lakes Region, which remains the most violent and explosive region of the African continent. The eastern part of the Democratic Republic of Congo (DRC) and the neighbouring countries of Rwanda, Burundi, and Uganda remain the archetypical regional conflict formation,[6] comparable in its potential to generate inter-ethnic violence to the Balkans of the 1990s. The civil war in the DRC, which began in 1998 and cost the lives of an estimated three million people while displacing a further three million, surpasses the death toll of the Rwandan genocide. Although formally concluded in 1999, the Lusaka Peace Accords, which were meant to end the war and lead to the withdrawal of all foreign troops, took years to implement. By 2003, the last regular foreign troops—from Uganda—were repatriated, but the proxy forces of several foreign governments remained in the country. By the same token, the DRC is used as a safe haven for rebel groups opposing neighbouring governments. Since 1994, some of the militias responsible for the genocide in Rwanda have been based in the DRC and launched regular attacks across the border. This prompted Rwanda, together with Burundi and Uganda, to back rebels who ousted President Mobutu Sese Seko, in the hope that the new government under Laurent Kabila would curb the incursions, but also with a relatively clear and predatory economic agenda in view of the rich resources, especially in the eastern part of the DRC. This, however, did not happen, and tensions escalated to such a point that, in December 2004, Rwandan troops attacked rebel strongholds in the eastern DRC, prompting significant DRC troop deployments in the volatile border region. The close ethnic, economic, political, and military ties that link the countries of the Great Lakes Region also make it prone to domino-principle-like destabilization. With the peace process in Burundi still not concluded and Rwanda still struggling to come to terms with the consequences of its genocide 10 years ago, the future may well continue to be one characterized by instability in this part of Africa, the consequences of which will, as ever, be borne for the most part by innocent civilians.

If we look to south and south-east Asia, the picture is similarly mixed. Resolved ethnic conflicts, or conflicts close to resolution, contrast sharply with those where attempts at a settlement have repeatedly failed or where no such attempts have been made. Indonesia, for example, underwent tremendous change following the fall of its long-term dictator Suharto. Many saw the independence of East Timor as the first step in the disintegration of a country of 210 million people spread across 14,000 islands. Unsurprisingly, ethnic and religious tensions soon engulfed the country, leading to thousands of people being killed and driven from their homes, and to churches and mosques being destroyed to serve as a 'reminder' of whichever group considered itself the rightfully dominant population in a particular area. Decades of internal migration, especially of Javanese, who make up about half of Indonesia's population, have created a colourful mosaic of ethnic and religious groups across the archipelago. Yet, rather than the crown jewel of a multicultural democracy, this has become a major peril for political stability in Indonesia's transformation process after decades of military rule. Privileges for Javanese migrants, displacement of minorities, exploitation of natural resources for the benefit of the country's dominant population group, and the brutal repression of any ethnic or religious opposition over three decades created a legacy that has proved a major burden in Indonesia's shaky transition to more democratic political processes. East Timor may have been, for a long time, the most obvious separatist province in Indonesia, but it never was the only one. Its successful drive for independence has, if anything, radicalized independence-seeking movements elsewhere in Indonesia.

Aceh was conquered by the Dutch and 'included' in Indonesia when the country became independent. Resistance to Dutch colonial rule had never ceased, and it flared up again when Indonesia transformed into a unitary state with a strong and increasingly repressive central government after 1950. In 1976, Aceh declared itself an independent state, and a guerrilla war has been fought in the province until 2005, supported by a wealthy diaspora in Malaysia and Thailand. Any attempt to come to an agreement between separatists and the central government failed—neither power sharing nor wealth sharing were pursued seriously, and the fact that, since May 2003, following the collapse of a 2002 peace agreement, there was a renewed military campaign of the Indonesian armed forces against the so-called Free Aceh Movement did not hold the promise of an impending political solution. Yet, within eight months of the tsunami disaster of December 2004, a comprehensive peace agreement was concluded between government and rebels in August 2005.

Other rebellious provinces include Papua, the Spice Islands (Moluccas), and Riau, in all of which, just like in Aceh, ethnic, religious, political, and economic grievances overlap to a significant extent. Especially Aceh and Papua, as well as Riau, are rich in natural resources, and Indonesia is unlikely to accept their secession. In the Spice Islands, another dynamic has emerged since 2000: a civil war is fought on many of the approximately 1,000 islands between Islamic militants, pursuing their own version of Jihad, and Christians. Some of these Islamic militants fought as mujahedin in Afghanistan in the 1980s and 1990s and continue to have ties to radical Islamic groups elsewhere in the region and in the Middle East.

Ethnic conflict also plagues some of Indonesia's other provinces, even though the main demand here may not be for secession. In Kalimantan, local Christian, animist, and Muslim groups bonded together to stop the further influx of migrants from Madura. The violence that ensued and went largely unchecked included the most vicious incidents that Indonesia had experienced since the end of the Suharto regime, leading to some 500 deaths in 2001 alone. In a similar vein, Sulawesi has also seen significant levels of violence between local and immigrant groups, but, as in Kalimantan, this is driven less by a secessionist agenda than by resentment towards privileged immigrant groups and a central government that supports them.

Indonesia may be the most potentially explosive area for ethnic conflicts in Asia, but it is not the only one by far. The conflict in Sri Lanka between ethnic Tamil separatists and the government in Colombo was tantalizingly close to a solution in early 2004, but Norwegian-brokered negotiations failed to reach a successful conclusion. Since then, fighting between the Tamil Tigers and the government, as well as among different Tamil factions, has intensified again, with no solution likely in the near future, especially after the government in Colombo rejected rebel demands for a resumption of unconditional peace talks at the end of 2004.

What is interesting about both Sri Lanka and Aceh is the apparent, but short-lived, boost that both conflicts received towards a settlement following the tsunami that struck both areas at the end of 2004. Initially, many observers were hopeful that, at least in the short term, these two decade-long civil wars would be 'suspended' in the wake of the devastating tsunami waves that hit the region in late December 2004. And indeed, the Tamil Tigers in Sri Lanka, the Free Aceh Movement, and the governments of both countries respectively, showed early signs of cooperation with each other and international relief organizations. It appeared that there was now a window of opportunity upon which further peace efforts could be built once a certain degree of normality returned. A degree of optimism prevailed—even though these conflicts had been ongoing for decades and killed tens of thousands of people, and there is very little evidence that 'disaster diplomacy' really has long-term positive effects. The main reasoning behind this positive outlook was that the sheer scale of the disaster might make people who would have normally supported violence rethink their priorities.

Two weeks later and this optimism appeared largely shattered by the reality of resuming violence and an escalating war of words between the conflict parties in both Sri Lanka and Indonesia. In Aceh, with a long history of Indonesian soldiers and rebels cashing in on the conflict by exerting control over legal and illegal businesses, including logging and marijuana sales, both sides announced ceasefires in the immediate aftermath of the tsunami, but there were many reports of renewed violence and killings. Rebels and military levelled accusations against each other of exploiting the disaster situation for their own purposes, as well as mounting new attacks against each other, extending control over populations and territory, and attacking aid convoys. Although there was little direct evidence of serious disruption to the international relief effort as a consequence of this, the security situation remained tense. A dialogue between government and rebels nevertheless got started, and initial indications were that real progress could be made, the first since a ceasefire agreement between the parties collapsed in 2003. The peace agreement signed in August 2005 is an indication that this optimism was justified.

In Sri Lanka, Tamil Tiger rebels and the government had initially cooperated in specially formed task forces in rebel-held territories in the north and east of the country, but distrust between the two sides, grown over decades of bloody civil war, remained high and made it obvious that any hope for a longer-lasting boost to the stalled peace process may have been easily misplaced. Elected parliamentary members of the political wing of the rebels, the Tamil National Alliance, refused to join an all-party parliamentary committee to coordinate the relief effort. The Tamil Tigers also protested against government plans to have the army manage relief camps in areas under their control. They also made accusations against the government that aid was not distributed fairly. Rebel demands to receive aid directly from donors, on the other hand, were rejected by the Sri Lankan government who protested strongly against a decision by the Italian government to hand aid over directly to the Tamil Tigers. This stand-off continued for months to the detriment of civilians desperately in need of aid. When UN Secretary General Kofi Annan was refused permission by the Sri Lankan government to visit Tamil Tiger-controlled areas in the north-east of the country, all the signs were that Sri Lanka had returned to its kind of 'normality'.

In Kashmir, occasionally hopeful signs of rapprochement between India and Pakistan are normally offset by events on the ground. Beginning in April 2003, India and Pakistan seemed to undertake serious steps towards resolving their almost 60-year-old conflict. The efforts continued through the change of government in India in May 2004, including Indian troop withdrawals from Kashmir, but otherwise have not yielded any concrete, mutually agreed results. Attacks by Kashmiri militants on Indian police forces and the army in early December 2004, killing close to 20 people, coincided with yet another round of talks between the two countries. The main difficulty remains that militant extremists are allowed to operate from inside Pakistani-controlled Kashmir-and thus retain the opportunity to undermine any progress that may be made between the two countries' leaders and to cast doubt on the sincerity with which the Pakistani leadership is engaged in these talks. The dynamics of this increasingly pivotal role that Pakistan is playing in the stability of peace and security in south Asia is also highlighted by the fact that its western borderlands continue to be a zone of operation for the Taliban and some of the remnants of al-Qaeda, which in turn has implications for the future of Afghanistan.

Talking of borderlands, December 2004 also saw an escalation of fighting in the India–Burma border region. A number of the approximately 20 rebel groups in north-east India fighting for more rights have bases in neighbouring Burma from which they launch attacks on Indian government forces. Following a visit to New Delhi in October by Burma's military dictator Than Shwe, Indian and Burmese forces almost simultaneously launched large-scale offensives, involving 6,000 and 8,000 troops respectively, against Assamese and Nagaland rebel groups' bases on both sides of the two countries' common border. Internationally shunned because of its atrocious human rights violations, the Burmese junta came under increased criticism at the end of 2004 when internal purges brought to power more hard line elements in the military regime. Although the country's human rights record in general remains poor, a ceasefire with one of the main rebel forces—the Karen National Union—has largely remained intact since early 2004 and considerably eased tensions between Burma and Thailand, which reached their peak in 2001 when Burmese and Thai regular army units clashed following Burmese incursions into Thailand, allegedly in pursuit of rebel forces.

Thailand, in the meantime, has experienced a serious and violent escalation of tensions between Buddhists and Muslims in the south of the country, killing more than 100 people in the first half of November 2004 alone, out of a total of some 500 for the year up to then. Muslim demonstrations for greater rights and a greater share in the country's economic development met with a violent response by the police, who killed about 80 Muslims, sparking revenge killings of around 30 Buddhists. Following severe criticism of the government's handling of the crisis, including from Thailand's revered King Bhumibol Adulyadej, Prime Minister Thaksin Shinawatra, launched a campaign to fold 60 million origami paper birds to promote a message of unity. Made by students, housewives, and politicians across Thailand, some 100 million of them were dropped by 50 air force planes across the Muslim majority provinces of south Thailand amid renewed violence in early December 2004, including the assassination of a former prosecutor by Muslim militants and a bomb explosion killing a soldier. The strong and innovative peace initiative may well temporarily calm the situation in southern Thailand, but the grievances of the area's Muslim population are hardly addressed by this kind of gesture, nor does it necessarily rein in the often heavy-handed security forces or tackle the links that Muslim extremists in the Thailand–Malaysia borderlands have built with larger Islamic terrorist organizations in the region, such as Jemaah Islamiah, and with other separatists, such as the Free Aceh Movement in Indonesia.

Repression of Muslim protests—violent and non-violent—in Thailand and elsewhere in the region has increased in the wake of the USA's declaration of its 'war against terrorism', and especially since the Bali bombings of 2002. Non-Muslim governments were handed a convenient pretext to crack down hard on often-justified Muslim protests. This is a broader trend across and beyond Asia. Yesterday's freedom fighters have become today's terrorists. This was most obviously and literally the case in Afghanistan. Since then, many repressive governments have managed to find international favour again by couching their campaigns against ethnic and religious opponents in the terms of the 'war against terrorism'—from Mindanao in the southern Philippines, to Indonesia, Kashmir, Chechnya, and of course the Middle East. Rather than being pressed to seek a political solution with their challengers, incumbent governments' crack-downs are more widely tolerated, if not actively supported. As few ethnic conflicts are ever won militarily, if this trend takes hold it will mean conflicts are prolonged, mutual hatred will grow, and human rights violations and the suffering of civilians continue. Not only does this not bode well for the prospects of peace and stability on a local or regional level but it also bears the danger of turning into a self-fulfilling prophecy: increased repression and brutalization of minority groups will radicalize them even further and make them more susceptible to terrorist infiltration.

The implications of the 'global war on terrorism' for ethnic conflicts thus exist at several levels. In many ways, the new name of the game seems to be that stability trumps democracy, contrary to all White House pronouncements. Incumbent regimes are strengthened vis-à-vis protest movements and rebel organizations, regardless of how legitimate the grievances of the latter or how bad the human rights records of the former. American support for Indonesia, the Philippines, the central Asian successor states of the former Soviet Union, and the north African 'buffer' states of Chad, Niger, Mali, and Mauritania are evidence of that. More so than before, there is also a trend of partial or temporary disengagement from conflicts that are not deemed ready for a settlement. This is not a new strategy in how outsiders 'handle' ethnic conflicts, but it means that, in the absence of outside facilitation and potential security guarantees, security dilemmas for local conflict parties are exacerbated, and fighting often intensifies as a consequence. The Great Lakes Region in Africa and Sri Lanka serve as examples here, but the less than enthusiastic re-engagement of the USA in the Middle East conflict after the November 2004 re-election of George Bush does not bode too well for the future of this conflict either, despite the apparent progress achieved in Israeli–Palestinian relations in early 2005 following the election of Mahmoud Abbas to the helm of the Palestinian Authority. In contrast, however, outsiders will nevertheless continue to support conflict settlement initiatives where appropriate opportunities arise. Such constructive focus on conflict settlement can alleviate existing strategic dilemmas, empower moderate leaders, and address the causes of a given conflict. Kosovo and Cyprus offer the clearest opportunities in this respect in the near future. Sudan, on the other hand, is also an example of sustained, and ultimately successful international efforts to facilitate a deal between the government in Khartoum and the rebel organizations in the south. But this success served as an incentive for similarly aggrieved groups, in the west and east of the country, to launch their own campaigns for more rights and a more supportive development policy targeting their region. Initial international tolerance of the central government's crackdown on these new rebel movements was seen as the price for securing a peace agreement in the 30-year civil war between north and south.

More generally speaking, therefore, there can be little doubt that the international community, especially the UN, and regional organizations, such as the EU and the African Union (AU), will continue to have to intervene in internal conflicts. On one hand, this necessity arises from the complexity of the challenges faced. Individual states are less and less likely to be able to manage the security threats arising directly and indirectly from ethnic conflicts. Regional challenges require regional responses and strategies that treat causes rather than symptoms of conflicts. On the other hand, existing regional frameworks of political and economic integration have acquired an increasing security dimension, simply because viable and comprehensive security arrangements are inseparably linked to political, socioeconomic, and environmental issues. The Organization for Security and Cooperation in Europe (OSCE) and the Economic Community of West African States, to name but two such organizations, thus provide useful mechanisms that will make it easier for individual states—concerned about domestic and international perceptions of their actions, and the costs and risks involved—to support regional conflict management, including military intervention. Such a regional approach will also make it possible to bypass the UN, where China and Russia have traditionally opposed any challenges to the principle of non-intervention in the internal affairs of other countries. Even more so, it is likely that 'coalitions of the willing' will form on an ad hoc basis to intervene rapidly and decisively in emerging crises. Such a scenario has advantages in that it 'devolves' conflict management to a level where countries immediately concerned are able to act without dependence on Security Council decisions that are often driven by largely unrelated considerations of its member countries at any given time. The major disadvantage of such a system is that it is also likely to reinforce regional inequalities—the AU may be willing to begin to take care of its own conflicts, but unlike the EU it lacks the resources to do so. Unless there is continued and preferably increased international attention to Africa, further genocidal escalations of existing or newly emerging conflicts are likely—the conflict in Darfur since 2003 may have been but a taste of things to come.

Collective mechanisms either do not exist or are just in their infancy in the various regions of Asia, where tensions between different ethnic communities and between them and the states in which they live continue to plague all major states. China, Indonesia, the Philippines, Malaysia, India, Thailand, Afghanistan, and Iraq are all flashpoints of current conflicts that have the potential of serious local and regional escalation. Considering that China, India, and Pakistan are nuclear powers, outside intervention remains mostly limited to diplomatic initiatives. Their importance as major emerging markets puts further constraints on what other members of the international community are able and willing to do to mediate in ethnic conflicts within these states, and, as far as India and Pakistan are concerned, between them. The same goes for Russia: Chechnya remains a conflict in which outsiders restrict themselves to occasional criticisms of heavy-handed Russian 'counter-insurgency' tactics, but with Russia's increasing ability to portray Chechnya as yet another front in the USA-declared global war on terrorism, even these have declined considerably. In addition, Russia's continued influence across the former Soviet empire, with the exception of the Baltic republics, has led to a recognition of Russia's lead role in conflict management in many of this area's hotspots. Yet Russian peacekeepers in Georgia or Transdniestria are a euphemism at best—their major contribution has been the freezing of a status quo in Russia's favour.

In all these trouble spots in Europe, the former Soviet Union, Asia, and Africa, ethnic conflicts will also continue to become intertwined with transnational criminal networks of global aspirations and international terrorism. As economic desperation grows, as the gap between rich and poor widens, and as the disparity in development between the developed and developing worlds increases, religious fundamentalism and criminal intent will fall on fertile ground and exploit existing inter-ethnic tensions to build themselves political and territorial power bases from which to operate. Lack of imagination, patience, and resources on the part of the international community will constrain its responses, and weak states will be even more limited in responding constructively to the challenges of ethnic conflict. This in turn will increase the attractiveness of radical ideologies of global reach and with political agendas in the Tamil homelands of Sri Lanka, the Muslim-populated areas of Thailand and the Philippines, separatist regions in Indonesia, and across sub-Saharan Africa.

Thus, the near future is unlikely to see an end to ethnic conflicts. The root causes of ethnic conflict cannot simply be wished away overnight and, even where there are determined efforts to address them at a local, national, or regional levels, these efforts will have to be sustained for years to come and are certain to suffer setbacks. By the same token, political leaders, criminal entrepreneurs, ethnic activists, and religious fundamentalists will find ways to exploit existing problems to create the conditions in which their own agendas can come to fruition. Yet individual choice is a luxury that is afforded not only to those with an extremist, genocidal, or criminal agenda. The international community, too, makes choices about whether to turn a blind eye to another Bosnia or Rwanda in the making or to intervene early and decisively. This may not always be an option, and we need to be prepared to see international efforts limited to humanitarian aid rather than humanitarian intervention. Yet, if anything, the many failures and few successes in prevention, management, and settlement of ethnic conflicts, not only since the end of the Cold War but also over a much longer period before then, offer important lessons about the need for action, the conditions under which it can succeed, and the consequences of failure. The lessons are there; what is needed are enlightened political leaders willing and able to implement them, in Gaza and Kosovo, in the Tamil homelands of Sri Lanka and in Kashmir, in the eastern DRC and western Sudan, in Chechnya, and in Cyprus, as well as in Brussels, New York, and Washington.

Endnotes

Introduction

1. Rogers, Brubaker and Laitin, David D. (1998) Ethnic and nationalist violence. *Annual Review of Sociology* **24**: 425.
2. This is a conservative estimate by Stewart Patrick based on OECD, World Bank, UNDP and other sources covering the 1990s, `The Check is in the Mail: Improving the Delivery and Coordination of Post-Conflict Assistance', New York University: Center on International Cooperation, 1998, available online at: http://www.cic.nyu.edu/archive/pdf/The_Check_is_in_the_Mail.pdf. Note that these were funds pledged rather than actually available.

Chapter 1

1. See, for example, Eriksson, Mikael and Wallensteen, Peter (2004) Armed conflict 1989–2003. *Journal of Peace Research* **41**: 625–636.
2. This was a particularly prominent interpretation of the situation in the former Yugoslavia in the early 1990s. See Kaplan, Robert D. (1993) *Balkan Ghosts: A journey through history*. New York: St Martin's Press.
3. Amnesty International (1998) *A Human Rights Crisis in Kosovo Province, Drenica, February–April 1998: Unlawful killings, extrajudicial executions and armed opposition abuses*. New York: Amnesty International.
4. Amnesty International (2004) *Sudan: At the mercy of killers—destruction of villages in Darfur*. New York: Amnesty International.
5. Amnesty International (2004) *Victims of the War in Darfur Speak About their Plight*. New York: Amnesty International.
6. Amnesty International (1997) *In Search of Safety: The forcibly displaced and human rights in Africa*. New York: Amnesty International.
7. 'Taken over by Satan' (2004) Transcript from *Panorama: The Killers*, broadcast on BBC 1 on Sunday, 4 April 2004 at 22:15. Available at: http://news.bbc.co.uk/1/hi/programmes/panorama/3582011.stm

8. 'Living among the Dead' (2004) Transcript from *Panorama: The Killers*, broadcast on BBC 1 on Sunday, 4 April 2004 at 22:15. Available at: http://news.bbc.co.uk/1/hi/programmes/panorama/3582139.stm.

9. Amnesty International (1996) *To Bury My Brothers' Bones*. New York: Amnesty International.

10. Amnesty International (1996) *Turkey: No security without human rights*. New York: Amnesty International.

11. Human Rights Watch (2004) *D. R. Congo: War crimes in Bukavu*. New York: Human Rights Watch.

Chapter 2

1. On this point specifically, and for an accessible account of Bosnian history more generally, see Bieber, Florian (2005) *Ethnic Structure, Inequality and Governance of the Public Sector: Bosnia–Herzegovina*. Basingstoke: Palgrave, in press.

2. Ibid.

3. Connor, Walker (1994) *Ethnonationalism: The quest for understanding*. Princeton, NJ: Princeton University Press, p. 100.

4. Smith, Anthony D. (1991) *National Identity*. London: Penguin, p. 21.

5. Connor, Walker (1994) *Ethnonationalism: The quest for understanding*. Princeton, NJ: Princeton University Press, p. 104.

6. Esman, Milton J. (1994) *Ethnic Politics*. Ithaka, NY: Cornell University Press, p. 15.

7. Cf. Margaret Moore (1998) The territorial dimension of self-determination. In: Moore, Margaret (ed.), *National Self-Determination and Secession*. Oxford: Oxford University Press, pp. 134–157.

8. McGarry, John (1998) Orphans of secession: National pluralism in secessionist regions and post-secession states. In: Moore, Margaret (ed.), *National Self-Determination and Secession*. Oxford: Oxford University Press, pp. 215–232.

9. An excellent and critical treatment of economic interpretations of the causes of civil wars is Cooper, Neil and Pugh, Michael (2004) *War Economies in a Regional Context*. Boulder, CO: Lynne Rienner.

Chapter 3

1. For an excellent web-based collection of sources on the Solomon Islands, see Peter Murgatroyd, *Current Issues in the Solomon*

Islands: South Pacific Regional Security and Australian Interventionism, available online at: http://www.vanuatu.usp.ac.fj/library/Online/ Texts/Solomons/Solomon.htm.

2. Horowitz, Donald L. (1985) *Ethnic Groups in Conflict.* Berkeley, CA: University of California Press, p. 226.

3. Horowitz, Donald L. (1985) *Ethnic Groups in Conflict.* Berkeley, CA: University of California Press, p. 227.

4. Brown, Michael E. (ed.) (1996) The causes and regional dimensions of internal conflict. In: *The International Dimensions of Internal Conflict.* Cambridge, MA: MIT Press, pp. 577, 579.

5. Cf. Brown, Michael E. (2001) The causes of internal conflict. In: Brown, M. E., Coté, O. R. Jr, Lynn-Jones, S. M., and Miller, S. E. (eds.), *Nationalism and Ethnic Conflict,* revised edn. Cambridge, MA: MIT Press, pp. 15ff.

6. Brown, Michael E. (2001) The causes of internal conflict. In: Brown, M. E., Coté, O. R. Jr, Lynn-Jones, S. M., and Miller, S. E. (eds.), *Nationalism and Ethnic Conflict,* revised edn. Cambridge, MA: MIT Press, p. 17.

7. This point has been repeatedly made by Alan Kuperman. Cf., for example, Kuperman, Alan (2005) Suicidal rebellions and the moral hazard of humanitarian intervention. *Ethnopolitics* 4(2): 149–173.

8. Lake, David A. and Rothchild, Donald (1998) Spreading fear: The genesis of transnational ethnic conflict. In: Lake, D. A. and Rothchild, D. (eds.), *The International Spread of Ethnic Conflict: Fear, diffusion, and escalation.* Princeton, NJ: Princeton University Press, p. 8.

9. Ibid.

10. Ibid.

11. Lake, David A. and Rothchild, Donald (1998) Spreading fear: The genesis of transnational ethnic conflict. In: Lake, D. A. and Rothchild, D. (eds.), *The International Spread of Ethnic Conflict: Fear, diffusion, and escalation.* Princeton, NJ: Princeton University Press, p. 17

12. Walter, Barbara F. (1999) Introduction. In: Walter, B. and Snyder, J. (eds.), *Civil Wars, Insecurity and Intervention.* New York: Columbia University Press, pp. 4–8.

13. This dynamic has been well illustrated for the escalation of violence between Serbs and Croats in 1991–92 by: Figuero, Rui de and Weingast, Barry (1999) The rationality of fear: Political opportunism and ethnic conflict. In: Walter, B. and Snyder, J. (eds.), *Civil Wars, Insecurity and Intervention.* New York: Columbia University Press.

14. Kaufman, Stuart (2001) *Modern Hatreds: The symbolic politics of ethnic war*. Ithaka, NY: Cornell University Press.
15. Transcript of press statement by Gerry Adams. Available at http://news.bbc.co.uk/1/hi/northern_ireland/4417575.stm.
16. Walter, Barbara F. (2001) *Committing to Peace: The successful settlement of civil wars*. Princeton, NJ: Princeton University Press, p. 166.
17. Lake, David A. and Rothchild, Donald (1998) Spreading fear: The genesis of transnational ethnic conflict. In: Lake, D. A. and Rothchild, D. (eds.), *The International Spread of Ethnic Conflict: Fear, diffusion, and escalation*. Princeton, NJ: Princeton University Press.
18. Ibid.
19. Collier, Paul and Hoeffler, Anke, (1998) On economic causes of civil war. *Oxford Economic Papers* 50: 563–573.
20. Collier, Paul and Hoeffler, Anke (2001) *Greed and Grievance in Civil War*. Washington DC: World Bank Research Paper.
21. Ballentine, Karen and Sherman, Jake (2001) *The Political Economy of Armed Conflict: Beyond greed and grievance*. Boulder, CO: Lynne Rienner.
22. Pugh, Michael and Cooper, Neil (2004) *War Economies in a Regional Context*. Boulder, CO: Lynne Rienner.
23. Collier, Paul (2000) *The Economic Causes of Civil Conflict and Their Implications for Policy*. Washington DC: World Bank Research Paper.

Chapter 4

1. Human Rights Watch (2000) *'Welcome to Hell': Arbitrary detention, torture, and extortion in Chechnya*. New York, Washington, London, Brussels: Human Rights Watch.
2. Human Rights Watch (2000) *'No Happiness Remains': Civilian killings, pillage, and rape in Alkhan-Yurt, Chechnya*. New York, Washington, London, Brussels: Human Rights Watch.
3. Human Rights Watch (1995) *Stop Killings of Civilians*. New York, Washington, London, Brussels: Human Rights Watch.
4. Ibid.
5. I am grateful to Professor Brian Williams of the University of Massachusetts for sharing his insights into 'global jihadism' with me.

6. On rape as a war strategy, compare Mertus, Julie (2000) *War's Offensive On Women: The humanitarian challenge in Bosnia, Kosovo and Afghanistan*. West Hartford, CT: Kumarian Press.

7. Amnesty International (2004) *Democratic Republic of Congo: Mass rape —time for remedies*. New York: Amnesty International.

8. Cf. Kuperman, Alan J. (2004) Next steps in Sudan: To end the violence and aid refugees, reining in the Darfur rebels is essential. *Washington Post*, 28 September 2004, p. A27. Available at: www.washingtonpost. com/wp-dyn/articles/A55505-2004Sep27.html.

9. Amnesty International (2004) *Darfur: Rape as a weapon of war. Sexual violence and its consequences*. New York: Amnesty International.

10. Amnesty International (2004) *Victims of the War in Darfur Speak About Their Plight*. New York: Amnesty International.

11. Kuperman, Alan J. (2004) Next steps in Sudan: To end the violence and aid refugees, reining in the Darfur rebels is essential. *Washington Post*, 28 September 2004, p. A27. Available at: www.washingtonpost.com/ wp-dyn/articles/A55505-2004Sep27.html.

12. Lake, David A. and Rothchild, Donald (1998) Spreading fear: The genesis of transnational ethnic conflict. In: Lake, D. A. and Rothchild, D. (eds.), *The International Spread of Ethnic Conflict: Fear, diffusion, and escalation*. Princeton, NJ: Princeton University Press, p. 23.

13. See the organization's website at: www.makedonija.info.

14. On the criminalization of ethnic conflicts and the uneasy 'coexistence' of greed and grievance driven agendas in general see Cooper, Neil and Pugh, Michael (2004) *War Economies in a Regional Context*. Boulder, CO: Lynne Rienner; Kemp, Walter (2004) The business of ethnic conflict. *Security Dialogue* 35: 43–59; and Kemp, Walter (2005) Selfish determination: The questionable ownership of autonomy movements. *Ethnopolitics* 4(1): in press.

Chapter 5

1. Northern Ireland Office (1972) *The Future of Northern Ireland: A paper for discussion*. London: HMSO.

2. Cf. Hamilton, A., McCartney, C., Anderson T., and Finn, A. (1990) *Violence and Communities*. Coleraine: University of Ulster, Centre for the Study of Conflict.

3. Her Majesty's Government of the United Kingdom and Northern Ireland (1995) *A Framework for Accountable Government in Northern Ireland*. London: HMSO.
4. McGarry, John and O'Leary, Brendan (eds.) (1993) Introduction. The macro-political regulation of ethnic conflict. In: Ibid., *The Politics of Ethnic Conflict Regulation*. London: Routledge, p. 4.
5. Schneckener, Ulrich (2004) Models of ethnic conflict regulation: The politics of recognition. In: Schneckener, Ulrich and Wolff, Stefan (eds.), *Managing and Settling Ethnic Conflicts: Perspectives on successes and failures in Europe, Africa and Asia*. New York: Palgrave, pp. 18–39.
6. Weller, Marc (2005) Self-governance in interim settlements: The case of Sudan. In: Weller, Marc and Wolff, Stefan (eds.), *Autonomy, Self-governance and Conflict Resolution: Innovative approaches to institutional design in divided societies*. London: Routledge.
7. Compare Cordell, Karl and Wolff, Stefan (2005) *Germany's Foreign Policy towards Poland and the Czech Republic: Ostpolitik revisited*. London, New York: Routledge.

Chapter 6

1. Amnesty International (1999) *As Violence Descended: Testimonies from East Timorese refugees*. New York: Amnesty International.
2. Ibid.
3. Ibid.
4. Ibid.
5. World Bank (2000) *Transitional Support Strategy for East Timor*. Washington DC: World Bank.
6. McGarry, John and O'Leary, Brenda (2004) *The Northern Ireland Conflict: Consociational engagements*. Oxford: Oxford University Press, p. 31.
7. Press statement by Gerry Adams, 6 April 2005. Transcript available at: http://news.bbc.co.uk/1/hi/northern_ireland/4417575.stm.
8. Compare Paris, Roland (2004) *At War's End: Building peace after civil conflict*. Cambridge: Cambridge University Press.
9. Harris, Peter and Reilly, Benjamin (eds.) (1998) *Democracy and Deep-Rooted Conflict: Options for negotiators*. Stockholm: International Institute for Democracy and Electoral Assistance, Chapter 1. Available at: www.idea.int/publications/democracy_and_deep_rooted_conflict/home.htm.

10. The following enumeration of 'perils' draws on Sisk, Timothy D. (2001) Democratization and peacebuilding: Perils and promises. In: Crocker, Chester, Hampson, Fen Osler, and Aall, Pamela (eds.), *Turbulent Peace: The challenges of managing international conflict.* Washington DC: US Institute of Peace Press.

11. For details on the impact of drug trafficking on Afghanistan, see the contribution by Goodhand, Jonathan (2004) Afghanistan in Central Asia. In: Cooper, Neil and Pugh, Michael (eds.), *War Economies in a Regional Context.* Boulder, CO: Lynne Rienner.

12. Amnesty International (1996) *To Bury My Brothers' Bones.* New York: Amnesty International.

13. On the gacaca courts, see Joireman, Sandra (2003) Justice for genocide? *Global Review of Ethnopolitics* 2(2): 65–66.

14. Government of Australia (2004) AusAID. *Regional Mission To Solomon Islands: Facts and figures.* Available at: www.ausaid.gov.au/hottopics/solomon/solomons_ramsi_details.cfm.

Chapter 7

1. Central Intelligence Agency (2000) *Global Trends 2015: A dialogue about the future with nongovernment experts.* Washington DC: National Intelligence Council.

2. US Government (2002) *The National Security Strategy of the United States.* Available at: www.state.gov/documents/organization/15538.pdf.

3. Council of the European Union (2003) *A Secure Europe in a Better World: European security strategy.* Brussels: Council of the European Union. Available at: http://ue.eu.int/uedocs/cmsUpload/78367.pdf.

4. United Nations (2004) *A More Secure World: Our shared responsibility.* Report of the High-level Panel on Threats, Challenges and Change. New York: UN.

5. Definitions adopted from: www.cidcm.umd.edu/inscr/mar.

6. The term was coined by Barnett Rubin in 2001 in a talk to an International Peace Academy (IPA)-sponsored meeting for the UN Security Council on 'Regional Approaches to Conflict Management in Africa'. Transcript available at: www.un.int/colombia/english/consejo_seguridad/IPA-RegAproAfricaBarnett%20R_%20RubinAug08–01.htm.

A Guide to Further Reading

1. *Selected Internet Sources* (in alphabetical order; links live December 2006)

African Union [http://www.africa-union.org]
- Peace and Security Council [http://www.africa-union.org/root/au/organs/The_Peace_%20and_Security_Council_en.htm]

AlertNet [http://www.alertnet.org/]
- Crisis Profiles [http://www.alertnet.org/thenews/emergency/index.htm]

Amnesty International [http://www.amnesty.org/]

Armed Conflicts Report [http://www.ploughshares.ca/libraries/ACRText/ACR-TitlePageRev.htm]

Association of Southeast Asian Nations [http://www.aseansec.org/]
- Peace and Security [http://www.aseansec.org/92.htm]

Conciliation Resources [http://www.c-r.org/]
- Accord [http://www.c-r.org/accord/series.shtml]

Council of Europe [http://www.coe.int/]
- National Minorities [http://www.coe.int/T/E/human_rights/minorities/]

CRInfo: Gateway to Conflict Resolution Resources [http://www.crinfo.org/]

European Centre for Conflict Prevention [http://www.conflict-prevention.net/index.html]
- Searching for Peace [http://www.conflict-prevention.net/page.php?id=48]
- Conflict Surveys [http://www.conflict-prevention.net/page.php?id=40]

European Centre for Minority Issues [http://www.ecmi.de]

European Union Common Foreign and Security Policy [http://ec.europa.eu/comm/external_relations/cfsp/intro/index.htm]
- EU Conflict Prevention

[http://ec.europa.eu/comm/external_relations/cfsp/news/ip_01_560_en.htm]
- European Union Civilian Crisis Management
  [http://ec.europa.eu/comm/external_relations/cfsp/cpcm/cm.htm]
- European Union High Representative for the Common Foreign and Security Policy
  [http://www.consilium.europa.eu/cms3_applications/applications/solana/index.asp?lang=EN&cmsid=246]

European Union Institute for Security Studies
[http://www.iss-eu.org/]
- Chaillot Papers [http://www.iss-eu.org/public/content/chaile.html]

Forced Migration Online [http://www.forcedmigration.org/]

Human Rights Watch [http://www.hrw.org/]

INCORE (International Conflict Research)
[http://www.incore.ulst.ac.uk/]

International Crisis Group [http://www.crisisgroup.org/]

International Institute for Democracy and Electoral Assistance
[http://www.idea.int/]

International Peace Academy [http://www.ipacademy.org/]

Japan Center for Conflict Prevention
[http://www.jccp.gr.jp/eng/index.html]

Minority Rights Group International
[http://www.minorityrights.org/]

Organisation for Security and Cooperation in Europe
[http://www.osce.org/]
- Regional Activities [http://www.osce.org/regions/]
- Conflict Prevention [http://www.osce.org/activities/13035.html]
- High Commissioner on National Minorities
  [http://www.osce.org/hcnm/]
- Minority Rights [http://www.osce.org/activities/13045.html]

Specialist Group Ethnopolitics [http://www.ethnopolitics.org]

United Nations [www.un.org]
- Peace and Security [http://www.un.org/peace/]
- Human Rights [http://www.un.org/rights/]
- UNDP Democratic Governance [http://www.undp.org/governance/]
- UNDP Crisis Prevention and Recovery [http://www.undp.org/bcpr/]
  - Office for the Coordination of Humanitarian Affairs/OCHA
    [http://ochaonline.un.org/]
- Integrated Regional Information Networks [http://www.irinnews.org/]

- Offices and Missions [http://ochaonline.un.org/webpage.asp?
  Nav=_geography_en&Site=_geography]
- Research Institute for Social Development [http://www.unrisd.org/]
  - Ethnic Conflict and Development
    [http://www.unrisd.org/unrisd/website/projects.nsf/(httpProjects)/
    8C980DEAB3D2566B80256B640039E93B?OpenDocument]
  - Ethnic Diversity and Public Policies
    [http://www.unrisd.org/unrisd/website/projects.nsf/(httpProjects)/
    F4E9F9F4152150E280256B64003A2F13?OpenDocument]
  - Ethnic Structure, Inequality and Governance of the Public Sector
    [http://www.unrisd.org/unrisd/website/projects.nsf/(httpProjects)/
    913C94EA1C6A110BC1256C1D00383EEF?OpenDocument]

United States Institute of Peace [http://www.usip.org]
World Bank Research Program on 'The Economics of Conflict'
[http://econ.worldbank.org/programs/conflict/]

2. Selected General Sources on Conflict and Conflict Resolution

Adekeye, A. 2002. *Building Peace in West Africa: Liberia, Sierra Leone, and Guinea-Bissau.* Boulder, CO: Lynne Rienner.

Adeney, K. 2006. *Federalism and Ethnic Conflict Regulation in India and Pakistan.* Basingstoke: Palgrave.

Anderson, M. B. 1999. *Do No Harm: How Aid Can Support Peace—or War.* Boulder, CO: Lynne Rienner.

Arbatov, A. et al., eds. 1997. *Managing Conflict in the Former Soviet Union.* Cambridge, MA: The MIT Press.

Ballentine, K. and Sherman, J., eds. 2003. *The Political Economy of Armed Conflict: Beyond Greed and Grievance.* Boulder, CO: Lynne Rienner.

Bellamy, A. J., Willams, P. and Griffin, S. 2004. *Understanding Peacekeeping.* Cambridge: Polity Press.

Bercovitch, J., ed. 1996. *Resolving International Conflicts: The Theory and Practice of Mediation.* Boulder, CO: Lynne Rienner.

Berdal, M. R. 1993. *Whither on Peacekeeping?* London: International Institute for Security Studies (Adelphi Paper 281).

Bose, S. 2002. *Bosnia after Dayton: Nationalist Partition and International Intervention.* London: Hurst.

Bothe, M., Ronyitti, N. and Rosas, A., eds. 1997. *The OSCE in the Maintenance of Peace and Security: Conflict Prevention, Crisis Management and Peaceful Settlement of Disputes.* The Hague: Kluwer Law International.

Boutros-Ghali, B. 1992. *An Agenda for Peace: Preventive Diplomacy, Peace-making and Peace-Keeping.*New York: United Nations.

Brown, M. E., ed. 1996. *The International Dimensions of Internal Conflict.* Cambridge, MA: The MIT Press.

——2001. 'Ethnic and Internal Conflicts: Causes and Implications', in Crocker, Hampson and Aall, eds., *Turbulent Peace.*

—— and Ganguly, S. 1997. *Government Policies and Ethnic Relations in Asia and the Pacific.* Cambridge, MA: The MIT Press.

—— et al. 2001. *Nationalism and Ethnic Conflict.* Cambridge, MA: The MIT Press.

Buzan, B. and Wæver, O. 2003. *Regions and Powers.* Cambridge: Cambridge University Press.

Caplan, R. 2005. *International Governance of War-Torn Territories: Rule and Reconstruction.* Oxford: Oxford University Press.

Carment, D. and Schnabel, A. 2003. *Conflict Prevention: Path to Peace or Grand Illusion.* Tokyo: United Nations University Press.

Carr, F. and Callan, T. 2003. *Managing Conflict in the New Europe.* Basingstoke: Palgrave. Chs. 3, 6.

Chesterman, S. 2001. *Just War or Just Peace? Humanitarian Intervention and International Law.* Oxford: Oxford University Press.

Cohen, H. J. 2000. *Intervening in Africa: Superpower Peacemaking in a Troubled Continent.* Basingstoke: Palgrave.

Conversi, D., ed. 2004. *Ethnonationalism in the Contemporary World: Walker Connor and the Study of Nationalism.* London: Routledge.

Cordell, K. and Wolff, S., eds. 2004. *The Ethnopolitical Encyclopaedia of Europe.* Basingstoke: Palgrave.

Crawford, T. and Kuperman, A., eds. 2006. *Gambling on Humanitarian Intervention.* London: Routledge.

Crocker, C. A., Hampson, F. O. and Aall, P., eds. 2001. *Turbulent Peace: The Challenges of Managing International Conflict.* Washington, DC: United States Institute of Peace Press.

Darby, J. and McGinty, R. 2001. *Contemporary Peacemaking.* Basingstoke: Palgrave.

Diehl, P. F. 1994. *International Peacekeeping.* Baltimore: Johns Hopkins University Press.

—— and Lepgold, J., eds. 2003. *Regional Conflict Management.* Lanham, MD: Rowman & Littlefield.

Dobbins, J. et al. 2005. *The UN's Role in Nation-Building: From the Congo to Iraq.* Santa Monica: RAND Corporation.

218

Esman, M. J. and Telhami, S., eds. 1995. *International Organizations and Ethnic Conflict*. Ithaca: Cornell University Press.

Finin, G. A. and Wesley-Smith, Terence A. 2000. *Coups, Conflicts and Crises: A New Pacific Way?* Honolulu, HI: East–West Center Working Papers, Pacific Island Development Series, No. 13.

Freire, M. R. 2003. *Conflict and Security in the Former Soviet Union: The Role of the OSCE*. Aldershot: Ashgate.

Galtung, J. 1996. *Peace by Peaceful Means: Peace and Conflict, Development, and Civilisation*. London: Sage.

Gurr, T. R. 2000. *Peoples Versus States: Minorities at Risk in the New Century*. Washington, DC: United States Institute of Peace.

Hegarty, D. 2003. *Peace Interventions in the South Pacific: Lessons from Bougainville and Solomon Islands*. Honolulu, HI: Asia-Pacific Center for Security Studies, available online at: http://rspas.anu.edu.au/papers/conflict/hegarty_interventions.pdf

Heijmans, A., Simmonds, N. and van Veen, H., eds. 2004. *Searching for Peace in Asia Pacific*. Boulder, CO: Lynne Rienner.

Hogan-Brun, G. and Wolff, S., eds. 2003. *Minority Languages in Europe: Framework, Status, Prospects*. Basingstoke: Palgrave.

Holzgrefe, J. L. and Keohane, R., eds. 2003. *Humanitarian Interventions: Ethical, Legal, and Political Dilemmas*. Cambridge: Cambridge University Press.

Horowitz, D. L. 1985. *Ethnic Groups in Conflict*. Berkeley: University of California Press.

Hughes, J. and Sasse, G., eds. 2002. *Ethnicity and Territory in the Former Soviet Union: Regions in Conflict*. London: Frank Cass.

International Commission on Intervention and State Sovereignty. 2001. *The Responsibility to Protect*. Ottawa: International Development Research Centre.

Kaufman, S. J. 2001. *Modern Hatreds: The Symbolic Politics of Ethnic War*. Ithaca: Cornell University Press.

Kemp, W. 2001. *Quiet Diplomacy in Action: The OSCE High Commissioner on National Minorities*. The Hague, Boston, London: Kluwer Law International.

Keren, M. and Sylan, D. A., eds. 2002. *International Intervention—Sovereignty versus Responsibility*. London: Frank Cass.

King, C. 1997. *Ending Civil Wars*.London: International Institute for Security Studies (Adelphi Paper 308).

Lahneman, W. J., ed. 2004. *Military Intervention: Cases in Context for the Twenty-First Century.* Lanham, MD: Rowman & Littlefield.

Lake, D. A. and Rothchild, D., eds. 1998. *The International Spread of Ethnic Conflict.* Princeton: Princeton University Press.

Lijphart, A. 1977. *Democracy in Plural Societies.* New Haven: Yale University Press.

Lobell, S. and Mauceri, P. 2004. *Ethnic Conflict and International Politics.* Basingstoke: Palgrave.

McGarry, J. and Keating, M., eds. 2006. *European Integration and the Nationalities Question.* London: Routledge.

——— and O'Leary, B. 1993. *The Politics of Ethnic Conflict Regulation.* London: Routledge.

Mackinlay, J. and Cross, P., eds. 2003. *Regional Peacekeepers: The Paradox of Russian Peacekeeping.* New York: United Nations University Press.

Montville, J. V., ed. 1991. *Conflict and Peacemaking in Multiethnic Societies.* New York: Lexington Books.

Neuheiser, J. and Wolff, S., eds. 2002. *Peace at Last? The Impact of the Good Friday Agreement on Northern Ireland. With a Foreword by Lord Alderdice.* New York and Oxford: Berghahn.

Noel, S., ed. 2005. *From Powersharing to Democracy: Post-Conflict Institutions in Ethnically Divided Societies.* Montreal and Kingston: McGill-Queen's University Press.

O'Flynn, I. and Russell, D., eds. 2006. *Powersharing: New Challenges for Divided Societies.* Ann Arbor: University of Michigan Press.

Paris, R. 2004. *At War's End: Building Peace after Civil Conflict.* Cambridge: Cambridge University Press.

Power, S. 2002. *A Problem from Hell: America and the Age of Genocide.* London: Flamingo.

Regan, P. 2003. *Civil Wars and Foreign Powers: Outside Intervention in Intrastate Conflict.* Ann Arbor: University of Michigan Press.

Reilly, B. 2001. *Democracy in Divided Societies: Electoral Engineering for Conflict Management.* Cambridge: Cambridge University Press.

Roe, P. 1999. 'The Intrastate Security Dilemma: Ethnic Conflict as a "Tragedy"?' *Journal of Peace Research,* vol. 36, no. 2 (March 1999).

Roeder, P. G. and Rothchild, D., eds. 2005. *Sustainable Peace: Power and Democracy after Civil Wars.* Ithaca: Cornell University Press.

Rudolph, J. R. 2003. *Encyclopaedia of Modern Ethnic Conflicts.* Westport, CT: Greenwood.

Sahadevan, P. 1999. *Ethnic Conflict in South Asia*. Chicago: Joan B. Kroc Institute for International Peace Studies, available online at http://www.ciaonet.org/wps/sap01/index.html.

Scherrer, C. P. 2003. *Structural Prevention of Ethnic Violence*. Basingstoke: Palgrave.

Schneckener, U. and Wolff, S., eds. 2004. *Managing and Settling Ethnic Conflicts: Perspectives on Successes and Failures in Europe, Africa, and Asia*. New York: Palgrave.

Simons, P. C. 2002. 'Humanitarian Intervention: A Review of Literature', *Ploughshares Working Paper 01–2*, available online at http://www.ploughshares.ca/libraries/WorkingPapers/wp012.html.

Sisk, T. 1996. *Powersharing and International Mediation in Ethnic Conflicts*. Washington, DC: United States Institute of Peace Press.

Smith, M. and Timmins, G., eds. 2001. *Uncertain Europe: Building a New European Security Order?* London: Routledge.

Sriram, C. L. and Wermester, K. 'From Promise to Practice: Strengthening UN Capacities for the Prevention of Violent Conflict', available online at http://www.ipacademy.org/PDF_Reports/PROMISE_TO_PRACTICE_FINAL.pdf

____ Schnabel, A., Packer, J. and Toure, A. 2002. 'Sharing Best Practices on Conflict Prevention: The UN, Regional and Subregional Organizations, National and Local Actors', available online at: http://www.ipacademy.org/PDF_Reports/SHARING_BEST_PRAC.pdf

Stedman, J., Rothchild, D. and Cousens, E. M., eds. 2002. *Ending Civil Wars: The Implementation of Peace Agreements*. Boulder, CO: Lynne Rienner.

Suski, M. n.d. *Constitutional Options for Self-Determination: What Works?* Åbo: Åbo Akademy University, available online at http://www.unausa.org/newindex.asp?place=http://www.unausa.org/issues/kosovo/rome/suksi.asp.

Tellis, A. J. et al., eds. 1997. *Anticipating Ethnic Conflict*. Santa Monica, CA: Rand.

Tishkov, V. 1997. *Ethnicity, Nationalism and Conflict in and after the Soviet Union: The Mind Aflame*. London: Sage.

Varshney, A. *Ethnic Conflict and Civic Life: Hindus and Muslims in India*. New Haven: Yale University Press.

Walter, B. 2002. *Committing to Peace: The Successful Settlement of Civil Wars*. Princeton: Princeton University Press.

Walter, B. F and Snyder, J., eds. 1999. *Civil Wars, Insecurity and Intervention.* New York: Columbia University Press. Ch. 2.

Weller, M. and Wolff, S., eds. 2005. *Autonomy, Self-Governance and Conflict Resolution: Innovative Approaches to Institutional Design in Divided Societies.* London: Routledge.

Welsh, J., ed. 2004. *Humanitarian Intervention and International Relations.* Oxford: Oxford University Press.

Wheeler, N. J. 2000. *Saving Strangers: Humanitarian Intervention in International Society.* Oxford: Oxford University Press.

Wolff, S. 1999. 'Ethno-Territorial Cross-Border Conflict in Western Europe', in *The European Legacy*, vol. 4, no. 5 (1999).

____ 2001. ' "Bilateral" Ethnopolitics after the Cold War: The Hungarian Minority in Slovakia, 1989–1999', *Perspectives on European Politics and Society*, vol. 2, no. 2 (Summer 2001).

____ 2001. 'The Road to Peace? Conflict Resolution in Northern Ireland 1972–1998', *World Affairs*, vol. 163, no. 4 (Spring 2001).

____ 2002. 'Conflict Management in Northern Ireland', *Journal on Multicultural Societies*, vol. 4, no. 1 (Summer 2002), available online at http://www.unesco.org/most/jmshome.htm

____ 2002. 'The Peace Process in Northern Ireland since 1998: Success or Failure of Post-Agreement Reconstruction?', *Civil Wars*, vol. 5, no. 1 (March 2002).

____ 2002. 'Western Standards? Eastern Realities? The Practicalities of Minority Protection in Central and Eastern Europe', *Journal on Ethnopolitics and Minority Issues in Europe*, Issue 4/2002, available online at http://www.ecmi.de/jemie/

____ 2003. *Disputed Territories: The Transnational Dynamics of Ethnic Conflict Settlement.* New York and Oxford: Berghahn.

____ 2004. 'Can Forced Population Transfers Resolve Self-Determination Conflicts? A European Perspective', *Journal for Contemporary European Studies*, vol. 12, no. 1 (Spring 2004).

____ 2004. 'The Institutional Structure of Regional Consociations in Brussels, Northern Ireland, and South Tyrol', *Nationalism and Ethnic Politics*, vol. 10, no. 3 (Autumn 2004).

Zartman, I. W. 1985. *Ripe for Resolution: Conflict and Intervention in Africa.* Oxford: Oxford University Press.

____ 1995. *Elusive Peace: Negotiating an End to Civil Wars.* Washington, DC: Brookings Institution Press.

_____ 2001. *Preventive Negotiation: Avoiding Conflict Escalation*. Lanham, MD: Rowman & Littlefield.

_____ and Kremenyuk, V. 2005. *Peace Versus Justice: Negotiating Forward- and Backward-Looking Outcomes*. Lanham, MD: Rowman & Littlefield.

3. Sources on Selected Conflicts

3.1. Europe

Cyprus

- Guney, A. 2004. 'The USA's Role in Mediating the Cyprus Conflict: A Story of Success or Failure?' *Security Dialogue*, vol. 35, no. 1, pp. 27–42.
- Necatigil, Z. 1993. *The Cyprus Question and the Turkish Position in International Law*. Oxford: Oxford University Press.
- Richmond, O. P. 2006. 'Shared Sovereignty and the Politics of Peace: Evaluating the EU's "Catalytic" Framework in the Eastern Mediterranean', *International Affairs*, vol. 82, no. 1, pp. 149–76.

Finland/Åland Islands

- Daftary, F. 2001. 'Insular Autonomy: A Framework for Conflict Resolution? A Comparative Study of Corsica and the Åland Islands', *Ethnopolitics*, vol. 1, no. 1.
- Loughlin, J. and Daftary, F. 1999. '*Insular Regions and European Integration: Corsica and the Åland Islands Compared*', Flensburg: European Centre for Minority Issues.
- Tiilikainen, T. 2002. *Åland, Finland and European Security*. Mariehamn: The Åland Islands Peace Institute.

Italy/South Tyrol

- Steininger, R. 2003. *South Tyrol: A Minority Conflict of the Twentieth Century*. Brunswick, NJ: Transaction Publishers.
- Wolff, S. 2003. *Disputed Territories: The Transnational Dynamics of Ethnic Conflict Settlement*. New York and Oxford: Berghahn.
- Yaqoob, A. 2006. 'South Tyrol as a Model for Conflict Resolution in Jammu and Kashmir: A Critical Assessment', *Regional Studies*, vol. 24, no. 1, pp. 25–53.

Moldova

- King, C. 2000. *The Moldovans: Romania, Russia, and the Politics of Culture.*
- Protsyk, O. 2004. *Federalism and Democracy in Moldova.* Flensburg: European Centre for Minority Issues.
- Van Meurs, W. 2004. *Moldova ante portas: The EU Agendas of Conflict Management and Wider Europe.* Munich: Center for Applied Policy Research.

Spain/Basque Country

- Idoiaga, G. E. 2006. *The Basque Conflict: New Ideas and Prospects for Peace.* Washington, DC: United States Institute of Peace Press.
- Mansvelt-Beck, J. 2005. *Territory and Terror: Conflicting Nationalisms in the Basque Country.* London: Routledge.
- Mees, L. 2003. *Nationalism, Violence and Democracy: The Basque Clash of* Identities. Basingstoke: Palgrave.

Ukraine/Crimea

- Chase, P. 1995. 'Conflict in Crimea: An Examination of Ethnic Conflict under the Contemporary Model of Sovereignty', *Columbia Journal of Transnational Law*, vol. 34, no. 1, pp. 219–54.
- Sasse, G. 2002. 'The Theory and Practice of Conflict Prevention in a Transition State: The Crimean Issue in Post-Soviet Ukraine', *Nationalism and Ethnic Politics*, vol. 8, no. 2, pp. 1–26.
- Stewart, S. 2001. 'Autonomy as a Mechanism for Conflict Regulation: The Case of Crimea', *Nationalism and Ethnic Politics*, vol. 7, no. 4, pp. 113–41.

United Kingdom/Republic of Ireland/Northern Ireland

- Gilligan, C. and Tonge, J., eds. 2003. 'Northern Ireland', *The Global Review of Ethnopolitics*, vol. 3, no. 1.
- McGarry, J. and O'Leary B. 2004. *The Northern Ireland Conflict: Consociational Engagements.* Oxford: Oxford University Press.
- Wilford, R., ed. 2001. *Aspects of the Belfast Agreement.* Oxford: Oxford University Press.

Western Balkans

- Caplan, R. 2005. *Europe and the Recognition of New States in Yugoslavia.* Cambridge: Cambridge University Press.

- Morton, J. S. et al., eds. 2004. *Reflections on the Balkan Wars*. Basingstoke: Palgrave.
- Woodward, S. L. 1995. *Balkan Tragedy*. Washington, DC: Brookings Institution Press.

Kosovo

- Bieber, F. and Daskalovski, Z., eds. 2003. *Understanding the War in Kosovo*. London: Frank Cass.
- Independent International Commission on Kosovo. 2000. *The Kosovo Report: Conflict, International Response, Lessons Learned*. Oxford: Oxford University Press.
- Judah, T. 2000. *Kosovo: War and Revenge*. New Haven: Yale University Press.

Bosnia and Herzegovina

- Burg, S. L. and Shoup, P. S. 1999. *The War in Bosnia-Herzegovina: Ethnic Conflict and International Intervention*. Armonk, NY: M. E. Sharpe.
- Chandler, D. 1999. *Bosnia Faking Democracy after Dayton*. London: Pluto.
- Weller, M. and Wolff, S., eds. 2006. *Bosnia and Herzegovina Ten Years after Dayton* (Special Issue of *Ethnopolitics*, vol. 6, no. 1).

3.2. Africa

Burundi

- Abrams, J. S. 1995. 'Burundi: Anatomy of an Ethnic Conflict', *Survival*, vol. 37, no. 1, pp. 144–64.
- Bhavnani, R. and Backer, D. 2000. 'Localized Ethnic Conflict and Genocide: Accounting for Differences in Rwanda and Burundi', *Journal of Conflict Resolution*, vol. 44, no. 3, pp. 283–306.
- Lemarchand, R. 1996. *Burundi: Ethnic Conflict and Genocide*. Cambridge: Cambridge University Press.

Democratic Republic of Congo

- Clark, J. F., ed. 2002. *The African Stakes of the Congo War*. Basingstoke: Palgrave.
- Edgerton, R. 2002. *The Troubled Heart of Africa: A History of the Congo*. New York: St. Martin's Press.

- Nest, M. W. 2006. *The Democratic Republic of Congo: Economic Dimensions of War and Peace*. Boulder, CO: Lynne Rienner.

Nigeria

- Nnoli, O. 1995. *Ethnicity and Development in Nigeria*. Aldershot: Ashgate
- Omeje, K. 2004. 'The State, Conflict and Evolving Politics in the Niger Delta, Nigeria', *Review of African Political Economy*, vol. 31, no. 101, pp. 425–40.
- Suberu, R. T. 2001. *Federalism and Ethnic Conflict in Nigeria*. Washington, DC: United States Institute of Peace Press.

Rwanda

- Adelman, H. and Suhrke, A., eds. 1999. *The Path of a Genocide: The Rwanda Crisis from Uganda to Zaire*. London: Transactions Publishers.
- Dallaire, R. A. and Beardsley, B. 2003. *Shake Hands with the Devil: The Failure of Humanity in Rwanda*. New York: Carroll & Graf.
- Njoku, R. C. 2005. 'Deadly Ethnic Conflict and the Imperative of Power Sharing: Could a Consociational Federalism Hold in Rwanda?', *Commonwealth and Comparative Politics*, vol. 43, no. 1, pp. 82–101.

Sudan

- Johnson, D. H. 2004. *The Root Causes of Sudan's Civil Wars*. Oxford: The International African Institute.
- Prunier, G. 2005. *Darfur: The Ambiguous Genocide*. London: Hurst and Company.
- Strauss, S. 2005. 'Darfur and the Genocide Debate', *Foreign Affairs*, January/February 2005, pp. 123–33.

3.3. Continental Asia and the Middle East

Azerbaijan/Armenia/Nagorno Karabakh

- Carley, P. 1998. *Nagorno-Karabakh: Searching for a Solution*. Washington, DC: United States Institute of Peace Press.
- Coppieters, B., ed. 1996. *Contested Borders in the Caucasus*. Brussels: VUB-Press.

- Malek, M. 2006. 'State Failure in the South Caucasus: Proposals for an Analytical Framework', *Transition Studies Review*, vol. 13, no. 2, pp. 441–60.

Bangladesh

- Arens, J. and Chakma, K. N. 2002. *Bangladesh: Indigenous Struggle in the Chittagong Hill Tracts*. The Hague: European Centre for Conflict Prevention.
- Mohsin, A. 2002. *The Chittagong Hill Tracts, Bangladesh: On the Difficult Road to Peace*. Boulder, CO: Lynne Rienner.
- Sisson, R. 1991. *War and Secession: Pakistan, India, and the Creation of Bangladesh*. Berkeley: University of California Press.

Burma

- Kramer, T. 2005. *Burma/Myanmar: Military Rule and Ethnic Conflict*. The Hague: European Centre for Conflict Prevention
- Smith, M. 1993. *Burma: Insurgency and the Politics of Ethnicity*. London: Zed Books.
- South, A. 2002. *Mon Nationalism and Civil War in Burma*. London: Routledge Curzon.

Georgia

- Coppieters, B., Nodia, G. and Anchabadze, Y., eds. 1998. *Georgians and Abkhazians: The Search for a Peace Settlement*. Brussels: VUBPress.
- Cornell, S. E. 2002. *The South Caucasus: A Regional Overview and Conflict Assessment*. Stockholm: Cornell Caspian Consulting and Swedish International Development Agency.
- Welt, C. 2005. 'Balancing the Balancer: Russia, the West, and Conflict Resolution in Georgia', *Global Dialogue*, vol. 7, nos. 3–4, pp. 22–36.

India

- Bose, S. 2003. *Kashmir: Roots of Conflict, Paths to Peace*. Cambridge, MA: Harvard University Press.
- Chadda, M. 1997. *Ethnicity, Security and Separatism in South Asia*. New York: Columbia University Press.
- Singh, G. 2000. *Ethnic Conflict in India*. Basingstoke: Palgrave.

Malaysia

- Brown, G. K. 2005. 'Playing the (Non)Ethnic Card: The Electoral System and Ethnic Voting Patterns in Malaysia', *Ethnopolitics*, vol. 4, no. 4 (November 2005), pp. 429–45.
- Hefner, R. W. ed., 2001. *The Politics of Multiculturalism: Pluralism and Citizenship in Malaysia, Singapore, and Indonesia*. Honolulu, HI: University of Hawaii Press.
- Teik, K. B. 2004. *Managing Ethnic Relations in Post-Crisis Malaysia and Indonesia: Lessons from the New Economic Policy?* Geneva: UNRISD, available online at
  http://www.unrisd.org/published_/pp_/icc_/khoo/content.htm

Russia/Chechnya

- Kramer, M. 2004/05. 'The Perils of Counterinsurgency: Russia's War in Chechnya', *International Security*, vol. 29, no. 3 (Winter 2004/05), pp. 5–63.
- Lieven, A. 1999. *Chechnya: Tombstone of Russian Power*. New Haven: Yale University Press.
- Tishkov, V. 2004. *Chechnya: Life in a War-Torn Society*. Berkeley: University of California Press.

Sri Lanka

- Moolakkattu, J. S. 2005. 'Peace Facilitation by Small States: Norway in Sri Lanka', *Cooperation and Conflict*, vol. 40, no. 4, pp. 385–402.
- Rotberg, R. I., ed. 1999. *Creating Peace in Sri Lanka*. Washington, DC: Brookings Institution Press.
- Sislin, J. and Pearson, F. 2006. 'Arms and Escalation in Ethnic Conflicts: The Case of Sri Lanka', *International Studies Perspectives*, vol. 7, no. 2, pp. 137–58.

Thailand

- Aphornsuvan, T. 2004. *Origins of Malay Muslim 'Separatism' in Southern Thailand*. Asia Research Institute Working Paper Series, no. 32/2004. Singapore: National University of Singapore.
- De Silva, K. M. et al., eds. 1988. *Ethnic Conflict in Buddhist Societies: Sri Lanka, Thailand and Burma*. Boulder, CO: Westview Press.

- Yegar, M. 2002. *Between Integration and Secession: The Muslim Communities of the Southern Philippines, Southern Thailand, and Western Burma/Myanmar.* Lanham, MD: Lexington Books.

Turkey

- Barkey, H. J. and Fuller, G. E. 1998. *Turkey's Kurdish Question.* Lanham, MD: Rowman & Littlefield.
- Cline, L. E. 2004. 'From Ocalan to Al Qaida: The Continuing Terrorist Threat in Turkey', *Studies in Conflict and Terrorism*, vol. 27, no. 4, pp. 321–36.
- Kirişçi, Kemal and Winrow, M. 1998. *The Kurdish Question and Turkey: An Example of Trans-State Ethnic Conflict*, London: Frank Cass.

The Middle East

- Adam, H. and Moodley, K. 2005. *Seeking Mandela: Peacemaking Between Israelis and Palestinians.* Philadelphia: Temple University Press.
- Bickerton, I. J. and Klausner, Carla L. 2004. *A Concise History of the Arab-Israeli Conflict*, fourth edition. New Jersey: Prentice Hall.
- Milton-Edwards, B. 2003. *Conflicts in the Middle East since 1945.* London: Routledge.

3.4. Pacific Asia

East Timor

- Chesterman, S. 2001. *East Timor in Transition: From Conflict Prevention to State-Building.* Washington, DC: International Peace Academy.
- Martin, I. 2001. *Self-Determination in East Timor: The United Nations, the Ballot, and International Intervention.* Boulder, CO: Lynne Rienner.
- Salla, M. E. 1997. 'Creating the "Ripe Moment" in the East Timor Conflict', *Journal of Peace Research*, vol. 34, no. 4, pp. 449–66.

Indonesia

- Bertrand, J. 2004. *Nationalism and Ethnic Conflict in Indonesia.* Cambridge: Cambridge University Press.
- Coppel, C. A. 2005. *Violent Conflicts in Indonesia: Analysis, Representation, Resolution.* London: Routledge.

- Lloyd, G. 2000. *Indonesia's Future Prospects: Separatism, Decentralisation and the Survival of the Unitary State*. Parliament of Australia: Parliamentary Library (Current Issues Brief 17/1999–2000).

Papua New Guinea/Bougainville

- Carl, A. and Garasu, L., eds. 2003. *Weaving Consensus: The Papua New Guinea–Bougainville Peace Process*. London: Conciliation Resources.
- Regan, A. 2002. 'The Bougainville Political Settlement and the Prospects for Sustainable Peace', *Pacific Economic Bulletin*, vol. 17, no. 1, pp. 114–29.
- Regan, A. and Griffin, H., eds. 2005. *Bougainville before the Crisis*. Canberra: Pandanus Books.

Philippines/Mindanao

- McKenna, T. M. 1998. *Muslim Rulers and Rebels: Everyday Politics and Armed Separatism in the Southern Philippines*. Berkeley: University of California Press.
- Schiavo-Campo, S. and Judd, M. 2005. *The Mindanao Conflict in the Philippines: Roots, Costs, and Potential Peace Dividend*. Washington, DC: World Bank (Social Development Papers, paper no. 24/2005).
- Stankovitch, M. 2003. *Compromising on Autonomy: Mindanao in Transition*. London: Conciliation Resources.

Solomon Islands

- Dinnen, S. 2002. 'Winners and Losers: Politics and Disorder in the Solomon Islands 2000–2002', *The Journal of Pacific History*, 37 pp. 285–98.
- Moore, C. 2005. *Happy Isles in Crisis: The Historical Causes for a Failing State in Solomon Islands, 1998–2004*.Canberra: Asia Pacific Press.
- Ponzio, R. 2005. 'The Solomon Islands: The UN and Intervention by Coalitions of the Willing', *International Peacekeeping*, vol. 12, no. 2, pp. 173–88.

Index

CPSIA information can be obtained at www.ICGtesting.com
Printed in the USA
LVOW102244110112

263336LV00004B/16/P